Lecture Notes of the Institute for Computer Sciences, Social Informatics and Telecommunications Engineering 560

T0177969

The LNICST series publishes ICST's conferences, symposia and workshops.
LNICST reports state-of-the-art results in areas related to the scope of the Institute.
The type of material published includes

- Proceedings (published in time for the respective event)
- Other edited monographs (such as project reports or invited volumes)

LNICST topics span the following areas:

- General Computer Science
- E-Economy
- E-Medicine
- Knowledge Management
- Multimedia
- Operations, Management and Policy
- Social Informatics
- Systems

Martin Clayton · Mauro Passacantando ·
Marcello Sanguineti

Editors

Intelligent Technologies for Interactive Entertainment

14th EAI International Conference, INTETAIN 2023
Lucca, Italy, November 27, 2023
Proceedings

Editors
Martin Clayton ⓘ
Durham University
Durham, UK

Mauro Passacantando ⓘ
University of Milano Bicocca
Milan, Italy

Marcello Sanguineti ⓘ
University of Genova
Genoa, Italy

ISSN 1867-8211   ISSN 1867-822X (electronic)
Lecture Notes of the Institute for Computer Sciences, Social Informatics
and Telecommunications Engineering
ISBN 978-3-031-55721-7   ISBN 978-3-031-55722-4 (eBook)
https://doi.org/10.1007/978-3-031-55722-4

Preface

We are delighted to introduce the proceedings of the 14th edition (2023) of the European Alliance for Innovation (EAI) International Conference on Intelligent Technologies for Interactive Entertainment (EAI INTETAIN 2023). This year's edition of EAI INTETAIN focused on the several ways in which modern technologies inspired by game science are changing how humanity interacts with reality. The conference sought innovative contributions regarding methods (e.g., machine learning, movement analysis), computer-based systems (e.g., architectures, software, algorithms) and devices (e.g., digital cameras, smartphones) that enhance either intelligent human interaction or entertainment experience. The conference attracted several submissions from researchers, developers and practitioners around the world.

The technical program of EAI INTETAIN 2023 consisted of 16 full papers (15 of which appear in these conference proceedings). The conference sessions were on: Games and Game-Based Learning; Motion Capture; Sports and Competitions; Interfaces and Applications. Aside from the high-quality technical paper presentations, the technical program also featured one keynote talk on "Music and AI: What's Going On?". The keynote speaker was François Pachet (French scientist, composer and director of the Spotify Creator Technology Research Lab).

Coordination with the general chair, Giorgio Gnecco, and with the local chair and general co-chair, Francesco Biancalani, was essential for the success of the conference. We sincerely appreciate their constant support and guidance. It was also a great pleasure to work with the organizing committee team for its hard work in organizing and supporting the conference, and with the technical program committee for the peer-review process and selection of the technical program. We are also grateful to the conference manager, Marica Scevlikova, for her support, and to all the authors who submitted their papers to this edition of the EAI INTETAIN conference.

We strongly believe that the EAI INTETAIN conference provides a good forum for researchers, developers and practitioners interested in all science and technology aspects that are relevant to interactive entertainment. We also expect that the future editions of the EAI INTETAIN conference will be as successful and stimulating, as indicated by the contributions presented in this volume.

March 2024

Martin Clayton
Mauro Passacantando
Marcello Sanguineti

Organization

Steering Committee

Leonardo Boncinelli   University of Florence, Italy

Organizing Committee

General Chair

Giorgio Stefano Gnecco   IMT School for Advanced Studies, Lucca, Italy

General Co-chairs

Francesco Biancalani   IMT School for Advanced Studies, Lucca, Italy
Peter Keller   Western Sydney University, Australia
Narcís Parés   Universitat Pompeu Fabra, Spain

TPC Chair and Co-chairs

Gustavo Cevolani   IMT School for Advanced Studies, Lucca, Italy
Martin Clayton   Durham University, UK
Gabriele Costa   IMT School for Advanced Studies, Lucca, Italy
Benjamin R. Knapp   Virginia Tech, USA
Daniele Masti   IMT School for Advanced Studies, Lucca, Italy
Fabio Pinelli   IMT School for Advanced Studies, Lucca, Italy

Sponsorship and Exhibit Chair

Tiziano Antognozzi   IMT School for Advanced Studies, Lucca, Italy

Local Chair

Francesco Biancalani   IMT School for Advanced Studies, Lucca, Italy

Workshops Chair

Daniele Masti   IMT School for Advanced Studies, Lucca, Italy

Publicity and Social Media Chairs

Enno Bilancini   IMT School for Advanced Studies, Lucca, Italy
Roberto Di Paolo   IMT School for Advanced Studies, Lucca, Italy
Massimo Riccaboni   IMT School for Advanced Studies, Lucca, Italy

Publications Chair

Rodolfo Metulini   University of Bergamo, Italy

Web Chair

Federico Nutarelli   Bocconi University, Italy

Technical Program Committee

Mohammed Abdelsamea   Birmingham City University, UK
Salvatore Andolina   Polytechnic University of Milan, Italy
Francesco Angelini   University of Bologna, Italy
Davide Bacciu   University of Pisa, Italy
Frédéric Bevilacqua   IRCAM, France
Leonardo Boncinelli   University of Florence, Italy
Davide Bottari   IMT School for Advanced Studies, Lucca, Italy
Eleonora Ceccaldi   University of Genoa, Italy
Cristiano Cervellera   National Research Council, Genoa, Italy
Alessandro D'Ausilio   University of Ferrara, Italy
Patrizio Dazzi   University of Pisa, Pisa, Italy
Eyad Elyan   Robert Gordon University, UK
Mauro Gaggero   National Research Council, Genoa, Italy
Letterio Galletta   IMT School for Advanced Studies, Lucca, Italy
Claudio Gallicchio   University of Pisa, Italy
Ming Li   Zhejiang Normal University, China
Marco Lippi   University of Modena and Reggio Emilia, Italy
Danilo Macciò   National Research Council, Genoa, Italy
Niccolò Maggioni   IMT School for Advanced Studies, Lucca, Italy
Maurizio Mancini   Sapienza University of Rome, Italy
Vittorio Mattei   IMT School for Advanced Studies, Lucca, Italy

Stefano Melacci	University of Siena, Italy
Claudio Antares Mezzina	University of Urbino, Italy
Radoslaw Niewiadomski	University of Trento, Italy
Luca Oneto	University of Genoa, Italy
Mauro Passacantando	University of Milano-Bicocca, Italy
Zhenyue Qin	Australian National University, Australia
Fabio Raciti	University of Catania, Italy
Marcello Sanguineti	University of Genoa, Italy
Stefano Sebastio	Collins Aerospace Applied Research & Technology, Ireland
Gianna Vivaldo	National Research Council, Pisa, Italy
Gualtiero Volpe	University of Genoa, Italy
Zhiqiang Wang	Shanxi University, China
Bing Yang	China Jiliang University, China
Hailiang Ye	China Jiliang University, China

Contents

Sports and Competition

Interfaces and Applications

Games and Game-Based Learning

Toward a Better Measurement of Strategic Skills: The Multiple Choice Strategic Quotient (McSQ)

Andrea Piazzoli[1,3], Gianpietro Sgaramella[2,3], and Alan Mattiassi[3(✉)]

[1] Department of Economics and Statistics, University of Siena, 53100, Siena, Italy
[2] AXES Unit, IMT School for Advanced Studies Lucca, Piazza San Francesco 19, 55100 Lucca, Italy
[3] GAME Science Research Center, IMT School for Advanced Studies Lucca, Piazza San Francesco 19, 55100 Lucca, Italy
alan.mattiassi@gmail.com

Abstract. This paper develops the strategic quotient construct and its measure, the Strategic Quotient (SQ), a test to assess actual strategic competencies. While the developmental and refinement work is still in progress, here we document the process of rethinking the foundations of the test and the concepts it is based on, in order to design a novel version of the SQ, the "multiple choice Strategic Quotient" (mcSQ).

Keywords: strategic quotient · strategic ability · strategic interaction · games

1 Introduction

1.1 Aims and Goals

In the scientific literature, the definition and conceptualization of strategic ability varies from study to study. Recently, the concept of strategic quotient has been developed and presented (Bilancini et al. 2019). The strategic quotient has been conceived as separate from general intelligence and from the intelligence quotient (Deary 2012). While certain intelligent quotient measuring tools primarily assess cognitive abilities related to problem-solving and reasoning, the strategic quotient encompasses additional dimensions such as social intelligence, theory of mind, and the ability to understand and respond to strategic interactions. Conversely, it does not assess areas such as knowledge, perception, motor or practical skills that are considered by intelligent quotient tests (Otero et al. 2022), although it could in principle be affected by language and verbal skills, memory, and attention. Inhibition and possibly other executive functions are hypothesized to be critical for the strategic quotient. Additionally, and crucially, social skills such as empathy, perspective-taking, and understanding social cues play an important role in the concept of strategic quotient, but less so in the intelligence quotient. Overall, the conceptualization of the strategic quotient emphasizes its multidimensional nature, combining cognitive and social skills to assess and respond to strategic interactions in different decision-making contexts.

M. Clayton et al. (Eds.): INTETAIN 2023, LNICST 560, pp. 3–19, 2024.
https://doi.org/10.1007/978-3-031-55722-4_1

While strategic behavior had previously been studied extensively (Camerer et al. 2015; Weyhrauch and Culbertson 2014; Gill et al. 2023), no measure of strategic behavior or ability had previously been proposed before the introduction of the strategic quotient concept in the aforementioned work (Bilancini et al. 2019). In that paper, the authors presented the validation of a novel measure of strategic abilities called "Strategic Quotient", a test that we will refer to as SQ hereon (vs. the concept strategic quotient, lowercase). The authors conducted an experiment that was designed to create a strategic context, i.e. the context in which the outcome of a choice does not depend solely on the individual choice but on the combination of choices of all participants (Stahl and Wilson 1995). Indeed, the participants played games from the behavioral economic literature (Guala and Mittone 2010) in which they were required not only to understand the structure and payoffs of the games but also to assess and predict the behavior of other participants and try to choose the optimal response given the predicted choices of others.

Here we start by observing a number of shortcomings that we found by working with the SQ since its publication and then present a number of possible solutions that allowed us to develop a new version of the test that introduces, among other novelties, multiple choice-type responses and is as such called "mcSQ" (multiple-choice Strategic Quotient). Our goal is not to present a novel iteration of the test but rather to document the refining process of the test in order to simplify it, make it more coherent, and, most importantly, we propose a number of indicators that could empower the interpretation of the measured behavior.

1.2 Conceptualization of the Strategic Quotient

While Bilancini et al. (2019) first proposed the term "Strategic Quotient" both as the concept of strategic ability and as the name of its measuring tool, there are antecedents in the scientific literature that preceded it and led to its construction (Jelenc and Swiercz 2011). The historical development and evolution of the concept of strategic quotient in literature can be traced through several key milestones and research contributions. Here are some notable and contributing developments:

1. Game Theory: The basis for the study of strategic interactions can be traced back to the emergence of game theory in the mid-20th century (Von Neumann and Morgenstern 2007). Game theory provided a formal framework for analyzing strategic decisions and understanding how individuals reason and strategize in competitive situations.
2. Social Intelligence and Theory of Mind (ToM): In the 1980s and 1990s, research on Social Intelligence and ToM gained prominence (Wellman et al. 2001). These areas of study focused on the ability of individuals to understand and interpret the thoughts, emotions, and intentions of others. The inclusion of social intelligence as a component of strategic thinking contributed to the development of the strategic quotient foundations (Parales-Quenza 2006).
3. Experimental Studies: Experimental studies began to investigate individual differences in strategic thinking and decision-making (Golman et al. 2020) (Bayer and Renou 2012). Researchers developed various experimental games and tasks to measure participants' strategic abilities, often focusing on aspects such as anticipation

(Gill and Prowse 2016), prediction (Otero et al. 2022), and decision-making in competitive settings (Camerer et al. 2004). These studies provided empirical evidence that can be categorized as a significant step in the development of the strategic quotient.

4. Conceptualization of the Strategic Quotient: The term 'strategic quotient' began to receive attention in 2016 with the research of Boncinelli, Bilancini, and Mattiassi, published in 2019. The researchers sought to define and conceptualize it as a distinct construct, separate from general intelligence measures such as IQ. The focus shifted from logical items to understanding decision-making, performance, and success in interactions with the sample.

1.3 Features of the SQ Test

The main feature of the SQ, which also establishes how it is different from intelligence quotient measures, is that the correctness of the answer to most items of each game depends on the distribution of choices that all participants make. By using the pool of responses given by the entire sample of participants, the authors were able to calculate a score for each game and a general score that allowed them to rank the participants in order of strategic ability, i.e. from those who won the most to those who won the least. Since winning and losing were defined by the ability to estimate the behavior of other participants, each game had no *a priori* correct answer, but it varied depending on the responses of the whole sample. Participants with higher Strategic Quotient scores, then, were the ones who chose the most advantageous option based on a better assessment of the competence of others' behavior and on the best prediction of their behavior.

The SQ is particularly interesting also because it allows for repeated administrations: since it is possible to correctly estimate the behavior of others, and since each population has its own profile of actions, a participant can play against different populations and rank differently. As an anecdotical example, during one of the first administrations of SQ at a game fair, a participant obtained a low rank when playing against the entire population of participants playing at the fair but obtained one of the top ranks when repeating the test against participants from the high IQ society Mensa. It is worth noting that other means of ability estimation lose their validity when used a second time. This peculiarity of the SQ makes it possible to use the test in a competitive context such as human resources hiring, for example, to find the best candidate or the person who can best estimate the behavior of several groups or a specific group, etc.

Additionally, and most importantly, the SQ does not measure intelligence quotient. In their paper, the SQ authors examined the possible correlation between the SQ score and the Raven APM matrices and found it to be non-significant.

The SQ test is designed to assess not only an individual's ability to understand games and to perform rational problem-solving but also the ability to evaluate the skills of others and to predict their actions. To obtain a high score in the SQ, the following skills are thought to be important:

- Critical Thinking: involves the analysis of complex information. This competency is important for evaluating available information and formulating effective strategies.
- Metacognition: is concerned with being aware of one's thinking and learning process. Metacognition helps identify one's own knowledge gaps and develop effective learning strategies.

– Self-regulation: is about the ability to monitor one's behavior and adapt it to the demands of the situation. This implies mental flexibility and the ability to modify one's strategies based on the feedback received.
– Perspective-Taking: refers to the cognitive ability to understand and adopt the point of view, thoughts, feelings, and intentions of others. It involves mentally simulating the experiences of others and taking into account their unique perspectives, beliefs, and motivations. This process enables individuals to empathize with others, make accurate attributions, and engage in prosocial behaviors. Perspective-taking plays a crucial role in social interactions, interpersonal relationships, and the development of empathy, compassion, and cooperation.

Accordingly, the SQ test has been built using three kinds of items:

– Rationality items: these items have the form of a question that uses the game rules but presents a perfectly rational competitor, and as such do not consider the answers of the rest of the participants ("What would you choose if you were to play a game against a perfectly rational robot?"). Here, a correct answer exists, and the player needs to find it to score the maximum points: as such, these items measure by design the rational skills of the participant.
– Items related to the proficiency in predicting others' rationality: these items comprise the largest part of the SQ items and have the form of the traditional question posed by the game in the behavioral economic literature ("What do you choose in this game?"). There is also a secondary form of these items that relates to the same indicator: the one in which the participant is asked to play the same game in another role, such as the proposer and the responder in the ultimatum game ("What would you choose as the other player?"). These items measure by design the ability to understand the interaction of participants' choices; however, they do not measure rationality alone nor predict skills alone but have also a component of perspective-taking.
– Items related to the proficiency in predicting the prediction of others: these items ask participants to predict what other participants think that other participants will do – or the predicting ability of the other participants. These items take the form of a question that asks what the other participants did in a previous game or in a previous item of the same game, as such considering not only the prediction of the others' performance but also the prediction of the other's prediction ("what do you think the other participants predicted?"). These items are indeed focused on metacognition and perspective-taking.

All items require critical thinking and self-regulation; however, while critical thinking is considered in the original SQ paper, we argue that self-regulation has been left on the sidelines, when it should be better emphasized.

2 Methods

First, we identify a number of shortcomings of the version of SQ that has been published and used since publication. Then we propose a number of improvements and discuss the constructs at the foundations of the test in order to rediscuss them to drive the development of a new version.

2.1 Identified Shortcomings

Since the Bilancini, Boncinelli, and Mattiassi paper was published, the SQ has been used in several contexts and developed in multiple iterations. Here are some shortcomings that were found and some considerations on the weaknesses that might drive the design of a novel version of the test.

Items Too Time Costly or Too Difficult to Understand.   Several items have been found to be problematic because they seem to be too difficult to understand, badly worded, or just too time-consuming.

Response Modality.   Participants have been found to answer in multiples of five. Indeed, any responder that tries to figure out a response is thought to accumulate evidence until a particular response is obtained; however, evidence accumulates by using multiple "anchors" that function as reference points (see for example Kvam et al. 2022).

The Arbitrary Threshold for Points Earning.   In the previous version of SQ, the interval of responses that earned participants points was arbitrary. The formula with which each game was scored considered the distribution of answers of all participants and identified an interval that was considered representative of a good answer in relation to the distribution profile of answers. Unfortunately, different games elicited different distributions of responses, thus rendering them non-comparable.

Pre-test Section.   The first SQ aimed at measuring the strategic quotient with a set of games very different from each other, divided into two parts: a pre-test and a test based on the pre-test. As such, participants had to switch continuously between different pages in order to solve the games and this procedure took a lot of time.

Very Different Games.   The difference between the games is aimed at including all the faces of strategic thinking related to the strategic processes, but this aim is very difficult to achieve, especially through only one item for every indicator, which is not in line with the psychometric literature.

Consistency Between the Data-Driven Approach and the Constructs.   A matrix of correlation to aggregate the indicators into four main constructs was used to extract four factors. Correlations, however, have weak explanatory power for the internal consistency of a construct in psychometrics. The authors tried to explain the measure with two main indicators: mentalization and rationality. While generally rationality allows individuals to grasp the structure of the game and its payoff, mentalization allows players to predict other players' behavior. One could wonder if these two indicators are sufficient in order to account for the complexity of strategic skills.

Classic Game-Theoretical Payoffs.   Payoffs were calculated and presented in a classical game theory manner, but people attribute spontaneously payoffs based on their preferences about implicit goals that diverge from the optimization of gains (Gavetti 2012). However, the problem of suboptimal gain in favor of preferred behaviors is endogenous in rationality: e.g., if others' choices are perceived as not fair, it "feels" rational to punish that behavior even at a personal cost. On the contrary, if emotions or other preferences are considered exogenous to rationality (Alaoui and Penta 2016), then one should enforce a more rational interpretation of strategic ability that is not connected to the real competencies that are needed to predict others' behavior in society: e.g., a chess master can make very solid predictions on the next actions in a game but what if he has to predict emotions that can drive other's actions (Capra 2004)? This interpretation of the typical behavioral games used in economics can be an excellent tool to explore the difference between a more descriptive approach to *rationality* in which we can consider as rational the emotions that drive a specific behavior more than the maximum gain, and *hyper-rationality*, defined as a reduction of reality only in strictly logical terms like in classical game theory (Alos-Ferrer and Buckenmaier 2018). Fairness (Suleiman 2022) and punishment (Xiao and Houser 2005) are two preferred behaviors that override the rational preference for an optimization strategy at a personal cost.

2.2 Proposed Improvements

The main possible improvements to the SQ, in our opinion, are:

- Simplification of the questions (to reduce the probability of errors in responses)
- Homogeneity of the measured constructs (to be able to limit the range of skills measured to fewer constructs with more indicators, and not more constructs with few items each)
- Progressive adjustments of the questions to stay within the psychometric validity thresholds.
- Inclusion of a dual interpretation of the results of the test (people attributing rational or hyper-rational styles to others).

One first change we introduced in the novel version of the SQ is the response modality, changing it from a continuous scale to a discrete Likert scale of twenty-one points (from 0 to 100 or 0% to 100% in multiples of five), facilitating the choice between anchors and representing them in graphical form (as a list of ordered possible choices). As such, we also increased the probability of picking the right interval to score points by attributing points to the two percentages choices near the average choice of the whole participants' sample (one full score for picking one of the two percentages nearest to the *a posteriori* correct response and a half score for picking the percentages near those). A lot of people reported a certain confusion about the questions with intensive use of percentages after the conclusion of the test. The phrasing of many items was too convoluted. Reference to other items required too many elements to elaborate, and as such we introduced a more direct approach like "What do you think is the average percentage expressed in the previous question?".

To fix the homogeneity among very different games and items, we consistently introduced three kinds of items for each game (with only a few exception). Indeed, the internal coherence of the test should be favored by the constant use of three kinds of games. The items of the first kind consist of one of the typical Discrete Choice Experiments (or DCEs) economic games (Straub and Murnighan 1995): participants are asked to play the game by choosing one of the possible answers. The items of the second kind consist of a question asking the participant to estimate the average choice of the other subjects to the previous question. The items of the third kind ask the participant to estimate the average response to the second part. The first kind of item requires a multiple-choice response (in which rationality or hyper-rationality is measured) while the second and third parts evaluate the answers given by the sample with precision intervals around the average, giving points to the responder scores with the abovementioned method.

For the third improvement, the sample of participants needs to be extended to see if the standardization in the scoring can be distributed in a normal way in some of the questions. This is a work in progress and out of the scope of the present paper.

As for the last improvement, participants can be divided with respect to the tendency towards rationality or hyper-rationality. This is, as well, out of the scope of the present paper.

2.3 Additional Construct Contributions

In the original SQ article, the authors used two different approaches to understand the data from an exploratory analysis: data-driven and theory-driven. Here, we start from the validation of that SQ version and develop a set of constructs that might improve the SQ's ability to describe the behavior of the participants, its interpretability, and its easiness of use. We changed many of the original questions to these goals, in order to also improve its construct validity.

Construct #1: The evaluation of logical competencies. This is a classical approach to the first part of every game that we have in this test. Some games in the test have a correct answer that can be only identified by using logic-related capabilities. These items are useful to evaluate logic-related competencies (Weyhrauch 2016) and consequentially to see the estimation capability that we will talk about later in this section.

• Logic-related skills

Construct #2: The difference between emotional vs rational estimation and logical competence (van Dijk and Vermunt 2000). Usually, the economics literature considers anything prioritized with respect to a strictly material gain approach as an emotion-based bias (Kahneman 2003). This way of thinking conflicts with the variants of game theory that tried to include as endogenous factors the psychology of individuals (Athanasiou et al. 2015). So, if these factors can be considered inside the system to evaluate payoffs, then "hyper-rational people" are those who exclude these psychological factors in their estimations. This reasoning works in talking about games that can have different answers based on the preferences of people (Tisserand et al. 2015) and that are not *a priori* right or wrong. If the base games had right or wrong answers, another indicator could be used based on the estimation of logic-related competencies or incompetencies (Dhir et al. 2018). Indicators could be conceived in this way:

• Rationality vs hyper-rationality
• A good vs a bad estimation of other's logic-related capabilities

Construct #3: Pattern of responses in generalization of one competence to the rest of the participants. Some stable patterns emerged in the answers of individuals. In some cases, with respect to a rational approach to the tendency toward a mean, people tended to generalize to others their competencies in all the questions, or with a tendency to attribute more extreme competencies. Thus, two indicators could be conceived as:

- Overestimation or underestimation
- Approximation or extremization

In summary, we propose five continuous indicators as mentioned before, to evaluate the answers of participants along with the general score that they provide.

3 Experimental Procedure

Here we present the results of a pilot study with a version of the mcSQ that started to integrate the proposed changes and that has been more focused on the five indicators mentioned in the previous section. The goal is not to validate the test but to show how the changes affected its psychometric properties.

3.1 Sampling Strategy and Participant Selection

The sample is composed by 160 participants, of which 47.12% were females, 46.88% were males, 1.25% were non-binaries and 3.75% preferred not to answer. The mean age is 25.06 y.o. with a standard deviation of 8.2 years.

Participants were recruited at the University of Firenze in an economic course, at PLAY: Festival del Gioco fair in Modena, and online on social networks.

3.2 Data Analysis and Interpretation Techniques

Participants took the mcSQ in different settings, ranging from in-class to online, constituting a convenience sample with no control over the setting. However, the mcSQ was implemented in Google Forms, and as such data were collected automatically. We applied the scoring that was presented in par.1.5 and performed correlation analyses on the results between all items.

3.3 Results and Findings

Descriptive Statistics

The distribution between the 4 education levels registered (from having completed the high school to having 1 or 2 degrees and finally being a PhD condidate) is: 73.12% high school (level one), 7.5% bachelor's degree (level 2), 16.25% master's degree (level 3) and 3.13% Ph.D. (level 4).

Those who came from an economics, statistics and mathematics background were further divided into four levels, being no education at all (13.75% - level 0), marginally educated (22.55% - level 1), partially educated (33.75% - level 2) and educated in the subjects previously mentioned (30% - level 3).

Table 1. and Fig. 1 represent differences between the average scores of participants pertaining to different levels of education, while Table 2. and Fig. 2 represent different levels of education specifically in ESM disciplines.

Both the data on education and on ESM education need to be considered descriptive only, since the scarce numerosity of the groups with second, third, and fourth levels of

Table 1. Scores for education level

Total points				
	Lev 1	Lev 2	Lev 3	Lev 4
Valid	117	12	26	5
Mean	12.333	12.333	14.231	13.600
Std. Deviation	2.586	2.103	2.804	3.362
Minimum	7.000	8.000	10.000	10.000
Maximum	21.000	15.000	21.000	19.000

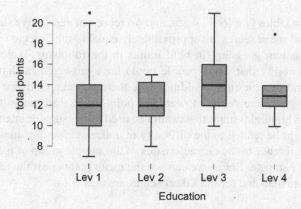

Fig. 1. Boxplot representation of scores by education level.

Table 2. Scores for ESM education levels

Total points				
	0	1	2	3
Valid	22	36	54	48
Mean	12.545	12.111	12.500	13.375
Std. Deviation	3.113	2.550	2.369	2.856
Minimum	7.000	7.000	8.000	9.000
Maximum	21.000	18.000	20.000	21.000

general education and the biased sampling method (0 levels of ESM education participants were mainly recruited online, while educated participants came from the same university courses) would render any statistical inference invalid.

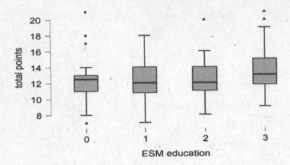

Fig. 2. Boxplot representation of scores divided by ESM education level.

The following tables (Tables 3., 4., 5., and 6.) represent descriptive statistics of each item. Many items' mean scores are approximately equal to the expected value obtained in the case of random guessing (in bold italics in the following Tables). This result suggests the possibility that many people could have answered randomly or did not clearly understand the questions. Additionally, there is some evidence in descriptive statistics that suggests a regression toward the point in the distribution that represents randomness. This highlights items that cannot be used to measure the intended construct. The problem might be related to the difficulty in understanding the questions or in the absence of any reference to the characteristics of the sample group of participants with which they must compete. Below we can see the mean points near the casuality, which for some items are 0.50 and for the Likert scales are near 0.14.

Table 3. Point means and standard deviations

	1.1	2.1	3.1	4.1	5.1	7.1	8.1	9.1	10.1	11.1	12.1
Mean	0.23	0.82	0.57	0.91	0.85	0.93	*0.21*	0.11	0.27	0.28	*0.58*
Std. Deviation	0.42	0.38	0.49	0.28	0.36	0.26	0.36	0.31	0.45	0.40	0.50

Table 4. Point means and standard deviations

	1.2	2.2	3.2	4.2	5.2	6.2	7.2	9.2	10.2	11.2	12.2
Mean	0.37	0.28	*0.19*	0.25	*0.16*	0.20	0.39	*0.19*	0.43	*0.17*	*0.47*
Std. Deviation	0.43	0.41	0.35	0.40	0.32	0.37	0.39	0.39	0.50	0.34	0.50

It is also worth noting that all the items result non-normally distributed following supporting evidence provided by the Shapiro-Wilk test (all $ps < 0.001$). The same applies to the distribution of the total scores (general SQ score) by every participant, showed below in the Fig. 3.

Table 5. Point means and standard deviations

	1.3	2.3	3.3	4.3	5.3	7.3	8.3	9.3	10.3	11.3	12.3
Mean	0.28	0.25	0.26	*0.19*	0.24	*0.18*	*0.15*	0.20	*0.53*	0.22	0.24
Std. Deviation	0.38	0.40	0.43	0.35	0.39	0.31	0.32	0.36	0.50	0.36	0.40

Table 6. Point means and standard deviations

	6.4	9.4	10.4
Mean	0.28	*0.19*	0.53
Std. Deviation	0.38	0.36	0.50

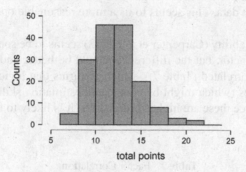

Fig. 3. Distribution of the total scores

The distribution of total scores is positively skewed, suggesting that people with greater strategic reasoning and who use that capability in a fruitful way are distributed in the right tail.

Scores and Measures of Strategic Quotient and Related Constructs
Based on a theory-driven approach we divided the indicators as follows:

- LC = Logic related competence (1.1, 2.1, 3.1, 4.1, 5.1, 7.1, 8.3, 9.1, 10.2)
- hRT = Hyper-rational type (1.1, 3.1, 6.2, 6.4, 9.2)
- eLC = Estimation of LC (1.2, 2.2, 3.2, 4.2, 5.2, 7.2, 8.1, 9.3, 10.1, 11.1, 12.1)
- eeC = Estimation of estimations capabilities (1.3, 2.3, 3.3, 4.3, 5.3, 7.3, 8.1, 9.4, 10.4, 11.2, 11.3, 12.2, 12.3)

3.4 Exploratory Factor Analysis

Since some games were slightly changed along with the underlying dimensions, we chose to explore the latent structure of data with an exploratory factor analysis. The Bartlett test p-value ($X2 = 924.13$, df $= 703$, p < 0.001) allowed us to have supporting evidence for the feasibility of the factor analysis.

Two factors emerged using the parallel analysis ($X2 = 714.67$, df $= 628$, p < 0.009), differently from what we theoretically assumed. It is worth noting that almost every item has a very high uniqueness (Table 8.), with some that are very close to one and correlating with no factor at all (in bold), leading to several considerations. The first is that some of the items could be subject to elimination in future versions, considering both uniqueness and average response near random guessing. On the other hand, since strategy can be composed of many different competencies and the games presented could require different combinations of them, a model with more factors or considering many items as measuring different abilities might be a possibility that we will try to test in the future if supported by data. This seems to us a more reasonable option for most of the games considered.

The logic-related ability (Carpenter et al., 2013) seems to be somewhat distinguishable from the other factor, but the difference should be better understood. These two are substantially uncorrelated (Table 7.), which confirms that logic-related ability and the other competences (which might be considered estimation skills) pertain to different latent factors. Since these are higher-order skills, it is likely to find items related to multiple factors.

Table 7. Factor Correlations

	Factor 1	Factor 2
Factor 1	1.000	0.095
Factor 2	0.095	1.000

Furthermore, typical questions with respect to risk aversion and trust refer to preferences and components of social order, so they are not just pure "calculation" skills (Chen et al. 2017). This is another point that will need to be developed further to reconcile theory and empirical results. To date, the two-factor model looks the best when looking at the data.

Collectively, these findings show that the design of the mcSQ needs additional iterations to satisfy psychometric validity.

Table 8. Factor Loadings over a threshold of 0.15.

	Factor 1	Factor 2	Uniqueness
V0.1		0.390	0.846
V0.2		0.284	0.919
V1.1	0.314		0.891
V1.2	0.275	0.175	0.889
V1.3			**0.973**
V2.1		0.191	**0.961**
V2.2			**0.990**
V2.3	0.160		**0.970**
V3.1	0.373		0.861
V3.2			**0.975**
V3.3		−0.166	0.971
V4.1		0.253	0.914
V4.2	−0.284	0.488	0.694
V4.3			**0.989**
V5.1	0.176	0.405	0.798
V5.2	0.160	0.160	0.946
V5.3			**0.996**
V6.2	0.236		0.941
V6.4			**0.990**
V7.1		0.214	0.945
V7.2		0.468	0.778
V7.3			**0.972**
V8.1			**0.998**
V8.3	0.204	0.310	0.857
V9.1	0.548		0.678
V9.2	0.656		0.557
V9.3			**0.975**
V9.4		0.243	0.941
V10.1	0.224	−0.203	0.913
V10.2			**0.990**
V10.3	0.235		0.930
V10.4			**0.987**
V11.1			**0.990**
V11.2		−0.280	0.911
V11.3			**1.000**
V12.1	−0.266		0.923
V12.2	−0.227		0.948
V12.3	0.151		0.977

Note. Applied rotation method is promax

4   Discussion and Conclusion

The latest SQ version, the mcSQ, is a test that requires multiple-choice responses to estimate the behavior of others. It builds upon the SQ and the strategic quotient concept in evaluating an individual's rationality, ability to estimate others' rationality, and ability to predict others' predictions. Thus, they are designed to measure an individual's ability to analyze and evaluate information, formulate and implement strategies, solve problems, and adapt to changing situations. However, the particular emphasis on skill estimation and action prediction makes them a unique and useful kind of test for those seeking to assess leadership potential in highly interacting contexts. The tests are particularly useful for assessing the ability to evaluate the competencies that are important in leadership or management roles. They can also be used to identify an individual's areas of strength and weakness and develop a personalized development plan and used to evaluate the effectiveness of training and development programs. While certainly the development and the refinement of the mcSQ is still a work in progress, the considerations that have been made on its strengths and weaknesses shed important light on the constructs of the test and its complexity.

Firstly, the underlying constructs of the SQ might be reconsidered. By re-designing the test with a theory-driven focus, one could expect to better measure strategic skills. However, the psychometric properties of the mcSQ are not yet acceptable, so further development needs to be implemented. Items need to be modified through subsequent evidence-based design-test cycles to improve internal coherence, item uniqueness and obtain better factor loadings.

Secondly, the mcSQ introduces a discrete multiple-choice response mode, that should help participants in anchoring the evidence accumulation for each alternative and choose the identified answer in a more time-efficient way and possibly with lower cognitive cost.

Thirdly, both the wording and the very heterogeneous structure of the SQ test might be improved. We designed mcSQ for this purpose by using the same three-part structure for the items of all games and simplified the wording on many items.

As mentioned, the development and refining process is still in progress and requires further research.

4.1   Limitations and Future Directions for Research

While the concept of strategic quotient has garnered attention and research interest, there are several criticisms, limitations, and gaps in the literature. These include:

Lack of Consensus.   Different studies employ varying definitions of strategic ability and methodologies and measures to measure it, making it challenging to compare findings across studies and establish a standardized framework for the concept.

Contextual Specificity.   Many studies examining strategic skills focus on specific games, such as the "Dictator Game". However, it remains unclear whether the findings and conclusions derived from these specific contexts can be generalized to different or real-world strategic decision-making scenarios.

Limited External Validity.   Most research on the strategic quotient has been conducted in voluntary samples, which may not fully capture the complexity and nuances of real-life strategic interactions. This raises concerns about the external validity and applicability of findings to real-world situations.

Lack of Longitudinal Studies.   The existing literature primarily relies on cross-sectional data, providing limited insight into the stability, development, and potential changes in strategic quotient over time. Longitudinal studies tracking individuals' strategic quotient across different stages of life or in response to interventions are needed to better understand its dynamics.

Relationship with Other Constructs.   We need to explore the relationship between strategic quotient and other cognitive or social constructs, such as intelligence or social intelligence, the nature of these relationships is still not well understood. Further research is needed to clarify the interplay between strategic quotient and related constructs.

Cultural and Individual Differences.   Principal strategic quotient research has been conducted in Western cultural contexts with WEIRD samples, raising questions about its universality and applicability across diverse cultural backgrounds. In some literature, there is evidence that different countries use different strategic approaches, so exploration of cultural effects is due.

Practical Applications.   Although there is potential for strategic quotient to have practical applications in various domains, such as education, business, and policymaking, the literature has not yet fully explored this opportunity.

Addressing these criticisms, limitations, and gaps in the literature will be crucial for further advancing the understanding of strategic quotient and its implications in various fields.

References

Alaoui, L., Penta, A.: Endogenous depth of reasoning. Rev. Econ. Stud. **83**(4), 1297–1333 (2016). https://doi.org/10.1093/restud/rdv052

Alos-Ferrer, C., Buckenmaier, J.: Cognitive sophistication and deliberation times. SSRN Electron. J. (2018). https://doi.org/10.2139/ssrn.3218928

Athanasiou, E., London, A.J., Zollman, K.J.S.: Dignity and the value of rejecting profitable but insulting offers. Mind **124**(494), 409–448 (2015). https://doi.org/10.1093/mind/fzu186

Bayer, R.C., Renou, L.: Logical abilities and behavior in strategic-form games. SSRN Electron. J. (2012). https://doi.org/10.2139/ssrn.1743515

Bilancini, E., Boncinelli, L., Mattiassi, A.: Assessing actual strategic behavior to construct a measure of strategic ability. Front. Psychol. **9**, 2750 (2019). https://doi.org/10.3389/fpsyg.2018.02750

Camerer, C.F., Ho, T.-H., Chong, J.K.: A psychological approach to strategic thinking in games. Curr. Opin. Behav. Sci. **3**, 157–162 (2015). https://doi.org/10.1016/j.cobeha.2015.04.005

Camerer, C.F., Ho, T.-H., Chong, J.-K.: A cognitive hierarchy model of games. Q. J. Econ. **119**(3), 861–898 (2004). https://doi.org/10.1162/0033553041502225

Capra, C.M.: Mood-driven behavior in strategic interactions. Am. Econ. Rev. **94**(2), 367–372 (2004). https://doi.org/10.1257/0002828041301885

Carpenter, J., Graham, M., Wolf, J.: Cognitive ability and strategic sophistication. Games Econom. Behav. **80**, 115–130 (2013). https://doi.org/10.1016/j.geb.2013.02.012

Chen, Y.-H., Chen, Y.-C., Kuo, W.-J., Kan, K., Yang, C.C., Yen, N.-S.: Strategic motives drive proposers to offer fairly in ultimatum games: an fMRI study. Sci. Rep. **7**(1), 527 (2017). https://doi.org/10.1038/s41598-017-00608-8

Dhir, S., Dhir, S., Samanta, P.: Defining and developing a scale to measure strategic thinking. Foresight **20**(3), 271–288 (2018). https://doi.org/10.1108/FS-10-2017-0059

Gavetti, G.: PERSPECTIVE—toward a behavioral theory of strategy. Organ. Sci. **23**(1), 267–285 (2012). https://doi.org/10.1287/orsc.1110.0644

Gill, D., Knepper, Z., Prowse, V.L., Zhou, J.: How cognitive skills affect strategic behavior: cognitive ability, fluid intelligence and judgment. SSRN Elect. J. (2023). https://doi.org/10.2139/ssrn.4465561

Gill, D., Prowse, V.: Cognitive ability, character skills, and learning to play equilibrium: a level-k analysis. J. Polit. Econ. **124**(6), 1619–1676 (2016). https://doi.org/10.1086/688849

Golman, R., Bhatia, S., Kane, P.B.: The dual accumulator model of strategic deliberation and decision making. Psychol. Rev. **127**(4), 477–504 (2020). https://doi.org/10.1037/rev0000176

Guala, F., Mittone, L.: Paradigmatic experiments: the dictator game. J. Socio-Econ. **39**(5), 578–584 (2010). https://doi.org/10.1016/j.socec.2009.05.007

Deary, I.J.: Intelligence. Annu. Rev. Psychol. **63**(1), 453–482 (2012). https://doi.org/10.1146/annurev-psych-120710-100353

Jelenc, L., Swiercz, P.M.: Strategic thinking capability: conceptualization and measurement. SSRN Electron. J. (2011). https://doi.org/10.2139/ssrn.2747927

Kahneman, D.: Maps of bounded rationality: psychology for behavioral economics. Am. Econ. Rev. **93**(5), 1449–1475 (2003). https://doi.org/10.1257/000282803322655392

Kvam, P.D., Marley, A.A.J., Heathcote, A.: A unified theory of discrete and continuous responding. Psychol. Rev. **130**, 368 (2022)

Otero, I., Salgado, J.F., Moscoso, S.: Cognitive reflection, cognitive intelligence, and cognitive abilities: A meta-analysis. Intelligence **90**, 101614 (2022). https://doi.org/10.1016/j.intell.2021.101614

Parales-Quenza, C.J.: Astuteness, trust, and social intelligence. J. Theory Soc. Behav. **36**(1), 39–56 (2006). https://doi.org/10.1111/j.1468-5914.2006.00295.x

Stahl, D.O., Wilson, P.W.: On players' models of other players: theory and experimental evidence. Games Econom. Behav. **10**(1), 218–254 (1995). https://doi.org/10.1006/game.1995.1031

Straub, P.G., Murnighan, J.K.: An experimental investigation of ultimatum games: information, fairness, expectations, and lowest acceptable offers. J. Econ. Behav. Organ. **27**(3), 345–364 (1995). https://doi.org/10.1016/0167-2681(94)00072-M

Suleiman, R.: Economic harmony—a rational theory of fairness and cooperation in strategic interactions. Games **13**(3), 34 (2022). https://doi.org/10.3390/g13030034

Tisserand, J.-C., Cochard, F., Gallo, J.L.: Altruistic or strategic considerations: a meta-analysis on the ultimatum and dictator games ∗ (2015)

Van Dijk, E., Vermunt, R.: Strategy and fairness in social decision making: sometimes it pays to be powerless. J. Exp. Soc. Psychol. **36**(1), 1–25 (2000). https://doi.org/10.1006/jesp.1999.1392

von Neumann, J., Morgenstern, O.: Theory of Games and Economic Behavior (60th Anniversary Commemorative Edition): Princeton University Press (2007). https://doi.org/10.1515/9781400829460

Wellman, H.M., Cross, D., Watson, J.: Meta-analysis of theory-of-mind development: the truth about false belief. Child Dev. **72**(3), 655–684 (2001). https://doi.org/10.1111/1467-8624.00304

Weyhrauch, W.S.: A mindset for strategic thinking: Developing a concept and measure (2016)

Weyhrauch, W.S., Culbertson, S.S.: A mindset for strategic thinking: conceptual synthesis of the capacity for strategic insight. Acad. Manag. Proc. **2014**(1), 12988 (2014). https://doi.org/10.5465/ambpp.2014.12988abstract

Xiao, E., Houser, D.: Emotion expression in human punishment behavior. Proc. Natl. Acad. Sci. **102**(20), 7398–7401 (2005). https://doi.org/10.1073/pnas.0502399102

Exploring the Effectiveness of Game-Based Learning in Teaching the 2030 Agenda to Middle School Students

Pietro Cappelli[1]([⊠]), Christian Tarchi[2], and Leonardo Boncinelli[3]

[1] Psychological Sciences and Techniques, Majoring in Developmental Psychology,
University of Florence, Florence, Italy
pietro.cappelli@unifi.it

[2] Developmental and Educational Psychology, Department of Education, Languages,
Interculture, Literatures and Psychology, University of Florence, Florence, Italy
christian.tarchi@unifi.it

[3] Economic Policy Department of Economics and Business,
University of Florence, Florence, Italy
Leonardo.boncinelli@unifi.it

Abstract. This experimental research aimed to investigate the use of a board game for improving argumentation and counter-argumentation skills related to the 2030 Agenda in middle school students. The study involved two different classroom conditions, one where a board game was used, and another where a frontal lesson was held using slides. Pre-test and post-test questionnaires were administered to investigate the students' interest and knowledge of the 2030 Agenda before and after the experience. Each student was then asked to write an argumentative essay, about their favorite topic of the 2030 Agenda, illustrating the reasons why it was important for them.

The results showed that the board game condition led to higher interest and better learning outcomes than the frontal lesson condition, but both conditions showed significant improvement in interest and knowledge of the 2030 Agenda. This highlights the importance of developing argumentative and counter-argumentative skills in middle school students and the potential of games as practical tools to make learning more engaging and effective.

The findings also suggest that there should be a synergy between traditional teaching approaches and innovative approaches such as games to improve learning outcomes. Future research could explore the long-term effects of such interventions and the potential of games for improving other soft skills in students. Overall, this study contributes to the growing literature on the effectiveness of games for education and highlights the importance of incorporating innovative approaches in education to improve learning outcomes.

Keywords: Gamification · argumentation and counter-argumentation skills · 2030 Agenda

M. Clayton et al. (Eds.): INTETAIN 2023, LNICST 560, pp. 20–30, 2024.
https://doi.org/10.1007/978-3-031-55722-4_2

1 Introduction

In recent years, gamification has become an increasingly popular approach to learning, particularly in educational contexts. Gamification refers to the use of game design elements and principles in non-game contexts, such as education, to motivate and engage learners. In particular, gamification has been shown to be effective in enhancing learning outcomes by improving students' motivation, engagement, and knowledge retention.

According to Deterding et al. (2011), gamification refers to the use of game design elements, such as points, levels, and rewards, in non-game contexts, to motivate and engage learners. Gamification has also emerged as an innovative and engaging approach to improve learning outcomes in various educational settings.

The development of argumentation and counter-argumentation skills has been identified as a critical aspect of academic success and life-long learning (Kuhn and Udell 2003). These skills enable individuals to effectively communicate their ideas, evaluate evidence, and engage in critical thinking Dawson and Venville 2010). Several studies have explored the effectiveness of argumentation-based approaches in enhancing students' critical thinking and reasoning skills (Bromme et al. 2011; Hmelo-Silver et al. 2007; Osborne and Patterson 2011).

Gamification and argumentation-based approaches share a common goal of enhancing students' engagement and motivation in the learning process. By integrating gamification elements into argumentation-based activities, educators can create an engaging and challenging learning environment that fosters the development of argumentation and counter argumentation skills. According to Koivisto and Hamari (2019), gamification can enhance students' motivation and engagement in learning, leading to improved learning outcomes. Similarly, Dawson and Venville (2010) suggested that argumentation-based approaches can promote students' engagement and participation in the learning process.

Several studies have investigated the potential of gamification in improving argumentation and counter argumentation skills in various educational settings. For instance, Huang et al. (2017) found that a gamified argumentation-based learning approach improved students' argumentation and critical thinking skills in a college-level course. Similarly, Borges et al. (2018) reported that a gamified online discussion platform enhanced students' argumentation and collaborative skills in a university-level course. These findings suggest that gamification can be an effective tool for enhancing argumentation and counter argumentation skills in higher education.

However, few studies have explored the potential of gamification in improving argumentation and counter argumentation skills, or soft skills generally, in middle school students. Lee et al. (2019) underline how gamification has the potential to support middle school students' engagement, motivation, and learning outcomes, emphasizing the potential of gamification as a tool for improving science education in middle school, while Chen et al (2019) investigated the effects of a gamified argumentation approach on middle school students' argumentation performance and cognitive load., using a gamified argumentation system called Game-based Argumentation Instruction (GAI) and compared its effectiveness with a non-gamified argumentation approach. Results showed that students in the experimental group had significantly better argumentation performance and lower cognitive load than those in the control group, proving that the gamified approach is an effective way to enhance middle school students' argumentation skills.

Given the importance of developing soft skills, such as argumentation and counter argumentation skills, in middle school students, it is critical to investigate the potential of gamification in enhancing these skills in this age group. The present study aims to fill this gap by investigating the effectiveness of a board game on improving argumentation and counter argumentation skills in middle school students.

By developing argumentative and counter-argumentative skills, middle school students can better understand the complexities of the world around them, communicate their ideas effectively, help to think critically, reason logically, and engage in productive discourse with others (Kuhn and Udell 2003, p. 1245). These skills are essential for success both academically and professionally, making it crucial to incorporate them into middle school education. Teaching argumentation skills to middle school students is important because it can help them to understand complex issues, think critically about the world around them, and communicate their ideas effectively to others (Dawson and Venville 2010, p. 464).

Soft skills are essential for success in academic, personal, and professional pursuits, and it is important to foster their development in children from a young age. In recent years, gamification has emerged as a practical tool to interest children in learning while promoting the development of important skills such as problem-solving, critical thinking, and collaboration. However, it is important to note that gamification should not replace traditional lessons completely. Instead, there should be a synergy between the two approaches, with gamification being used as a supplement to traditional teaching methods. By combining these two approaches, students can benefit from the engaging and interactive nature of games while also receiving the foundational knowledge and skills necessary for academic success. In this study, we sought to explore the potential benefits of incorporating gamification into traditional lessons and the importance of balancing the two approaches to achieve optimal learning outcomes for middle school students.

One of the key areas where gamification has been applied is in the context of sustainable development education. Sustainable development education is a critical area of education, particularly given the current global environmental challenges. The United Nations has recognized this by adopting the 2030 Agenda for Sustainable Development, which sets out a comprehensive framework for global sustainable development. The 2030 Agenda includes 17 Sustainable Development Goals (SDGs), which are aimed at ending poverty, protecting the planet, and promoting prosperity for all.

Given the complexity of the SDGs and the need for broad-based public engagement in their implementation, it is essential to develop innovative and effective educational approaches to promote awareness and understanding of the SDGs. One promising approach is gamification, which can help to engage and motivate learners, and promote the development of important skills such as critical thinking, problem-solving, and collaboration.

Therefore, the present study aims to investigate the effectiveness of a gamified app-roach for teaching the 2030 Agenda to middle school students. Specifically, the study will focus on the use of a board game designed to improve argumentation and counter-argumentation skills related to the 2030 Agenda. The study will compare the effec-tiveness of the board game approach with a more traditional frontal lesson approach. By doing so, the study will provide valuable insights into the potential of gamification as an effective educational tool for the development of soft skills, such as argumenta-tive and counter-argumentative skills, and for a sustainable development education, and contribute to the broader literature on gamification in education.

2 Method

2.1 The Game

The board game used in this study was inspired by "Summit 2030" (Ligabue et al. 2016) but was modified to place a greater emphasis on debate and argumentation skills. In the modified game, participants were required to make and defend their arguments while also responding to opposing viewpoints. The game consisted of several rounds of debate on different aspects of the 2030 Agenda, and the winner of each round was determined based on their ability to make and defend their arguments effectively. By using this modified game, the study aimed to foster the development of argumentation skills and to promote interest in the 2030 Agenda among middle school students.

2.2 Participants

The study involved 44 middle school students, with 22 students in each class. All students were from the same school and were in the same grade: second grade of middle school.

2.3 Design

A pre-test/post-test control group design was used to evaluate the effectiveness of a board game on the development of argumentative and counter-argumentative skills, as well as on the students' interest in the 2030 Agenda.

2.4 Measures

Two different types of measures were used: a multiple-choice test to assess the students' prior knowledge and interest in the 2030 Agenda, and an argumentative essay assignment to evaluate their argumentative and counter-argumentative skills. The multiple-choice test consisted of 8 questions, with 4 questions related to prior knowledge and 4 questions related to interest in the 2030 Agenda. The essay assignment asked students to write about their favorite topic from the 2030 Agenda and provide a justification for why it was an important point of the Agenda for them.

2.5 Interventions

The study involved two interventions: a board game and a frontal lesson. The board game intervention was designed to promote the development of argumentative and counter-argumentative skills, as well as to increase students' interest in the 2030 Agenda. The frontal lesson intervention served as a control condition. Each intervention lasted one hour, and both were conducted in the same classroom environment.

2.6 Procedure

The study was conducted in two phases. In the first phase, both groups completed a pretest consisting of the multiple-choice test and the essay assignment. After the pretest, one group played the board game while the other group received the frontal lesson, after that they both completed a posttest consisting of the same multiple-choice test. In the second phase, both groups did the essay assignment in an hour of time. The essay assignment was conducted approximately one week after the first part of the experiment, and was rated by giving a grade between five and nine.

2.7 Data Analysis

The data collected from the pre-test and post-test were analyzed using descriptive statistics and t-tests to determine if there were significant differences between the experimental and control groups in terms of learning outcomes and interest in the 2030 Agenda. The argumentative themes were also analyzed using descriptive statistics and independent-samples t-tests to determine if there were significant differences in argumentation and counter-argumentation skills between the experimental and control groups.

3 Results

Based on the results it can be concluded that the use of a board game can be an effective tool for improving argumentation and counter-argumentation skills in middle school students. This conclusion stems from the observation that the treatment class obtained better grades than the control class with regard to the essay assignment (Mean Contr. $6.667 <$ Mean Treatm. 7.221). We observe that both classrooms showed high levels of interest and good learning outcomes, suggesting that even a slightly implemented frontal lesson, in this case seen with the use of slides in the control classroom, can have a positive impact. Regarding the t-test analysis we note that there are no particularly significant differences between the two groups, but this can be traced back to the small number of the sample, 19 students in one class and 21 in the other. Since the distributions are not normal (see Shapiro-Wilk test) I also did the Whitney-Mann test.

Overall, these findings suggest that incorporating gamification and argumentative writing tasks into classroom activities can be an effective approach to enhance soft skills of middle school students (Figs. 1, 2 and 3).

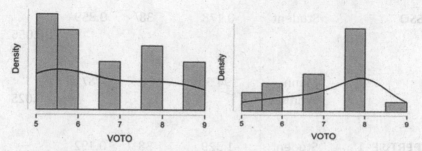

Fig. 1. Distribution of votes to the argumentative text. On the left the control group, on the right that of the intervention group.

	EXPERTISE_1		TALK		ABOUT		LEARNING INTEREST		EXPERTISE_1.1		LIKE		INTEREST		VOTE	
	CONTROL	TREATMENT	CONTROL	TREATMENT	CONTROL	TREATMENT	CONTROL	TREATMENT	CONTROL	TREATMENT	CONTROL	TREATMENT	CONTROL	TREATMENT	CONTROL	TREATMENT
Valid	21	19	21	19	19	17	17	18	18	18	17	18	21	19
Missing	0	0	0	0	2	2	4	1	3	1	4	1	0	0
Mean	2.333	2.632	1.524	1.526	3.684	3.588	3.000	2.944	3.833	3.722	2.941	2.944	6.667	7.211
Median	2.000	3.000	1.000	1.000	4.000	4.000	3.000	3.000	4.000	4.000	3.000	3.000	6.000	8.000
Mode	3.000	3.000	1.000	1.000	4.000	4.000	3.000	3.000	4.000	4.000	3.000	3.000	5.000	8.000
Std. Deviation	0.730	0.684	0.928	0.772	0.820	0.712	0.791	0.639	0.924	1.127	1.088	0.802	1.461	1.134
Shapiro-Wilk	0.774	0.593	0.625	0.684	0.874	0.837	0.813	0.646	0.853	0.729	0.922	0.840	0.874	0.858
P-value of Shapiro-Wilk	$<.001$	$<.001$	$<.001$	$<.001$	0.017	0.007	0.003	$<.001$	0.009	$<.001$	0.160	0.006	0.012	0.009
Minimum	1.000	1.000	1.000	1.000	2.000	2.000	1.000	1.000	2.000	1.000	1.000	1.000	5.000	5.000
Maximum	3.000	3.000	4.000	3.000	5.000	5.000	4.000	4.000	5.000	5.000	5.000	4.000	9.000	9.000

Fig. 2. Descriptive Statistics

Independent Samples T-Test					
	Test	Statistic	df	p	Effect Size
SESSO	Student	-0.178	38	0.859	-0.056
	Mann-Whitney	194.500		0.871	-0.025
EXPERTISE_1	Student	-1.329	38	0.192	-0.421
	Mann-Whitney	151.000		0.136	-0.243
TALK	Student	-0.009	38	0.993	-0.003
	Mann-Whitney	189.500		0.756	-0.050
LEARNING	Student	0.373	34	0.712	0.124
	Mann-Whitney	170.000		0.783	0.053
EXPERTISE_1.1	Student	0.229	33	0.820	0.078
	Mann-Whitney	161.500		0.747	0.056

Fig. 3. Independent Samples T-Test

LIKE	Student	0.323	34	0.748	0.108
	Mann-Whitney	164.500		0.944	0.015
INTEREST	Student	-0.010	33	0.992	-0.003
	Mann-Whitney	153.500		1.000	0.003
VOTO	Student	-1.305	38	0.200	-0.413
	Mann-Whitney	154.000		0.210	-0.228
Q_1	Student	-0.092	37	0.927	-0.029
	Mann-Whitney	187.500		0.941	-0.013
Q_2	Student	-0.036	37	0.971	-0.012
	Mann-Whitney	189.500		1.000	-0.003
Q_3	Student	-1.504	37	0.141	-0.482

Fig. 3. (*continued*)

	Mann-Whitney	159.500			0.146	-0.161
Q_4	Student	NaN	a			
	Mann-Whitney	NaN	a			
Q_1.1	Student	-0.644	34		0.524	-0.215
	Mann-Whitney	151.000			0.659	-0.068
Q_2.1	Student	0.000	36		1.000	0.000
	Mann-Whitney	180.500			1.000	0.000
Q_3.1	Student	-0.541	35		0.592	-0.178
	Mann-Whitney	162.500			0.607	-0.050
Q_4.1	Student	NaN	b			
	Mann-Whitney	NaN	b			

Note. For the Student t-test, effect size is given by Cohen's d. For the Mann-Whitney test, effect size is given by the rank biserial correlation.

[a] The variance in Q_4 is equal to 0 after grouping on INF_CRON

[b] The variance in Q_4.1 is equal to 0 after grouping on INF_CRON

Fig. 3. (*continued*)

4 Discussion

This article discusses the use of gamification as an approach to learning, specifically in the context of sustainable development education, highlights the importance of developing effective educational approaches to promote awareness and understanding of the Sustainable Development Goals (SDGs) and for incentivising and enhancing argumentation and counter-argumentation skills. Gamification could be a promising approach to engaging and motivating learners and developing important skills such as critical thinking, problem-solving, and collaboration.

The use of game design elements and principles in non-game contexts has been shown to be effective in enhancing learning outcomes, including motivation, engagement, and knowledge retention. Additionally, the focus on developing important skills such as critical thinking, problem-solving, and collaboration is essential for success both academically and professionally, making it crucial to incorporate these skills into education.

One of the key strengths of gamification is its ability to engage and motivate learners, which is essential for promoting knowledge retention and improving learning outcomes. By incorporating game design elements such as points, levels, and rewards, gamification can create a more interactive and enjoyable learning experience that encourages active participation and fosters a sense of achievement.

Another important benefit of gamification is the possibility to provide students with opportunities to engage in productive discourse with others, and can help to develop argumentation and counter-argumentation skills that are essential for success both academically and professionally.

However, it is also important to note that gamification is not a one-size-fits-all solution and its effectiveness may depend on a range of factors such as the context of the learning environment, the age and developmental level of the learners, and the design and implementation of the gamified elements. Therefore, it is essential to conduct rigorous research to evaluate the effectiveness of gamification in different educational contexts and to develop evidence-based guidelines for its use.

The results of this study suggest that the use of a gamified approach, specifically a board game designed to improve argumentation and counter-argumentation skills, may be an effective educational tool for teaching the 2030 Agenda to middle school students. It's important to note that this study has a small sample size and is not an absolute test of the effectiveness. Rather, it serves as a basis for future work that can build upon these findings and refine the approach. In particular, future research could investigate the use of the gamified approach across multiple schools and with larger sample sizes, to determine whether the positive effects observed in this study are replicable. Additionally, it would be valuable to explore how the board game approach could be further developed and improved, potentially incorporating additional game design elements or adjusting the rules to better suit the learning objectives and preferences of middle school students.

Overall, the use of gamification in sustainable development education shows promise as an innovative and engaging approach to improving learning outcomes, particularly with respect to motivation, engagement, and the development of important skills such as critical thinking and problem-solving, or argumentation and counter-argumentation skills like in this study. More research is needed to fully understand the potential of this approach, and to develop and refine effective gamified educational tools that can support the achievement of the Sustainable Development Goals.

In conclusion, this study has the potential to contribute to the broader literature on gamification in education and to provide valuable insights into the effectiveness of gamification as an educational tool for sustainable development education. By developing innovative and effective educational approaches to promote awareness and understanding of the Sustainable Development Goals, we can help to create a more sustainable and just future for all.

References

Borges, L.M., Fernandes, C.M., Borges, M.C.: Gamified online discussion platform: Impact on argumentation and collaboration skills. Interact. Learn. Environ. **26**(5), 644–657 (2018)

Borges, B.H., Moreira, R.S., Junior, M.V., Souza, A.C.: Gamification in education: a systematic mapping study. J. Educ. Technol. Soc. **21**(3), 1–14 (2018)

Bromme, R., Hesse, F.W., Spada, H.: Barriers and biases in computer-mediated knowledge communication—and how they may be overcome. Appl. Cogn. Psychol. **25**(5), 763–773 (2011)

Chen, Y.-J., Chen, C.-M., Liu, Y.-H.: Effects of a gamified argumentation approach on middle school students' argumentation performance and cognitive load. J. Educ. Comput. Res. **56**(3), 393–417 (2019)

Dawson, V.M., Venville, G.J.: Introducing high school chemistry students to the practice of argumentation. Res. Sci. Educ. **40**(5), 611–634 (2010)

Dawson, V., Venville, G.: Teaching strategies for developing students' argumentation skills about socioscientific issues in high school genetics. Res. Sci. Educ. **40**(2), 133–148 (2010)

Deterding, S., Dixon, D., Khaled, R., Nacke, L.: From game design elements to gamefulness: defining gamification. In: Proceedings of the 15th International Academic MindTrek Conference: Envisioning Future Media Environments, pp. 9–15 (2011)

Deterding, S., Khaled, R., Nacke, L.E., Dixon, D.: Gamification: toward a definition. In: CHI 2011 Gamification Workshop Proceedings, pp. 1–4 (2011)

Hmelo-Silver, C.E., Marathe, S., Liu, L.: Fish swim, rocks sit, and lungs breathe: expert-novice understanding of complex systems. J. Learn. Sci. **16**(3), 307–331 (2007)

Huang, Y.M., Huang, T.C., Huang, Y.M., Lin, Y.T.: A gamification-based approach to improving college students' argumentation skills. Interact. Learn. Environ. **25**(6), 772–785 (2017)

Huang, W.H., Soman, D., Hsieh, Y.C.: A meta-analysis of the effect of gamification on student learning. J. Educ. Psychol. **109**(8), 1116–1134 (2017)

Koivisto, J., Hamari, J.: The rise of motivational information systems: a review of gamification research. Int. J. Inf. Manage. **45**, 191–210 (2019)

Kuhn, D., Udell, W.: The development of argument skills. Child Dev. **74**(5), 1245–1260 (2003)

Lee, H.-S., Linn, M.C.: The design of a gamified inquiry curriculum to support middle school students' argumentation. J. Educ. Comput. Res. **56**(3), 418–442 (2019)

Ligabue, A., Gandolfi, G., Bisanti, M.: Summit 2030: a board game to build the sustainable city of the future. In: Paracchini, P., Mazzola, P., Bruzzone, R., (Eds.) Advances in Intelligent Systems and Computing: Engineering Applications of Neural Networks, pp. 463–471. Springer International Publishing, Cham (2016). https://doi.org/10.1007/978-3-319-42118-6_47

Osborne, J., Patterson, A.: Scientific argument and explanation: a necessary distinction? Sci. Educ. **95**(4), 627–638 (2011)

Introducing a Videogame Project in a Mobile Software Development Academic Course

Fabrizio Balducci(✉) and Paolo Buono

Computer Science Department, University of Bari 'A. Moro',
via E. Orabona 4, 70125 Bari, Italy
{fabrizio.balducci,paolo.buono}@uniba.it

Abstract. In the 2020–2021 academic year, the 'videogame design' topic has been introduced in the 'Mobile Software Development' bachelor degree course. Consequently, it has been proposed to students a related project theme in addition to apps oriented towards productivity and mobile services. The *ArkanApp* project concerned the re-design and the introduction of specific features into an *Arkanoid* game clone; the other proposed apps were related to safe meeting organization, documents and project data management and a free-theme app. The exploration of data collected during the main part of the academic year related to student preferences and projects delivery, highlighted how leaving the choice about the theme, as well as the introduction of the videogame one, involved the majority of students to finish the project before the starting of the new course edition. Moreover, it also emerged that *ArkanApp* featured the highest female participation.

Keywords: videogame · education · mobile software

1 Introduction

This paper describes a case study related to the *Mobile Software Development* academic course held in the Computer Science (CS) dept. of the University of Bari 'A. Moro' (Italy). For the final exam assessment, this course requires the delivery of a practical project to be carried out in group and to be discussed in an oral presentation after a written test related to lecture contents. Each group of students has to design and develop an Android mobile app chosen in a pool of different themes and requirements, according to the explained topics.

In the 2020–2021 academic year, the *Mobile Software Development* lectures started in September 2020 and ended in December 2020 featuring 9 exam sessions allocated from January 2021 to May 2022. As the topic regarding videogame design and development was introduced, one of the proposed project theme consisted in a variant of the the 80's arcade game *Arkanoid*[1] where students were

---

[1] Arkanoid, https://en.wikipedia.org/wiki/Arkanoid, last visit: 2022-05-10.

© ICST Institute for Computer Sciences, Social Informatics and Telecommunications Engineering 2024
Published by Springer Nature Switzerland AG 2024. All Rights Reserved
M. Clayton et al. (Eds.): INTETAIN 2023, LNICST 560, pp. 31–39, 2024.
https://doi.org/10.1007/978-3-031-55722-4_3

asked to re-design and modify some aspects of the game introducing gameplay variations and interactive features; the other themes were 1) Covid-19 safe meeting organization; 2) school document and project management; 3) a free-theme app proposed by a group and approved by the teacher.

To depict how a specific theme like 'videogames' influences academic student preferences, it was decided to collect data about their work organization and timing for deliver the app within the main exam sessions of the academic year, before lectures of the new course edition. The description of a real use case in a CS academic course aims to provide advices on project themes to propose to students, focusing on the introduction of videogames production and design topics with the best mode to propose it to students.

Related works regarding videogame topics in educational institutions are reported in Sect. 2. Section 3 illustrates the proposed project themes while comparisons and considerations coming from student data are depicted in Sect. 4. Conclusions and future work are illustrated in Sect. 5.

2 Related Work

Kurkovsky et al. [7,8] inquire the relationships between mobile games and student interest in CS, considering the game development as a motivational and learning context and supporting such ideas through practical case studies while Boudreaux et al. [5] target handled platforms as the *Game Boy Advance* exposing students to programming environments. The adoption of the videogame topic in American computer science courses is faced in Yue and Shan [16] while Rankin et al. [10] analyzed the effect of game design on student attitudes in attaining a CS degree. In Rodrigues et al. [12] are depicted guidelines adopted in 2010 for the first game development bachelor degree in Portugal, pointing out the importance of project themes that promote entrepreneurship and provide practical professional experiences.

In their work, Wood and Costello [15] perform two analyses on setting, mood and aesthetic data exploiting outcomes coming from five-years of a game design course where student groups developed videogames at school, highlighting their creativity and involvement. It is know that videogames can elicit satisfaction and emotions not only in those who create them but also in people who play such creations [2,3]. Almeida et al. [1] introduce a pilot experiment about computer games creation by primary school students while Doran et al. [6] present a CS course exploiting the *Game Maker* framework for middle school ones. Moreover, the relationship between technology and female students through videogame development is faced in [4] where game design within the *Coding4Girls* project is considered as a method to addresses equal opportunities in CS professions regardless gender or background.

Aspects relating to an industry-academia alliance for game development are in [14] and in [9] in which is described an educational curriculum created by the International Game Developers Association (IDGA); in the work of Sato et al. [13] there is the proposition of the TRIAD education model which sees together contributions from academy and industry. Finally, Restrepo and

Figueroa [11] propose a videogame development curriculum in Colombia with a postgraduate program that aims to respond industry needs and reach a wide audience through a blended learning model.

3   Project Themes

Mobile Software Development is a fundamental course (86 lecture hours) held in the third year at the first semester of the *Computer Science and Software Development Technologies* Bachelor Degree. The main topics covered in this course are the Android Studio IDE, the Android framework with the Operating System architecture, app components, sensors and connectivity managements, graphic features, data persistence and Material Design guidelines for interaction and User eXperience. In the 2020–2021 academic year the *Transmedia products* and *Videogame design and development* topics, specifically declined for the mobile environment, have been added.

The third year is the final one of the bachelor degree and students had already faced courses like *Database Design, Computer Networks, Software Engineering, Object-Oriented Programming, Operating Systems and Computer Organization*; in this way they have all the necessary knowledge to develop a complete app exploiting the Android Studio IDE. The exam assessment consists of: a) written test about the theoretic part of the course, accessed after the delivery of a complete app (created in a group ranging from 3 to 4 members), and b) oral presentation, in which each student explains the part of the project he dealt with, answering any question and doubt of the teacher.

In the 2020–2021 the following themes have been proposed:

– *ArkanApp*: a variant of the japanese *Arkanoid* (1986) videogame created by Taito[2]. Since the Android documentation and repositories contains many exercises and working examples, to balance the difficulty of those who start from scratch with this topic a game template has been provided through a github project[3].

It must be noticed that it only contains a fixed screen with four brick rows and a paddle that moves through the accelerometer, very far from what is required for the exam delivery that is: 1) a navigation structure with panels (splash-screen, menus, options section, ..); 2) at least one multiplayer mode (asynchronous, cooperative, massive, local, ..); 3) game editor that allows to save and load the creations; 4) at least one gameplay variant (behaviours, events, ...) and almost a power-up; 5) at least one alternative control system (touch, slider, virtual gamepad, ..); 6) difficulty modes (in addition to the default one related to the ball speed); 7) leaderboard that allows sharing scores with external services through connectivity (Bluetooth, WiFi, Internet); 8) audio and music features (absent in the template); 9) new graphics (open source collections allowed).

---

[2] Taito corporation, https://www.taito.co.jp/en/, last visit: 2022-05-10.

[3] Arkanoid github, https://github.com/Ludovit-Laca/Arkanoid-android-game, last visit: 2022-05-10.

- *ManagerApp*: a social network-like app that allows to organize, consult and promote student projects, sharing heterogeneous materials (also by their teachers) that accumulates year after year and that can be managed at different levels. The app must allow the following: 1) advanced user profiles management (guest, teacher, developer, group, ..) each with specific functions (registration, projects creation, upload or download materials, ..); 2) groups management (by people, exams, grades, ..); 3) permissions management; 4) projects evaluations and reviews; 5) search modes; 6) sharing of information with personalized communications and posts (screenshots, text, ..) through external services and apps.
- *ContagionApp*: similar to the tracking apps used by governs in the COVID-19 pandemic outbreak, it exploits inter-personal dynamics to provide and verify health statuses and allow to securely organize meetings and events using a dynamic health score. The app must offer the following: 1) manage user profiles (single person or a group); 2) provide and verify the health status i.e. a dynamic score assigned by the system, depending on events and meetings attended and on official communications (like a Covid-19 test online notification); 3) meetings management where participants can be accepted as single or group by an organizer, depending on the suggestion provided by the app and related to a 'risk score'; 4)communication between devices through connectivity to a) check the user status (for privacy the information are not visible to other people) and b) real-time communication about risky encounters.
- *FreeChoiceApp*: a group can propose its own idea taking into account the originality, the relevance and its feasibility, following the requirements and instructions given by the teacher; if not well-motivated the proposal can be rejected or modified.

Regardless of the chosen project all groups must meet specific delivery requirements, in fact the app must be developed through the Android Studio IDE and no external tools or frameworks are allowed; it is possible to call services like server-side databases, Google Play and localization services as long as they are transparently documented. The aim is to replicate the business pipeline of a company that has to design, develop, test and promote a software product

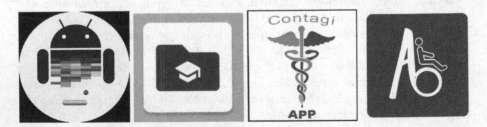

Fig. 1. Examples of app icons delivered for the evaluation of ArkanApp, ManagerApp, ContagionApp and FreeChoiceApp projects.

Fig. 2. Examples of material for the project evaluation: flyers with advertising taglines for ArkanApp, ManagerApp, ContagionApp and FreeChoiceApp.

into an app store and so, the materials required for the exam assessment aim to simulate the *Play Store* publication:

- Android Studio project (code, resources, libraries, data, external services) where the code must be self-explanatory, commented and organized in an intuitive and orderly way;
- the design document for the app *Product Icon* (Fig. 1), following the Material Design guidelines and explaining motivation, colors, approach, meaning and inspirations also through hand-drawing and sketches;
- user manual that describes the app features;
- absent or limited connectivity management, providing appropriate feedback and alternatives;
- at least two type of users (guest, paying, ...);
- multilingual features;
- a flyer featuring advertising taglines (Fig. 2) that would be distributed in conventions, social events or a website;
- screenshots showing peculiar aspects of the app;
- short video (2 to 4 min) about significant interactive session of the app, optionally with editing, graphic and sound effects (trailer);
- signed release APK file.

In Fig. 3 there are screenshots coming from some of the projects delivered by the groups, featuring two examples for each of the four themes: starting from the top-left there are ArkanApp and ManagerApp images, followed in the bottom row by ContagionApp and FreeChoiceApp respectively. From such screens emerges how students introduced peculiar features regarding user interface, graphics, visual organization, style and colors, for example the ArkanApp images show a boss fight and a space environment while the ContagionApp images features symbols related to Covid-19 and medical recommendations.

Fig. 3. Screenshots from delivered projects: by the top-left there are two images for each ArkanApp, ManagerApp, ContagionApp and FreeChoiceApp.

4   Projects Exploration

At May 2022 the academic year related to the 2020–2021 course can be considered concluded, in fact the four months of lectures and laboratory activities started in September 2020 have been followed by 9 exam sessions scheduled as: three between January and February 2021, one at May and July 2021, two in September 2021, one at November 2021 and between April an May 2022.

In Table 1 are collected information regarding the 2020–2021 assigned projects but where the 'Delivered Projects' and 'Involved Students' metrics are specific for those between January and July 2021; this time interval in fact, represents half of the time period to complete the exam and contains 5 of the total exam sessions; since in September lectures for the new academic year will start again, this interval can be considered as the reference one for the evaluation of

Table 1. Data about the projects of the main five 2020–2021 exam sessions ('F' means Female gender). All data have been collected at July 2021.

	ArkanApp	ManagerApp	ContagionApp	FreeChoiceApp
Scheduled Groups	17	12	5	6
Scheduled Students	62 (F:9)	42 (F:7)	17 (F:1)	22 (F:3)
Delivered Projects	9 (52.9%)	6 (50%)	2 (40%)	5 (83.3%)
Involved Students	37 (59.7%, F:7)	20 (47.6%, F:3)	8 (47%, F:0)	19 (86.4%, F:2)

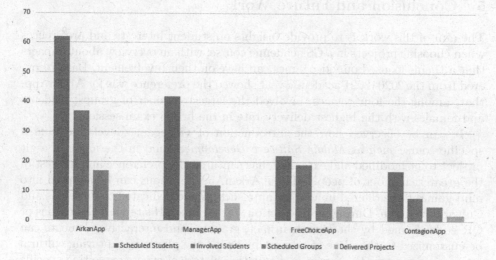

Fig. 4. Comparison of the four project themes where the 'Delivered Projects and 'Involved Students' refer to the main 5 exam sessions (January 2021-July 2021).

the delivery time goodness. It is important to underline that all the Scheduled Groups delivered their projects over time (there were no dropouts).

Scheduled Groups are considered those who sent the registration email indicating the chosen project and the participants list. It can be noticed that there have been 40 scheduled groups (for a total of 143 involved students) and their main preference (17 groups) was ArkanApp i.e. the project themes related to videogames; the others in fact were chosen from a number of groups less than or equal to 2/3 of the preferred one.

Considering the *Scheduled Students*, the majority (62) worked on ArkanApp and this project turns out to be the favorite by female members, confirming that nowadays the interest in videogames no longer knows gender limits. Unfortunately, it can be noticed that the female component is very limited (14%) within the overall course.

The *Delivered Projects* (i.e. scheduled, delivered and evaluated by July 2021) were 22 of which FreeChoiceApp and ArkanApp achieved the highest percentage in relation to their scheduled groups (83.33% and 52.94%) while, in absolute numbers, the latter represents the greatest delivery volume (9 vs. 5 groups). About the *Involved Students* in the Delivered Projects at July 2021, it is confirmed what seen before with the majority of students belonging to the videogame project (37 vs. 20 of ManagerApp vs. 19 of FreeChoiceApp).

In Fig. 4 are compared the data depicted in Table 1. It can be observed how ArkanApp presents the highest values for the four metrics i.e. related to groups who have chosen and delivered this project and to the related enrolled people.

5   Conclusion and Future Work

The aim of this work is to provide insights on student interests and preferences when choosing projects in a CS academic course, with an overview about impacts that a theme focused on videogames can have on their involvement. Data recovered from the 2020–2021 academic year showed the preference was for ArkanApp, that, among the four themes, involved the largest number of groups, students and females with the highest delivery rate in the first 5 exam sessions.

It can be observed how the introduction of videogame development in a specific course such as *Mobile Software Development* and in the mode of a git project to be modified and extended, has captured the preference and interest of the greatest number of people. These ArkanApp iterations can be adapted into mini-games to be offered in a larger app, such as one dedicated to museums and Cultural Heritage. During an interaction started in a CH site via IoT beacons or QR codes framed by the visitor, in fact, graphics and interactive elements can be customized to the place of interest involving the player in capturing cultural artifacts moving on the screen or simulating historical events exploiting specific tools (arrows, cannons, ships, ropes, ..) instead of the actual bouncing ball.

Finally, future work will exploit the delivered materials to carry out different assessments, providing qualitative explorations and evaluation like the comparison of features and improvements introduced by the groups on the same videogame template; it will help to understand how much the creation of interactive software brings out CS students' creativity.

Acknowledgments. F. Balducci thanks the students of the 2020–2021 'Mobile Software Development' course and acknowledges the support by the REsearch For INnovation (REFIN) grant, CUP:H94I20000410008 cod.F517D521 POR Puglia FESR FSE 2014-2020 "Gestione di oggetti intelligenti per migliorare le esperienze di visita di siti di interesse culturale".

References

1. Almeida, R., Gomes, A., Bigotte, M.E., Pessoa, T.: iprog: getting started with programming: pilot experiment in two elementary schools. In: 2017 International Symposium on Computers in Education (SIIE), pp. 1–5 (2017)
2. Balducci, F., Grana, C.: Affective classification of gaming activities coming from rpg gaming sessions. In: Tian, F., Gatzidis, C., El Rhalibi, A., Tang, W., Charles, F. (eds.) E-Learning and Games, pp. 93–100. Springer, Cham (2017)

3. Balducci, F., Grana, C., Cucchiara, R.: Classification of affective data to evaluate the level design in a role-playing videogame. In: 2015 7th International Conference on Games and Virtual Worlds for Serious Applications (VS-Games), pp. 1–8 (2015)
4. Bevčič, M., Rugelj, J.: Game design based learning of programming for girls. In: 2020 43rd International Convention on Information, Communication and Electronic Technology, pp. 576–580 (2020)
5. Boudreaux, H., Etheredge, J., Roden, T.: Adding handheld game programming to a computer science curriculum. In: Proceedings of the 3rd International Conference on Game Development in Computer Science Education, pp. 16–20. GDCSE '08, Association for Computing Machinery, New York, NY, USA (2008)
6. Doran, K., Boyce, A., Finkelstein, S., Barnes, T.: Outreach for improved student performance: a game design and development curriculum. In: Proceedings of the 17th ACM Annual Conference on Innovation and Technology in Computer Science Education, pp. 209–214. ITiCSE '12, ACM, New York, NY, USA (2012)
7. Kurkovsky, S.: Can mobile game development foster student interest in computer science? In: 2009 Int. IEEE Consumer Electronics Society's Games Innovations Conference, pp. 92–100 (2009)
8. Kurkovsky, S.: Engaging students through mobile game development. In: Proceedings of the 40th ACM Technical Symposium on Computer Science Education, pp. 44–48. SIGCSE '09, Association for Computing Machinery (2009)
9. Mikami, K., et al.: Construction trial of a practical education curriculum for game development by industry/university collaboration. In: ACM SIGGRAPH ASIA 2009 Educators Program. SIGGRAPH ASIA '09, ACM (2009)
10. Rankin, Y., Gooch, A., Gooch, B.: The impact of game design on students' interest in cs. In: Proceedings of the 3rd International Conference on Game Development in Computer Science Education, pp. 31–35. GDCSE '08, ACM (2008)
11. Restrepo, A.M., Figueroa, P.: Designing a blended learning curriculum in the development of video games. In: 2014 IEEE Frontiers in Education Conference (FIE) Proceedings, pp. 1–3 (2014)
12. Rodrigues, N.F., Simões, R., Vilaça, J.L.: A digital game development education project. In: 2nd International Conference on Games and Virtual Worlds for Serious Applications, pp. 79–82 (2010)
13. Sato, Y., Hanaoka, H., Engström, H., Kurabayashi, S.: An education model for game development by a swedish-japanese industry-academia alliance. In: 2020 IEEE Conference on Games (CoG), pp. 328–335 (2020)
14. Stephenson, B., James, M., Brooke, N., Aycock, J.: An industrial partnership game development capstone course. In: Proceedings of the 17th Annual Conference on Information Technology Education, pp. 136–141. SIGITE '16, ACM (2016)
15. Wood, Z.J., Lovaglio Costello, E.: Not so different games: an exploration of five years of student game designers. In: IEEE Conference on Games (CoG), pp. 1–8 (2019)
16. Yue, Q., Shan, W.: Analyse of american academic game courses in computer science education and guidance for domestic universities. In: Int. Conf. on E-Health Networking Digital Ecosystems and Technologies (EDT). vol. 2, pp. 164–167 (2010)

Artificial Intelligence in Video Games 101: An Easy Introduction

Vittorio Mattei[(✉)]

IMT School for Advanced Studies Lucca, Lucca, Italy
vittorio.mattei@imtlucca.it

Abstract. This paper offers an easy introduction of Video Game Artificial intelligence (VGAI), i.e. the set of computational techniques embedded inside Non-Playable Characters (NPCs) that populate a video game and simulates the idea of playing against rational individuals. The two main pillars of VGAI will be briefly presented, namely pathfinding and decision-making, alongside an introduction and an explanation of the difference between academic AI research and video game AI. In summary, this paper delivers a solid but easy-to-understand introductory guide to this interesting and long-running research and industrial field without sacrificing mathematical formalism but not going into every detail, as the most industry-used books and academic references will be provided.

Keywords: Artificial Intelligence · Video games · Pathfinding · Decision-making

1 Introduction

In the realm of entertainment, the synergy between technology and creative expression has consistently given rise to novel paradigms, redefining both the medium and the experience. From blockbuster movies to electronic music, from video games to installation art, the entertainment industry is becoming more and more advanced and technology-dependent. Of every single member of the entertainment family, video games are the closest ones to computer science and the Information and Communication Technologies (ICT) domain: a video game is a software (SW) that runs on hardware (HW) and enables a Human-Machine Interaction (HMI) through one or more peripherals (e.g. a *Dualshock* or a *Kinect*). But video games are a lot more than just software: in recent years, outstanding creators managed to make video games an art form, such as Hideo Kojima, Hidetaka Miyazaki, Toby Fox, Ken Levine, Neil Druckmann and Yoko Taro, to name a few.

It is worth mentioning that, in addition to the artistic and technological importance, the video game industry is becoming more and more crucial for the overall entertainment industry. According to Wikipedia, as of July 2018, video games generated $ 134.9 billion annually in global sales and employed nearly 66000 direct employees and around 220000 in total. These numbers indicate the

M. Clayton et al. (Eds.): INTETAIN 2023, LNICST 560, pp. 40–51, 2024.
https://doi.org/10.1007/978-3-031-55722-4_4

importance of this industry in today's world and suggest that research work in this field will prove valuable in the future, enabling more people to work for and experience this industrial domain. For more advanced and complete information on Video Game AI (VGAI), plenty of literature is available in [1–5].

The paper is organized as follows. Section 2 will briefly discuss the differences between academic AI and Video Game AI (VGAI). In Sect. 3, we will introduce the concept and main techniques for decision-making. In Sect. 4, the pathfinding problem will be presented alongside the most common algorithms. In Sect. 5, more advanced applications will be briefly mentioned.

2 Difference Between Academic AI and Video Game AI (VGAI)

The first thing worth mentioning when talking about AI in video games is the difference between the academic world and video games. To be more specific, at least in the early stages, Video Game AI (VGAI) was very different with respect to AI techniques that we know and use nowadays. Academic AI is divided into two broad categories: *strong AI*, which aims to impersonate a human brain fully, and *weak AI*, which applies AI techniques to some restricted domains, such as robotics, automotive, finance and medicine, to name a few. Understanding that a unique definition does not exist, in this paper, we define an AI system as *the combination between a learning subsystem and a decision-making one*. To give a practical example, a self-driving car has a learning system that processes some input data and predicts some behaviour. Then, there is a decision-making system (e.g. a control system) responsible for taking an action, such as braking or changing lanes. In VGAI, this is not always the case, and some of the more industry-standard techniques are, in fact, deterministic and no learning is involved at all. We could say that VGAI does not respect the aforementioned definition, so it is not an AI system in the strictly academic sense, but this fact is perfectly fine, as the main purpose of VGAI is to be believable: a VGAI should not be intelligent in the sense of data-driven and adaptive, but it should create the illusion of intelligence, enabling the player to experience the game fully. In addition, modern gaming consoles have outdated HW, so implementing heavy AI techniques should be avoided if not strictly necessary. At its core, VGAI deals with two common and important problems when it comes to Non-Playable Characters (NPCs): decision-making, i.e. the action that the NPC should do at a certain time (e.g. attacking or escaping) and pathfinding, i.e. going from a starting point A to a stopping point B, avoiding any obstacles. As time goes by, new applications of VGAI are being developed, e.g. Procedural Content Generation (PCG) and Dynamic Difficulty Adjustment (DDA), to name a few, but still, the core of VGAI in most of modern videogames remains the combination of pathfinding and decision-making techniques, as not every game has procedural content or parameters that change dynamically, such as virtual climate or music (e.g. *Hi-Fi Rush*[1]).

---

[1] Tango Gameworks, *Hi-Fi Rush*, 2023.

3   Decision-Making

Decision-making in VGAI envelops the techniques that enable an NPC to behave in a certain way and to take some actions. Every video game with an option to play against the CPU has some decision-making rules coded inside that simulate the scenario of playing with other rational agents. The three most common decision-making models in VGAI are: rule-based systems [16], Finite State Machines (FSMs) [13], and Decision Trees [14]. The three of them will be briefly introduced in the following.

3.1   Rule-Based Systems

In the early stages of video game development, decision-making for AI entities relied on rule-based systems [16]. These systems employed an explicit set of conditions and corresponding actions, allowing non-player characters (NPCs) to respond predictably to predefined stimuli. Let $C = \{c_1, c_2, \ldots, c_n\}$ be a set of conditions, and $A = \{a_1, a_2, \ldots, a_m\}$ be a set of actions, we could implement a rule-based system in the following way:

```
if c1:
    a1;
else if c2:
    a2;
         .

         .

         .
else if cn:
    an;
```

Let us make a practical example. Suppose we want to code the famous little ghost from *Pac-Man*[2] using a rule-based system. The main idea behind the ghost's reasoning is that it goes forward until it finds a blocked path. In that case, it goes to the right if it is free, and it goes to the left if the right path is blocked. If both left and right are not accessible, it turns around and finds a new path. If we want to code this reasoning, the outcome should be something like the following:

```
if (ahead_free==TRUE):
    go_forward();
else if (ahead_free!=TRUE && right_free==TRUE):
    go_right();
else if (ahead_free!=TRUE && right_free!=TRUE && left_free==TRUE):
    go_left();
else if (ahead_free!=TRUE && right_free!=TRUE && left_free!=TRUE):
    go_back();
```

---

[2] Bandai Namco Entertainment, *Pac-Man*, 1980.

Rule-based systems can also be represented by tables, like the following:

c_1	$\cdots$	c_n	Actions
TRUE	$\cdots$	*	a_1
$\vdots$	$\ddots$	$\vdots$	$\vdots$
FALSE	$\cdots$	TRUE	a_n

Let us implement the little ghost's behaviour by using a table:

Ahead	Right	Left	**Actions**
Open	*	*	**Proceed forward**
Blocked	Open	*	**Turn right**
Blocked	Blocked	Open	**Turn left**
Blocked	Blocked	Blocked	**Turn around**

The main issue with rule-based systems is their scalability: as the NPC behaviour tends to become more complex, the size of the *if-else* chain becomes large, which is a problem regarding coding practices. This issue was one of the main reasons behind the adoption of more sophisticated techniques for decision-making in VGAI, namely Finite State Machines (FSMs) and Decision Trees.

3.2 Finite State Machines (FSMs)

As video games grew in complexity, finite state machines (FSMs) [13] gained prominence as a decision-making paradigm. FSMs are mathematically represented by graphs. From graph theory, we can define a graph G as an ordered pair $G = (S, E)$, where:

- $S = \{s_1, \ldots, s_n\}$ is a set of vertices (i.e. the states of the FSM);
- $E \subseteq \{\{s_i, s_j\}|s_i, s_j \in S \wedge i \neq j\}$ is a set of edges (i.e. the transitions of the FSM), which are unordered pairs of vertices (an edge connects two distinct vertices).

To be more specific, an FSM can be represented by a directed graph $G = (S, E)$, where:

- $S = \{s_1, \ldots, s_n\}$ is a set of vertices (i.e. the states of the FSM);
- $E \subseteq \{(s_i, s_j)|(s_i, s_j) \in S^2\}$ is a set of edges (i.e. the transitions of the FSM), which are ordered pairs of vertices (an edge connects two vertices). S^n denotes the set of n-tuples of elements of S, that is, ordered sequences of n elements that are not necessarily distinct.

Let us note that $i \neq j$ was removed in the definition of E to allow the existence of self-loops. We can describe a state transition with the following formalism:

$$s_i = T(s_j, e_k)$$

where $T(\cdot)$ is the transition function. A classical FSM is like the one in Fig. 1:

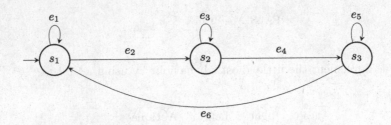

Fig. 1. A Finite State Machine (FSM) represented by a directed graph.

Let us make a practical example. Suppose we want to code an enemy NPC from a classical action or first-person shooter (FPS). The main idea behind the NPC reasoning is that it stays in the guard (G) state until the player character (PC) is near. In that case, it goes into the fight (F) state until the hit points (HP) are low (i.e. under a certain value). If the HP are low, the NPC goes into the escape (E) state until the PC is far away. An FSM that simulates this NPC behaviour should be something like Fig. 2:

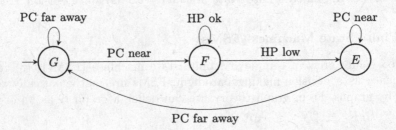

Fig. 2. A Finite State Machine (FSM) representing an NPC behaviour.

Despite their great versatility, FSMs come with some issues. The first one is the scalability, as new states must implement new situations or behaviours. The second one is sequentiality, since it is necessary to design, implement or modify transitions to change the state sequence. Another issue is parallelization, as an FSM can be in only one state at a given time. Since the number of states tends to increase with the complexity of the video game design, "spaghetti state machines" can become a reality and slow down the development process. These issues paved the way for Decision Trees, but FSMs remain useful for controlling the overall game cycle, the player states and controls.

3.3   Decision Trees

Decision Trees [14] are a powerful mathematical tool that lets us decide how and when to execute some actions. A typical decision tree in VGAI is like the one in Fig. 3:

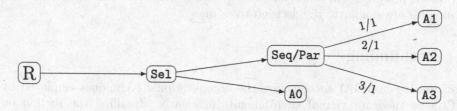

Fig. 3. A Decision Tree.

where:

- **R (Root):** initial state.
- **Sel (Selector):** selects one node.
- **Par (Parallel):** selects every node after it simultaneously.
- **Seq (Sequential):** selects every node after it following a given order.
- **A (Action):** task that has to be done or configuration that has to be taken.

Note that decision trees are evaluated from root to leaf (action), every time.

Let us make a practical example. Suppose we want to code the same enemy NPC from the FSMs subsection. A decision tree that simulates the NPC behaviour should be something like the one in Fig. 4:

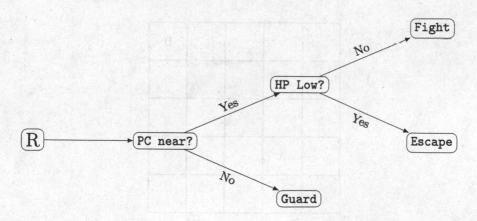

Fig. 4. A Decision Tree representing an NPC behaviour.

As we can see, decision trees overcome some limitations of FSMs, especially when dealing with more complex NPC behaviours. Another great advantage of decision trees is modularity: every task can be called from anywhere else in the tree and this helps when designing different behaviours, since it is only needed to change the sequence while keeping the same other blocks.

Note that there exists an extension of decision trees, i.e. Behaviour Trees [15], as they do not need to go back to the root node at every evaluation. They are more powerful and allow for more complex behavior, but the functioning principles are similar to the decision trees ones.

4 Pathfinding

Pathfinding in VGAI encompasses the computational techniques employed by NPCs to navigate virtual environments efficiently. Recalling the section on decision-making, when an NPC wants to find the PC or escape from it, it has to go from a point A in the virtual space to another point B. In the following, a simple scenario will be presented to understand the pathfinding problem intuitively, and after that, the two most used pathfinding algorithms will be briefly discussed, namely Dijkstra's Algorithm [11] and A* Algorithm [10].

4.1 A Simple Scenario

The developer is interested in finding the optimal route when coding pathfinding for a video game. Let us make an example to show this idea step by step. In the following, we assume that the cost of every 1-step movement (horizontally, vertically, diagonally) is 1.

Suppose an NPC should move from the starting point A to the ending point B, while avoiding the grey obstacles. This is represented in Fig. 5:

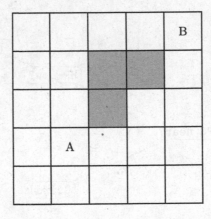

Fig. 5. Grid representing the space where the NPC can move.

Let us compute some possible paths and the costs associated with them. Let us consider the scenario represented in Fig. 6:

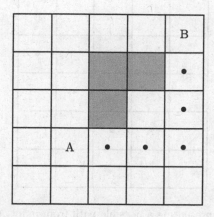

Fig. 6. Grid representing a possible path from point A to point B.

In this case, the cost is 6. Let us consider the scenario represented in Fig. 7:

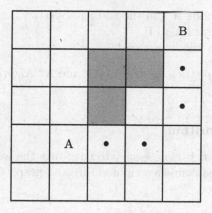

Fig. 7. Grid representing a possible path from point A to point B.

In this case, the cost is 5. Let us consider the scenario represented in Fig. 8:

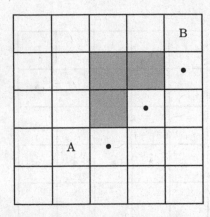

Fig. 8. Grid representing a possible path from point A to point B.

In this case, the cost is 4. We can state that, in the latest scenario, the path is the optimal one. A generic pathfinding algorithm works by iterating the same actions that were performed before:

1. Select the starting node A and the ending node B.
2. Locate every path from A to B.
3. Select the path with the lowest cost.

In the following, Dijkstra's Algorithm [11] and A* Algorithm [10] will be briefly presented.

4.2 Dijkstra's Algorithm

To find the optimal cost, it is necessary to introduce the weights in the previous graph definition. Let us define a weighted directed graph $G_W = (S, E, W)$ that allows self-loops, where:

- $S = \{s_1, \dots, s_n\}$ is a set of vertices;
- $E \subseteq \{(s_i, s_j) | (s_i, s_j) \in S^2\}$ is a set of edges;
- $W : E \to \mathbb{N}_0$ is a function assigning a non-negative weight $W(s_i, s_j)$ to every edge (s_i, s_j).

Here, the weight represents the distance, so $W(s_i, s_j)$ is the length of the edge (s_i, s_j). If $P = (A = s_1, s_2, \dots, s_n = B)$ is a directed path from point A to point B, then its length would be $L(P) = \sum_{k=1}^{n} W(s_k, s_{k+1})$ and the distance between A and B is defined as the minimum length of a directed path from A to B. Before writing Dijkstra's Algorithm, let us put $W(s_i, s_j) = +\infty$ when $(s_i, s_j) \notin E \wedge i \neq j$. We can now write Dijkstra's Algorithm [11]:

- **Step 0 (Preparation):** Let $n = |S|$. At each time step $k, k \in [1, n]$, the following quantities are computed:
  - A sequence $\Psi = (s_1, \ldots, s_k)$ where $A = s_1$. If $s_i \in \Psi$ then s_i is called *permanent vertex*, while if $s_j \notin \Psi$ then s_j is called *temporary vertex*.
  - $\forall s_i \in S$, a path $P = (A, \ldots, s_i)$ of length $L(s_i)$ is determined.
- **Step 1 (Initialization):** Set $k = 1$. Let $P = (A)$ be the trivial path and set $L(P) = L(A) = 0$, $s_1 = A$ and $\Psi = (s_1)$. Compute $L(x) = W(A, x), P = (A, x), \forall x \in S \wedge x \neq A$. Let x be a temporary vertex for which $L(x)$ is minimum. Set $s_2 = x$ and update $\Psi = (s_1, s_2)$. Set $k = k + 1$.
- **Step $k, k > 1$ (Recursion):** While $k < n$, $\forall x \notin \Psi$, set $L(x) = \min\{L(x), L(x) + W(s_k, x)\}$. If $L(x)$ is minimum, set $s_{k+1} = x$ and update $\Psi = (s_1, \ldots, s_k, s_{k+1})$. Set $k = k + 1$.

Dijkstra's Algorithm is recursive and always returns the shortest path, but only when the edge weights are all non-negative. However, it can fail when there are negative edge costs. To improve the efficiency, an extension of Dijkstra's Algorithm was developed: the A* Algorithm, which will be briefly introduced in the following.

4.3 A* Algorithm

A* Algorithm [10] is an extension of Dijkstra's Algorithm, obtained by adding some heuristics. To be more formal, A* Algorithm selects the path that minimizes:

$$f(s) = g(s) + \hat{h}(s)$$

where:

- $f(s)$ is the total cost of path through node s.
- $g(s)$ is the path's cost from the start node to s.
- $\hat{h}(s)$ is the estimated cost of the path starting from s to the end node.

A* algorithm concludes its execution under two conditions: when it extends a path that successfully connects the starting point to the goal, or when there are no remaining eligible paths to extend. The effectiveness of A* heavily relies on the problem-specific heuristic function $\hat{h}(\cdot)$. When this heuristic function adheres to the property of admissibility, meaning it never overestimates the true cost of reaching the goal, A* is assured to provide the least-cost path from the initial point to the goal. The main difference from Dijkstra's Algorithm is the heuristic function $\hat{h}(\cdot)$. The value of $\hat{h}(s)$ would ideally be equal to the cost of reaching the end node starting from s. Different heuristics can be used, but the most common are the Manhattan and the Euclidean distances.

Note that when $\hat{h}(s) = 0$, A* Algorithm becomes Dijkstra's Algorithm.

A lot of other algorithms exist in the literature, such as Best-first search algorithms (e.g. B* [12]), but both A* and Dijkstra's Algorithm remain an industry standard and have been implemented in a lot of video games.

5   Advanced VGAI Applications

Until now, we have presented the backbone of VGAI regarding the NPCs, but more advanced AI applications in video games exist.

One interesting frontiers of nowadays video games is Procedural Content Generation (PCG) [6,7]. Popular video games such as *Minecraft*[3], *No Man's Sky*[4] and *Bloodborne*[5] incorporate some PCG elements, and some of them rely entirely on them to build the overall gaming experience.

Procedural Content Generation (PCG) [6,7] refers to the automatic creation of game content (e.g. maps, quests, weapons, stories, terrains) through advanced machine and deep learning techniques. It is an opposing concept to the manual crafting of every game content, which remains the main way of developing games until now.

If we think about the applications in the video game development process, we can understand how big the impact of PCG techniques is on this industry: if PCG could help developers speed up the generation of game assets, they could focus more on the artistic and design side of the product, reducing the time spent on repetitive tasks and hopefully improving productivity and well-being at work.

Another interesting application of AI could be players' modelling [8]. Over the past years, the mobile gaming sector has taken center stage in the video game industry, particularly emphasizing the prevalence of free-to-play (e.g. *Clash Royale*[6]) or gatcha (e.g. *Genshin Impact*[7]) games. Companies could balance in-game elements and personalise non-free objects by profiling players' behaviours and personal preferences.

Moreover, the most famous recent application of AI in the video games world has been *AlphaGo* [17], the AI that plays Go developed by *DeepMind*. These game-playing AIs [9] substitute a human player since they have access to the same information and are a separate SW from the game (usually, they are developed after the game is released). In contrast with NPCs development, where the main focus is to create the illusion of intelligence, game-playing AIs' objective is to play well and, most of the time, outperform humans. Other examples of game-playing AIs are *OpenAI Five* [18], a game-playing AI that plays *Dota 2*[8] and *MarIQ*[9], an AI that plays *Super Mario Kart*[10].

---

[3] Mojang Studios, *Minecraft*, 2011.

[4] Hello Games, *No Man's Sky*, 2016.

[5] FromSoftware, *Bloodborne*, 2015.

[6] Supercell, *Clash Royale*, 2016.

[7] miHoYo, *Genshin Impact*, 2020.

[8] Valve, *Dota 2*, 2013.

[9] SethBling, *MarIQ - Q-Learning Neural Network for Mario Kart*, 2019.

[10] Nintendo EAD, *Super Mario Kart*, 1992.

References

1. Millington, I.: Artificial Intelligence for Games (2006)
2. McShaffry, M., Graham, D.: Game Coding Complete (2013)
3. Buckland, M.: Programming Game AI By Example (2004)
4. Muñoz-Avila, H., Bauckhage, C., Bida, M., Congdon, C.B., Kendall, G.: Learning and Game AI (2013)
5. Yannakakis, G.N., Togelius, J.: Artificial Intelligence and Games (2018)
6. Yannakakis, G.N., Togelius, J., Stanley, K.O., Browne, C.: Search-Based Procedural Content Generation: A Taxonomy and Survey (2011)
7. Yannakakis, G.N., Togelius, J.: Experience-Driven Procedural Content Generation (2011)
8. Pedersen, C., Yannakakis, G.N., Togelius, J.: Modeling Player Experience for Content Creation (2010)
9. Justesen, N., Bontrager, P., Togelius, J., Risi, S.: Deep Learning for Video Game Playing (2019)
10. Hart, P.E., Nilsson, N.J., Raphael, B.: A Formal Basis for the Heuristic Determination of Minimum Cost Paths (1968)
11. Dijkstra, E.W.: A Note on Two Problems in Connexion with Graphs (1959)
12. Berliner, H.: The B* Tree Search Algorithm. A Best-First Proof Procedure (1979)
13. Wang, J.: Formal Methods in Computer Science (2019)
14. von Winterfeldt, D., Edwards, W.: Decision trees (1986
15. Colvin, R.J., Hayes, I.J.: A semantics for Behavior Trees using CSP with specification commands (2011)
16. Alty, J.L., Guida, G.: The Use of Rule-based System Technology for the Design of Man-Machine Systems (1985)
17. Silver, D., et al.: Mastering the game of Go with deep neural networks and tree search (2016)
18. OpenAI et al., Dota 2 with Large Scale Deep Reinforcement Learning (2019)

Motion Capture

A Somaesthetics Based Approach to the Design of Multisensory Interactive Systems

Silvia Ferrando[✉], Gualtiero Volpe, and Eleonora Ceccaldi

Casa Paganini, InfoMus, DIBRIS, University of Genoa, Genoa, Italy
silvia.ferrando@edu.unige.it, gualtiero.volpe@unige.it,
eleonora.ceccaldi@dibris.unige.it

Abstract. This paper aims to analyse the state-of-the-art of somaesthetics, describing the scientific and philosophic basis of the discipline, in order to devise how to implement a soma-based design. The goal is to apply the somaesthetics approach to the design of multisensory interactive systems for the purpose of creating novel technology designs for people with disabilities that can foster their participation and improve their daily life and overall well-being. Somatics can be intended as a set of instrumental values to increase bodily awareness. It allows us to get in touch with our own inner states, which can lead to a personal evaluative dimension for the designer, which can be used to integrate existing methods for evaluating experiences. Paying attention to one's own bodily states is key as it can turn such states in desing material. This concept was further developed with Shusterman's somaesthetics, a theoretical framework for aesthetic experiences. In the paper, we present examples of somaesthetics approaches to the design of interfaces (e.g. the SomaMat, that uses heat stimuli to guide the user attention to different parts of his/her body and can be a support for exercising or a tool to increase the body awareness). Moreover, we illustrate existing practices to design such as Embodied Sketching or Moving and Making Strange that are based on the body as the starting point of the design process, usually preceded by techniques such as defamiliarization or Feldenkrais exercises. Then, we move on to our forthcoming research, aimed at applying a somaesthetics approach to create a system for two possible groups of users: (1) children who are patients at the Giannina Gaslini Institute (a pediatric hospital) and (2) visually impaired and blind people members of Unione Italiana Ciechi (an Italian association of blind people). The system will help users move together, to increase interaction between them as well as involve them in educational and creative activities. The work will be carried out under the PNRR RAISE project (*Robotics and AI for Socio-economic Empowerment*; https://www.raiseliguria.it/).

Keywords: Multi-sensory technologies · somaesthetics approach · full-body movement analysis

Supported by RAISE Liguria.

1   Introduction

While multisensory interactive systems increasingly find applications in many areas (e.g., education, rehabilitation, and entertainment), these systems are usually conceived as technologies that observe their users, analyze users' behavior (e.g., their motor behavior), and produce a suitable multisensory feedback. An issue with this approach is that analysis is grounded on a collection of features that are similar for every category of users and that do not necessarily reflect the inner state of the user, but rather correspond to what an external observer perceives. An approach that, instead, leverages awareness that users have of their body, by eliciting, identifying, and measuring the features that are most responsible of such awareness (thus reflecting the user's inner state) for each user (or category of users) may make the experience with the interactive system more effective and compelling. Along this direction, in this paper we present a novel methodology for the design of multisensory interactive systems based on: (1) a design approach grounded on theories from *somaesthetics*, and (2) computational techniques for automated analysis of movement and generation of multisensory feedback. Somaesthetics is used to give users awareness of their body so that the design process can identify both (1) the movements that are most suitable for a given task and class of users and (2) the multisensory feedback which is most appropriate to them. Then, automated approaches to movement analysis and feedback generation are applied to actually make the system. These techniques will need to go beyond currently popular mappings based on physical aspects (e.g., positions, distances, and energy) moving towards higher-level expressive qualities (e.g., lightness, fluidity, and fragility). Moreover, finding the most suitable movements/feedback for each class of users and making users aware of that will help overcome physical and cognitive barriers e.g., for users with disabilities. The design of the demonstrators for the PNRR RAISE project (https://www.raiseliguria.it/) will be taken as a test-bed for this novel approach. The RAISE project supports the development of an innovative ecosystem based on the scientific and technological domains of Artifical Intelligence and Robotics, focusing on the needs of a specific regional context, i.e., the Liguria Region. In this framework, we focus on the development of a collection of multisensory interactive systems intended to support inclusion in the classroom and at technology-extended playgrounds. Main objectives of the work will be to investigate somaesthetic designs, methodologies, and their state-of-the-art, to devise a somaesthetics approach to the design of multisensory interactive systems, and to apply and evaluate the proposed approach in the selected use-cases. This paper discusses the state-of-the-art of somaesthetics approaches to the design of the systems and our plan for research in this area.

2   State-of-the-Art and Existing Approaches

Somatic is a set of traditions centered on the body which are historically tied to the treatment of the body such as medicine, physiology, and performance [16].

Somatic gave start to research on how to build, change, and express themselves: it became a research field during the XIX and the XX century in Europe and America. One of its characteristics is to endorse subjective perception of the body [16]. Somatics is defined as the experience from within the lived body [3].

The idea of transformation at a bodily level is key in somatic approaches: the emphasis is on learning and cultivating experiential skills through doing. The checking-in, cross-referencing, and calibration process is continuous and it takes between the self-directed intentions embodied in physical action with an inner focus of attention, and the awareness of one's inner state as a shifting dynamic. For this reason, somatics is also intended as a set of instrumental values: self as a set of states, attention as an operator, experience as a skill, and inter-connectedness as empathy. Experienced teachers usually guide novices through techniques of practices, where observation of self and others are key elements [16]. By adjusting our sensorial focus and attention to energies of self and of others, we enter a cyclic process of consciousness, made up by somatic aware-ness. This phase should not be continuously maintained, as rest and recuperation phases are critical for learning of sensory-motor habits [5].

2.1   Theoretical Basis

Gendlin [6] states the body is on the edge of thinking, because it knows more than our rational mind. His technique for focusing wants to find a way to access implicit information in the body through supposition. By feeling the inner state of the body, it is possible to generate design concepts and qualities. Metaphors are usually used to articulate and describe the inner states, such as "feels like a crumbling rock" [16]. The body can also be described as a set of qualitative states, that can change continuously according to mental events and physio-logical states. If the focus of our attention is our internal state, we can notice and differentiate internal changes. When we shift the focus on external events without losing the connection with our inner ones, internal changes can be used to evaluate the experience of that interaction. Existing methods for evaluating experiences can be augmented by the evaluative dimension, allowing to acknowl-edging immediate impressions as well as the lingering effects of interaction [16]. The somatic perspective can contribute to first-person methods for understand-ing and valuating experience: it can make the designer or researcher feel an higher sense of their own presence [16].

According to Dewey [4], an aesthetic experience "has a unity that gives it its name, that meal, that storm, that rupture of a friendship. The existence of this unity is constituted by a single quality that pervades the entire experience in spite of the variation of its constituent parts". Aesthetic experiences, however, are not something outside the ordinary, because such experiences can be repeated or lived on a daily basis; scary or bad experiences can be considered aesthetic as well [9].

Richard Shusterman further developed Dewey's ideas with somaesthetics, a theoretical framework for aesthetic experiences [21]. The framework emphasizes the importance of bodily movements, sensations, and somatic training, as well as the aesthetic in these experiences [9]. Hannah defines somatics as the field which studies the soma: this means, the body as perceived from within by first-person perception. When a human being is observed from a third-person viewpoint, the human body is perceived as a phenomenon. When the same human being is observed from the first-person viewpoint of his own proprioceptive senses, a different phenomenon is perceived: the human soma. [23] Shusterman's somaesthetics is based on different body-work traditions and methodologies, such as yoga, tai chi, or more modern methods, such as the Alexander Technique [1] and the Feldenkrais Method [5]. These techniques focus on using touch and movement for learning coordination of the body, by emphasizing skills, which are innate or have already been acquired and are habitual or even unconscious. There is, however, the possibility of adopting bad habits that lead to restricted movements, causing a loss of perception of aesthetics in our own somatics [9]. Self-observation combined with intention gives life to self-agency and it is very important in somatics practice [9] because only when we move, we experience through our own somas [20] and when movements are limited, so are experiences [5].

The approach helps designers by providing them with tools that support mental, physical, and emotional health of users through enhanced perception of the body [16]. It gives designers the opportunity to work explicitly with experiences as material to base projects on: there is a causal nexus between attention and experience, because attention transforms material qualities of the experience. In somatics, through attention experience can become a pliable material [7]. Somatic techniques should be understood to be applied to technologies as well [10], in order to design new experiences. These insights can be considered as a resource for design practices [19]. Technologies require attention and somatic techniques can provide many useful strategies, in order to support greater attentional skills and awareness in users and designers. [19].

2.2   Examples of Soma Based Designs

Some examples of soma based designs follow; all designs have a playful approach, where everyday movements are altered. Another similarity in these examples is the design material, made up by two parts: digital mediated materials and our bodies. Both can be modified by mutual interaction [9]. The first example is BrightHearts, an interactive work of art and biofeedback application, developed to minimize pain and anxiety in children who undergo painful medical procedures. Their hearth-beat is monitored to change diameter and color of concentric circles: the more relaxed they are, less intense and warm are colors [13].

Another example is the SomaMat, that uses heat stimuli to guide the user attention to different parts of his/her body; it can be used alone or as a support to exercises to increase the user's body awareness. It is used together with an app with many pre-recorded audio sessions, with instructions guiding their bodies in very slow movements, while they are focused on different body parts and how these interact with each other [11].

GangKlang is an app that uses the rhythm of a person's walk to generate a soundscape. It emphasizes the physical dimension of who is walking by perceiving the user's movements and inserting them into the context. It translates their peculiarities into characteristics of the sound landscape in real time [8].

Soma based design is not only used for applications, for example Embodied Encounters Studio is a toolbox made up of 3 components: the Embodied Ideation Toolkit, which is a set of non-descriptive magnetic objects; Hexn, a tangible modular notation system composed of transparent hexagons with icons and Inspiration Cards, which are RFID-enabled cards with images related to database content, such as slides and videos that are shown on a stationary iPad [12]. The goal of this toolbox is to allow two or more participants to brainstorm together through playful encounters. This design supports nonverbal communication and social coordination in action, instead of a more dialogue-oriented discussion. [12].

Finally, The Tail and Ears are mechanical extensions of the body to be used in theatrical contexts. The tail moves as the hips do, using accelerometers and gyroscopes; the ears are controlled by sensors on gloves [22].

2.3   How to Implement Soma Based Designs

Before starting to create soma based designs, there are practices to adopt; the main one is defamiliarization, i.e., the disruption of habitual ways of moving, sensing, and feeling to give perception a new perspective or to create new connections by rearranging sensorimotor neural pathways [16]. Another practice is represented by *Feldenkrais*, i.e., exercises to increase awareness of the body, also helping to "slow down the brainstorming" [9]. It is necessary to holistically explore bodily and emotional aspects in the experience of movement to increase awareness [14].

Moreover, the designer has to articulate experiential qualities and strong concepts, in order to generalize from the specific insights gained and testing what has been learned [11]. An experiential quality describes the experience between user and system that the designer wants to achieve. A strong concept must be generative, from more than one application: it has to do with the interactive behavior of an application [11].

One practice involving designing bodily experiences early in the design process is called *Embodied Sketching*. It is based on five principles: (1) an activity-centred approach to ideation, (2) use of a complete setting as a design resource, (3) physical and practical involvement of the designers with an improvised and unplanned activity, (4) use of movement and play both as a method and a goal, and (5) the provision of an awareness-raising and planning space [17]. It is activity centred because the goal is to design enjoyable social and physical activities that are technologically-supported; contextual elements are used as design resources, while in other methods are just used as a backdrop, useful to evaluate ideas. This methodology focuses on initial explorative ideation phases as a way to open up the design space; in order to do so, using a physical and playful engagement is key, as it allows designers to engage in a mind-set conducive of exploration and creativity [17]. Another approach, called *Moving and Making Strange*, recognizes the central role of body in lived cognition. Making strange is a tactic used for disrupting habitual perceptions and ways of thinking. This methodology provides a set of principles, perspectives, methods, and tools for designing and evaluating movement based interactions with technology. This also provides a general framework for research and for designing technologies, based on an embodied approach that privileges the body as a source of movement and as a place of experience. [15]. A generic and summarized example of approach used to create soma based design is shown in Fig. 1.

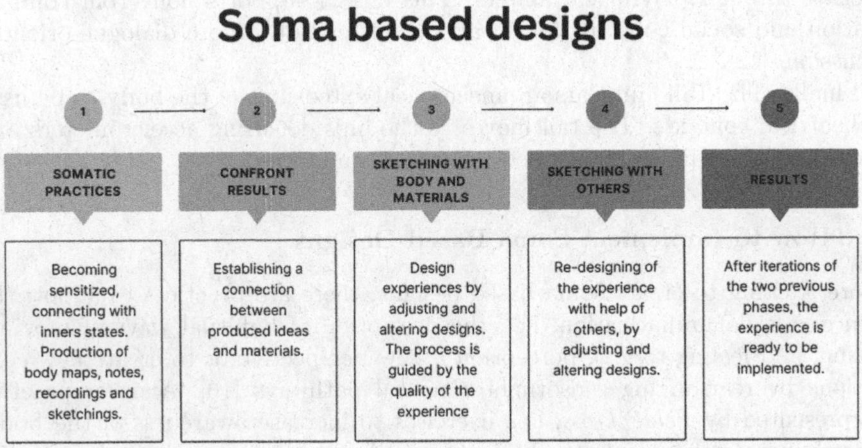

Soma based designs

Fig. 1. An example of soma based design timeline.

3 Forthcoming Research

We selected two possible classes of users: (1) children who are patients at the Giannina Gaslini Institute, a pediatric hospital, and who are receiving a rehabilitation treatment at home and (2) visually impaired and blind people members of Unione Italiana Ciechi. Applications developed for these users often rely on different design approaches, such as co-design [18] or participatory design [2]. For this project we will develop a system which allows users to create their own story, starting from preset elements which can be combined in different ways. We will use the same concept seen in the book "Six billions fables by Jean de la Fontaine", written by Nicola Ferrari. This book is structured in a way readers can mix and match sentences, thanks to the pages being cut in a non standard way; however the reader combines the sentences, the final story has the same structure but a different meaning. The goal of this system is to help users move together, for example children who attend frequently the hospital. This would increase a better interaction between patients, as well as the involvement in creative and educational activities. This system could be installed in part of the common areas of Giannina Gaslini Institute, which are dedicated and accessible to all patients.

For this project, we will first start to create designs mainly based on somaesthetics, develop the identified technology, and finally assess the obtained prototypes.

References

1. Alexander, F.M.: The use of the self. BMJ **1**(3728), 1149 (1932)
2. Chick, A.: Co-creating an accessible, multisensory exhibition with the national centre for craft & design and blind and partially sighted participants. In: REDO: 2017 Cumulus International Conference, 30 May - 2 June 2017 (2017)
3. Deikman, A.J.: The observing self. Beacon Press (1983)
4. Dewey, J.: Art as experience. penguin (2005)
5. Feldenkrais, M.: Awareness through movement, vol. 1977. Harper and Row, New York (1972)
6. Gendlin, E.T.: The primacy of the body, not the primacy of perception. Man and world **25**(3–4), 341–353 (1992)
7. Gendlin, E.T.: Focusing-oriented psychotherapy: A manual of the experiential method. Guilford Press (1998)
8. Hajinejad, N., Grüter, B., Roque, L., Bogutzky, S.: Gangklang: Facilitating a movement-oriented walking experience through sonic interaction. In: Proceedings of the Audio Mostly 2016. pp. 202–208. AM '16, Association for Computing Machinery, New York, NY, USA (2016). https://doi.org/10.1145/2986416.2986447
9. Höök, K., et al.: Embracing first-person perspectives in soma-based design. Informatics **5**(1) (2018). https://doi.org/10.3390/informatics5010008, https://www.mdpi.com/2227-9709/5/1/8
10. Hook, K.: Designing with the body: Somaesthetic interaction design. Mit Press (2018)
11. Höök, K., Ståhl, A., Jonsson, M., Mercurio, J., Karlsson, A., Johnson, E.C.B.: Cover storysomaesthetic design. Interactions **22**(4), 26–33 (jun 2015). https://doi.org/10.1145/2770888
12. Hummels, C., Trotto, A.: Designing in skills studio. In: Proceedings of the 8th International Conference on Tangible, Embedded and Embodied Interaction, pp. 357–360. TEI '14, Association for Computing Machinery, New York, NY, USA (2014). https://doi.org/10.1145/2540930.2567901
13. Khut, G.P.: Designing biofeedback artworks for relaxation. In: Proceedings of the 2016 CHI Conference Extended Abstracts on Human Factors in Computing Systems, pp. 3859–3862. CHI EA '16, Association for Computing Machinery, New York, NY, USA (2016). https://doi.org/10.1145/2851581.2891089
14. Lee, W., Lim, Y.k., Shusterman, R.: Practicing somaesthetics: Exploring its impact on interactive product design ideation. In: Proceedings of the 2014 Conference on Designing Interactive Systems, pp. 1055–1064. DIS '14, Association for Computing Machinery, New York, NY, USA (2014). https://doi.org/10.1145/2598510.2598561
15. Loke, L., Robertson, T.: Moving and making strange: an embodied approach to movement-based interaction design. ACM Trans. Comput.-Hum. Interact. **20**(1) (apr 2013). https://doi.org/10.1145/2442106.2442113
16. Loke, L., Schiphorst, T.: The somatic turn in human-computer interaction. Interactions **25**(5), 54–5863 (Aug 2018). https://doi.org/10.1145/3236675

17. Márquez Segura, E., Turmo Vidal, L., Rostami, A., Waern, A.: Embodied sketching. In: Proceedings of the 2016 CHI Conference on Human Factors in Computing Systems, pp. 6014–6027. CHI '16, Association for Computing Machinery, New York, NY, USA (2016). https://doi.org/10.1145/2858036.2858486
18. Melonio, A., Gennari, R.: Co-design with children: the state of the art. KRBD Research Centre for Knowledge and Data. University of Bozen, Italy (2012)
19. Schiphorst, T., Loke, L., Höök, K.: Designing for sensory appreciation: Cultivating somatic approaches to experience design. In: Extended Abstracts of the 2020 CHI Conference on Human Factors in Computing Systems, pp. 1–4. CHI EA '20, Association for Computing Machinery, New York, NY, USA (2020). https://doi.org/10.1145/3334480.3375056
20. Sheets-Johnstone, M.: The primacy of movement. The primacy of movement, pp. 1–606 (2011)
21. Shusterman, R.: Body consciousness: A philosophy of mindfulness and somaesthetics. Cambridge University Press (2008)
22. Svanaes, D., Solheim, M.: Wag your tail and flap your ears: the kinesthetic user experience of extending your body. In: Proceedings of the 2016 CHI Conference Extended Abstracts on Human Factors in Computing Systems, pp. 3778–3779. CHI EA '16, Association for Computing Machinery, New York, NY, USA (2016). https://doi.org/10.1145/2851581.2890268
23. Thomas, H., et al.: What is somatics? DH Johnson, Bone. North Atlantic Books, Berkeley, Breath & Gesture (1995)

GFTLSTM: Dynamic Graph Neural Network Model Based on Graph Framelets Transform

Shengpeng Yang[1], Siwei Zhou[1], Shasha Yang[1(✉)], and Jiandong Shi[2]

[1] Key Laboratory of Intelligent Education Technology and Application of Zhejiang Province, Zhejiang Normal University, Jinhua, China
{yangshengp,yangss}@zjnu.edu.cn
[2] School of Computer Science and Technology (School of Artificial Intelligence), Zhejiang Normal University, Jinhua, China

Abstract. There is currently a surge of interest in graph representation learning, with researchers increasingly focusing on methods and applications involving graph neural networks (GNNs). However, traditional GNN models for static graph data analysis have limitations in their ability to extract evolutionary patterns from dynamic graphs, which are more commonly observed in real-world data. Additionally, existing dynamic GNN models tend to prioritize low-frequency information while neglecting high-frequency information. To address these limitations, we introduce a dynamic graph neural network model that leverages graph framelet transforms, capitalizing on the benefits of traditional wavelets in multi-resolution analysis. The initial step involves constructing the graph framelet transform based on graph wavelet research, subsequently implementing multi-resolution graph convolution with both low-pass and high-pass filtering. Then, we incorporate the convolution operation into a long short-term memory (LSTM) network. As a result, we develop a dynamic GNN model founded on the graph framelet transform, which effectively uncovers the evolutionary information embedded within dynamic graphs. In our experiment evaluation, we compare our model with 11 widely used dynamic graph representation learning algorithms across three public datasets of discrete dynamic graph representation learning tasks (encompassing six groups of experimental data). Our model outperforms the alternatives in terms of accuracy on the majority of the datasets.

Keywords: graph representation learning · dynamic graph · graph framelets transform

1 Introduction

With the rapid development of digital technologies such as the Internet, the Internet of Things, and artificial intelligence, trillions of bytes of data are generated every day across all industries [14]. These diverse and complex data record

M. Clayton et al. (Eds.): INTETAIN 2023, LNICST 560, pp. 63–75, 2024.
https://doi.org/10.1007/978-3-031-55722-4_6

various aspects of people's daily lives. Analyzing this data and mining potentially valuable information is crucial for scientific study, commerce, and other industries [12,32]. For example, in recommendation systems, users' preferences can be discovered through their browsing history, resulting in targeted product recommendations that increase shopping efficiency [8,13]. Similarly, in intelligent transportation systems, road conditions can be analyzed using vehicle-to-everything information to provide optimal path suggestions for destinations, ultimately saving users' time [5,7].

Since deep-learning-based data analysis methods have made significant advancements in academia, many models that use deep learning techniques to analyze and process different types of data are currently used in a wide range of industries. However, the majority of these models primarily focus on Euclidean structured data. In the era of big data, characterized by diverse data representations, there is an increasing prevalence of non-Euclidean structured graph data represented by social networks, telecommunication networks and transportation networks [11,22,27,31], which process data into graph forms and contain rich relational information.

Real-world graph data does not exhibit an unchangeable static graph structure; instead, it displays an extremely complex temporal evolution, as observed in social network graphs on Facebook and user-video interaction graphs on YouTube, etc. These data not only contain various individual entity features but also relationships between various users that change over time, creating a dynamic graph structure that has caught the interest of numerous academics. The work in [19] proposes the Evolving-GCN model which uses a recurrent neural network (RNN) to train the parameters of GCN to capture dynamic graph features. The authors of [21] introduce an attention mechanism into dynamic graph representation learning to construct the temporal and spatial information of graph evolution at different times. A K-Core-based model [16] is integrated into GCN and RNN to further consider the local similar information from different aspects in the same snapshot of dynamic graphs, thus improving the efficiency of subsequent tasks. The Netwalk model presented in [28] re-encodes dynamic graph data based on a deep self-encoder, updating node features in real-time using a graph random walk. It gathers nodes with similar features closely in space to perform graph clustering analysis. By utilizing a node labeling function, the StrGNN model in [3] incorporates closed subgraph sampling for neighbor nodes of the target node within a specific dynamic graph time window. This novel subgraph sampling approach aims to find the shortest path between the target node and the source node. By considering both the global and local information of dynamic graph neural networks in the same snapshot as well as dynamic evolution information in various snapshots, the authors in [17] achieve the best results to date on several dynamic graph anomaly detection benchmark datasets.

In this paper, we propose a representation learning method for dynamic graphs because the existing feature extraction methods for Euclidean structures do not apply to non-Euclidean structures and the proposed models based on static graph representation learning are unable to capture the evolution features in dynamic graphs. GFTLSTM is a dynamic graph neural network model based on graph framelets transform. Given that wavelet analysis is more applicable to changing data, we attempt to combine wavelet analysis with dynamic graphs in the frequency domain before data reconstruction to achieve the effect of ReLU, after which we combine the long and short-term memory neural network model to capture the temporal features. We validate the effectiveness of our method by experimenting with two different parameter training methods on three benchmark datasets, finding that GFTLSTM outperforms the most dynamic graph neural network models in terms of performance. Furthermore, the ablation study and ReLU activation function comparison study also verify the model's performance. We summarize the contributions of this work as follows:

- We propose a dynamic graph neural network model based on graph framelets, representing an attempt to combine dynamic graphs with wavelet theory for processing node signals in the frequency domain.
- We consider both low-frequency and high-frequency information of the dynamic graph in the same snapshot, combining the low-pass filter with the high-pass filter and achieving activation functions in the frequency domain.
- As a new dynamic graph representation learning method, experiments on three public benchmarks demonstrate that GFTLSTM can capture dynamic information and outperform more current baseline models in dynamic graphs.

2 Dynamic Graphs

Based on how data is processed in time series, there are two main categories of dynamic graphs. The first category, discrete dynamic graphs, records graph data in fixed time snapshot as shown in Fig. 1(a); the second category, continuous dynamic graphs, records graph data in continuous time, as illustrated in Fig. 1(b). Based on the structure of discrete dynamic graph, they can be further classified into the following three types according to the dynamic characteristics of nodes and edges: (1) The first discrete dynamic graph is an ordered set of node features and graph structure, referred to as a static graph structure with a temporal signal, as shown in Fig. 2(a). In this type of dynamic graph, node features change over time, but the graph structure remains constant across all snapshots; (2) The second discrete dynamic graph is an ordered set of node features and

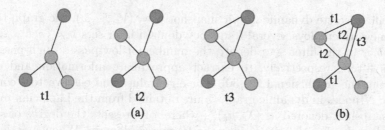

Fig. 1. (a) discrete dynamic graphs (b) continuous dynamic graphs.

graph structure, referred to as a dynamic graph structure with static features. In this case, node features remain unchanged, while the graph structure evolves over time, as seen in Fig. 2(b); (3) The third discrete dynamic graph is also an ordered set of node features and graph structure, wherein both node features and graph structure vary across different time snapshots. This type is known as a dynamic graph structure with a temporal signal, as shown in Fig. 2(c);

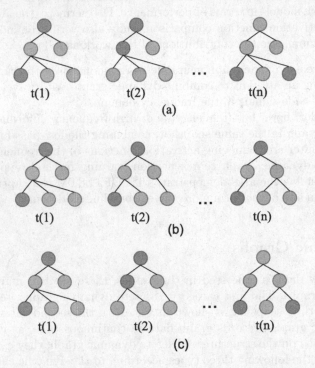

Fig. 2. (a) static graph with temporal signal (b) dynamic graph with static signal (c) dynamic graph with temporal signal.

3   Multi-resolution Framelets Analysis in Dynamic Graphs

In a specific discrete dynamic graph snapshot $\mathcal{G}_t = (V_t, E_t, \omega)$, the graph transform framework employs several frequency domain filter sets $\eta = \{a; b^1, ..., b^n\}$, where a, b, n in the filter sets denote the number of low-passes, high-pass and high-pass filters, respectively, to extract approximate information and other details from the graph signal [10,30]. The eigenvalues and eigenvectors consisting of the N nodes in dynamic graph $\mathcal{G}_t$ are obtained from the Laplacian matrix at each snapshot, denoted as $(\lambda_\ell, \mu_\ell)_j^N$, where j represents the degree of signal scaling when passing the signal into the frequency domain. When $n = 1, ..., r$, the signal of node p is transformed by the low-pass filter $\varphi_{j,p}$ and high-pass filters $\phi_{j,p}^r$ in a snapshot can be expressed as follows

$$\varphi_{j,p}(v) = \sum_{\ell=1}^{N} \widehat{\alpha}\left(\frac{\lambda_\ell}{2^j}\overline{\mu_\ell(p)}\mu_\ell(v)\right) \tag{1}$$

$$\phi_{j,p}(v) = \sum_{\ell=1}^{N} \widehat{\beta^{(n)}}\left(\frac{\lambda_\ell}{2^j}\overline{\mu_\ell(p)}\mu_\ell(v)\right) \tag{2}$$

where we exploit the Chebyshev polynomial approximation for the filters $\widehat{\alpha}$ and $\widehat{\beta^{(n)}}$. The process of projecting the original signal f to $\varphi_{j,p}$ and $\phi_{j,p}^r$ can be denoted as $<\varphi_{j,p}, f>$ and $<\phi_{j,p}^r, f>$, respectively, to obtain the final wavelet coefficients $v_{j,p}$ and $w_{j,p}$. Since the data used for deep learning training is in tensor form, the transformation of the graph signal can be achieved by the signal decomposition operator $\mathcal{W}$ and the signal reconstruction operator $\mathcal{V}$, described as

$$\mathcal{W} = \{\mathcal{W}_{r,j} \mid r = 1, \ldots, n; j = 1, \ldots J\} \cup \{\mathcal{W}_{0,j}\} \tag{3}$$

$$\mathcal{W}_{r,1} f = \mathcal{T}_r^k\left(2^{-J}\mathcal{L}\right) f \tag{4}$$

$$\mathcal{W}_{r,j} f = \mathcal{T}_r^k\left(2^{K+j-1}\mathcal{L}\right) \mathcal{T}_0^k\left(2^{K+j-2}\mathcal{L}\right) \cdots \mathcal{T}_0^k\left(2^{-K}\mathcal{L}\right) f \tag{5}$$

where $j = 2 \ldots J$, $\mathcal{T}_r^k$ is the r-degree Chebyshev polynomial, $\mathcal{L}$ is the graph Laplacian matrix, K is a constant satisfying $\lambda_{max} \le 2^K\pi$, $\mathcal{W}_{0,J} f = \{v_{J,p}\}_{p \in V_t}$ are the low-pass coefficients and $\mathcal{W}_{r,j} f = \{w_{j,p}^r\}_{p \in V_t}$ are high-pass coefficients of f, r is the number of high-pass filters. When the signal in the frequency domain is reconstructed, the reconstruction operator $\mathcal{V}$ is an arrangement reorganization of $\mathcal{W}$.

4   Dynamic Graph Neural Network Model Based on Graph Framelets Transform

A graph neural network is a powerful deep learning method. Most existing graph neural networks, such as GCN [9] and GAT [26], are based on spatial modeling. These models use spatial message passing to calculate information from neighboring nodes, then converge and integrate information from source to target nodes through graph convolution techniques. They are trained by multi-layer network stacking, ultimately achieving full graph feature learning. However, graph convolution models in the spatial domain are essentially low-pass filters and shallow graph convolution operations do not effectively propagate node labels. Deep graph convolution stacking can lead to excessive feature smoothing, and after multiple training iterations, similar information is sharpened more than once, making it difficult to distinguish between different classes of nodes. Using the Fourier transform to pass the signal into the frequency domain is another modeling technique. The spatial domain signal is projected onto the Fourier basis to determine the magnitude of the signal in the spectrogram. After performing a series of operations, the signal is transmitted back into the spatial domain by the inverse Fourier transform indiscriminately. This frequency domain-based data analysis and modeling method has significant limitations for non-smooth signals with frequencies that change over time.

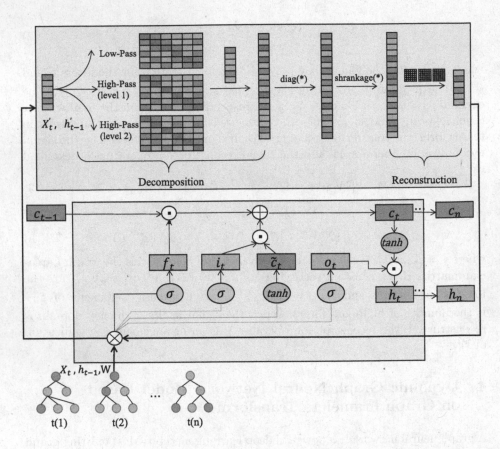

Fig. 3. The framework of GFTLSTM.

Due to the aforementioned shortcomings of modeling based on the spatial and frequency domains, we consider the wavelet transform, which is not only suitable for handling non-smooth signal characteristics (also a feature of dynamic graphs) but can also compensate for the drawbacks of the Fourier transform. We construct a frequency convolution model for dynamic graph signal extraction, GFTLSTM, based on the wavelet transform principle. The model structure is shown in Fig. 3. First, we project the spatial domain signal onto the wavelet basis, then filter the low-frequency and high-frequency signals differently and further compress the signal in the frequency space using the *Shrinkage* function while denoising. The final step is to merge the filtering results with a long short-term memory neural network to capture the evolving features and relationships in dynamic graphs.

4.1 Multi-resolution Graph Convolution Based on Graph Framelets Transform

Based on the above graph framelets transform steps, we can perform convolution operations in the frequency domain space, formulated as follows:

$$\mathcal{V}\left(Shrinkage\left(diag\left(\theta\right)\left(\mathcal{W}X_{t}^{'}\right)\right)\right), X_{t}^{'} = X_{t}W \tag{6}$$

$$\mathcal{V}\left(Shrinkage\left(diag\left(\theta\right)\left(\mathcal{W}h_{t-1}^{'}\right)\right)\right), h_{t-1}^{'} = h_{t-1}W \tag{7}$$

where $X \in R^{N \times d}$ represents the node feature in dynamic graphs at the current moment t, $W \in d \times d'$ denotes the trainable weight matrix, $X_{t}^{'}$ is the input feature matrix at this snapshot t after the transformation of the weight matrix W, θ is a network filter that multiplies each component value with the frequency domain framelet coefficients $\mathcal{W}X_{t}^{'}$ and $\mathcal{W}h_{t-1}^{'}$ to achieve the filtering operation, $Shrinkage$ denotes the signal compression function.

Activation functions for signal compression are typically applied in the spatial domain, which means the signal must be transferred back to the spatial domain without any loss before using the activation function. The conventional processing approach found in most activation functions does not meet our requirement for multi-resolution data analysis. In contrast, applying different filters to low-frequency and high-frequency signals in the frequency domain and then transferring them back to the spatial domain using the reconstruction operator accommodates the need for multi-resolution analysis while maintaining good performance. As shown in Fig. 3, three signal decomposition operators $\mathcal{W} = \{\mathcal{W}_{0,2}; \mathcal{W}_{1,1}, \mathcal{W}_{1,2}\}$ are obtained after portraying the signal with $j = 1, 2$ in a high-pass filter, followed by a low-pass filter and a high-pass filter. If the dimension of each decomposition operator is $N \times N$, then $W^{|X|} \in R^{3N \times d}$. After filtering the signal in the frequency domain through filter θ, the signal compression function $soft - shrinkage$ and $hard - shrinkage$ are used instead of the activation function to truncate the high-frequency components. The reconstruction operator $\mathcal{V} = (\mathcal{W})^{T}$ is then used to transfer the signal to the spatial domain. We perform the following signal compression function $Shrinkage$

$$Shrinkage - soft\left(x\right) = sgn\left(x\right)\left(|x| - \lambda\right)_{+}, \forall x \in R \tag{8}$$

$$Shrinkage - hard\left(x\right) = x\left(|x| - \lambda\right), \forall x \in R \tag{9}$$

4.2 Long Short-Term Memory Neural Network

One of the recurrent neural network models is the long short-term memory network (LSTM), which is primarily utilized to address gradient vanishing and gradient explosion issues during the training of long sequences [6]. We combine the graph convolution operation with the long short-term memory neural network, the multiplication operation of the input matrix X_t and temporal information h_{t-1} with the weight matrix W in the long and short-term memory network is replaced by the multi-resolution graph convolution based on the graph framelets transform. The specific processing is shown as follows:

$$i_t = \sigma \left(W_{xi} * gX_t + W_{hi} * gh_{t-1} + w_{ci} \odot c_{t-1} + b_i \right) \tag{10}$$

$$f_t = \sigma \left(W_{xf} * gX_t + W_{hf} * gh_{t-1} + w_{ci} \odot c_{t-1} + b_f \right) \tag{11}$$

$$c_t = f_t \odot c_{t-1} + i_t \odot tanh \left(W_{xc} * gX_t + W_{hc} * gh_{t-1} + b_c \right) \tag{12}$$

$$o_t = \sigma \left(W_{xo} * gX_t + W_{ho} * gh_{t-1} + w_{co} \odot c_{t-1} + b_o \right) \tag{13}$$

$$h_t = o_t \odot tanh \left(c_t \right) \tag{14}$$

where $*g$ represents the convolution operation, which is the graph framelets transform, b is the bias matrix, c_{t-1} represents the internal state of the previous snapshots, recording all the historical information in the time sequence up to the previous snapshot; i_t serves as an input gate to retain important data and reduce the amount of information being input for unimportant data; f_t acts as a forget gate, selectively forgetting information about the internal state of the previous snapshots, while remembering crucial information; c_t indicates the internal state at the current snapshot, updating the information that needs to be recorded. The role of the output gate o_t is to control how much information needs to be output to the external state h_t from the internal state c_t at the current snapshot.

5   Experiments

5.1   Datasets

To evaluate the performance of the proposed GFTLSTM, we conduct experiments using three public datasets: Chickenpox Hungary [20], Pedal Me Deliveries [20], Wikipedia Math [20].

Chickenpox Hungary: This is a spatiotemporal dataset about officially reported cases of chickenpox in Hungary between 2005 and 2015, with nodes being counties, edges indicating adjacencies between counties, and a prediction target of the number of illnesses in the following week.

Pedal Me Deliveries: This is a dataset about the number of weekly bicycle package deliveries by Pedal Me in London during 2020 and 2021. Nodes in the graph represent geographical units and edges are proximity-based mutual adjacency relationships.

Wikipedia Math: This is a dataset about the popular mathematics topics on Wikipedia where the edges denote the links from one page to another and the features describe the number of daily visits between 2019 and 2021 March.

5.2   Experiment Settings

We conduct experiments on each of the three dynamic graph datasets using two training methods: incremental and cumulative. For the incremental training method, we perform the $Shrinkage - hard$ function, while for the cumulative training method, we use the $Shrinkage - soft$ function.

Incremental Training Method: The losses and training weights are updated for each time series snapshot in the dynamic graph.

Cumulative Training Method: The losses in each temporal snapshot in the dynamic graph are accumulated and then backpropagated.

The hyperparameters in the model are summarized in Table 1, where *epoch* denotes the total number of training iterations; hiddenNN denotes the number of neurons in the intermediate layers; lr denotes the learning rate; $dropout(p)$ is a function that randomly deactivates the neurons with probability p; λ is used as a threshold value to control the affected signal components. In the high-frequency coefficients, the value of all signal components is set to 0 if their absolute value is less than the threshold value, thus compressing the signal.

Table 1. Experiment Settings.

Datasets	Training methods	Epoch	HiddenNN	Lr	Dropout(p)	λ
Chickenpox Hungary	Incremental	100	200	0.0001	P = 0.3	1e−4
Chickenpox Hungary	Cumulative	100	32	0.01	P = 0.3	1e−4
PedalMe London	Incremental	100	200	0.0001	P = 0.3	1e−2
PedalMe London	Cumulative	100	32	0.0001	P = 0.3	1e−4
Wikipedia Math	Incremental	100	200	0.0001	.P = 0.3	1e−4
Wikipedia Math	Cumulative	100	32	0.01	P = 0.3	1e−4

5.3   Evaluation Metrics

We use mean squared error (MSE) and standard deviation as the evaluation metrics. MSE is the expected value of the squared difference between the sample estimate and the true sample value which can be defined as

$$L_q = \frac{1}{N} \sum_{N}^{i=1} (q_i - o_i)^2 \tag{15}$$

where $o = \{o_1, ..., o_N\}$ represents the model's output and q_i denotes the true sample values. The precision of the data is indicated by the standard deviation, which is a measure of the dispersion around the average value, described as

$$S = \sqrt{\frac{\sum_{i=1}^{n} (x_i - \overline{x})^2}{n - 1}} \tag{16}$$

where $\bar{x}$ denotes the sample average value and x_i is the i-th sample data. A high standard deviation indicates that most of the values are different from their average value, conversely, they are close to the average value.

5.4   Performance Comparison

Using supervised learning methods, the dynamic graph data are input into our model in a specific temporal sequence, and then the prediction results for the next snapshot are output. The experiments are repeated 10 times for each dataset under two different training methods, and the prediction results of other models are compared longitudinally. MSE is introduced to evaluate the performance of the model and the standard deviation is calculated for auxiliary validation. The experiment results are shown in Table 2.

Table 2. The predictive performance of GFTLSTM and other spatiotemporal neural networks evaluated by average mean squared error and standard deviations around the average mean squared error from 10 experiment repetitions.

	Chickenpox Hungary		PedalMe London		Wikipedia Math	
	Incremental	Cumulative	Incremental	Cumulative	Incremental	Cumulative
DCRNN [15]	1.124 ± 0.015	1.123 ± 0.014	1.463 ± 0.019	1.450 ± 0.024	0.679 ± 0.020	0.803 ± 0.018
GConvGRU [23]	1.128 ± 0.011	1.132 ± 0.023	1.622 ± 0.032	1.944 ± 0.013	**0.657 ± 0.015**	0.837 ± 0.021
GConvLSTM [23]	1.121 ± 0.014	1.119 ± 0.022	1.442 ± 0.028	1.433 ± 0.020	0.777 ± 0.021	0.868 ± 0.018
GC-LSTM [4]	1.115 ± 0.014	1.116 ± 0.023	1.455 ± 0.023	1.468 ± 0.025	0.779 ± 0.023	0.852 ± 0.016
DyGrAE [24,25]	1.120 ± 0.021	1.118 ± 0.015	1.455 ± 0.031	1.456 ± 0.019	0.073 ± 0.009	0.816 ± 0.016
EGCN-H [19]	1.113 ± 0.016	1.104 ± 0.024	1.467 ± 0.026	1.436 ± 0.017	0.775 ± 0.022	0.857 ± 0.022
EGCN-O [19]	1.124 ± 0.009	1.119 ± 0.020	1.491 ± 0.024	1.430 ± 0.023	0.750 ± 0.014	0.823 ± 0.014
A3T-GCN [1]	1.114 ± 0.008	1.119 ± 0.018	1.469 ± 0.027	1.475 ± 0.029	0.781 ± 0.011	0.872 ± 0.017
T-GCN [29]	1.117 ± 0.011	1.111 ± 0.022	1.479 ± 0.012	1.481 ± 0.029	0.764 ± 0.011	0.846 ± 0.020
MPNN LSTM [18]	1.116 ± 0.023	1.129 ± 0.021	1.485 ± 0.028	1.458 ± 0.013	0.795 ± 0.010	0.905 ± 0.017
AGCRN [2]	1.120 ± 0.010	1.116 ± 0.017	1.469 ± 0.030	1.465 ± 0.026	0.788 ± 0.011	0.832 ± 0.020
GFTLSTM	**1.099 ± 0.001**	**1.067 ± 0.012**	**1.437 ± 0.027**	**1.401 ± 0.096**	0.708 ± 0.013	**0.653 ± 0.027**

The bolded values in Table 2 indicate the best experiment results of the various prediction models. It can be observed that the GFTLSTM model proposed in this paper outperforms most of the comparison models in processing discrete dynamic graph data and achieves the best results in most experiments. Although the GFTLSTM model doesn't achieve state-of-the-art results in the Wikipedia Math dataset using the incremental training method, it still outperforms the majority of the models. This demonstrates that the GFTLSTM model can better capture the evolutionary features of dynamic graphs, providing a valuable reference for dynamic graph representation learning.

5.5   Ablation Study

Ablation experiments are conducted to verify the effectiveness of the *Shrinkage* function introduced in the frequency domain space to replace the spatial domain activation function ReLU in the model. In these experiments, GFTLSTM-S represents the model proposed in this paper after removing the *Shrinkage − soft* and *Shrinkage − hard* functions. After conducting 10 trials, the experiment results are presented in Table 3.

Table 3. The predictive performance of GFTLSTM-S evaluated using average mean squared error and standard deviations around the average mean squared error from 10 experiment repetitions.

	Chickenpox Hungary		PedalMe London		Wikipedia Math	
	Incremental	Cumulative	Incremental	Cumulative	Incremental	Cumulative
GFTLSTM-S	1.103 ± 0.002	1.078 ± 0.009	1.449 ± 0.020	1.569 ± 0.167	0.717 ± 0.019	0.669 ± 0.017

As shown in the table above, the MSE of the experiment results exhibits varying degrees of improvement after removing the *Shrinkage* function in the frequency domain space. This result indicates that the model performance becomes worse, which verifies the usefulness of introducing the *Shrinkage* function to the model.

5.6 Comparison Experiment

To further verify the effectiveness of multi-resolution analysis in the model, the ReLU activation function is introduced in the spatial domain and the *Shrinkage* function in the frequency domain is removed to obtain the GFTLSTM_R model. The experiment results are shown in Table 4 after 10 repetitions.

Table 4. The predictive performance of GFTLSTM_R evaluated by average mean squared error and standard deviations around the average mean squared error from 10 experiment repetitions.

	Chickenpox Hungary		PedalMe London		Wikipedia Math	
	Incremental	Cumulative	Incremental	Cumulative	Incremental	Cumulative
GFTLSTM_R	1.103 ± 0.003	1.080 ± 0.012	1.472 ± 0.031	1.466 ± 0.119	0.720 ± 0.014	0.658 ± 0.018

As shown in Table 4, a comparison of the performance of the GFTLSTM model as detailed in Table 2 shows that the value of GFTLSTM_R in terms of MSE or standard deviation metrics also increases, indicating that the experiment results become worse again. Therefore, for the discrete dynamic graph dataset, better results are obtained by using the *Shrinkage* function in the frequency domain space instead of ReLU as the activation function. This verifies the value of using the *Shrinkage* function for multi-resolution analysis in dynamic graphs.

6 Conclusion

In this work, we propose a general framework for dynamic graph representation learning, representing a first attempt to combine wavelet analysis theory, multi-resolution analysis and dynamic graphs. We evaluate the model's effectiveness on several dynamic graph datasets. In future work, we hope to apply the model to dynamic graph structures with static features, dynamic graph structures with temporal signals, and continuous dynamic graphs within specific application scenarios. This will further verify the model's generality across various dynamic graph representation learning tasks.

References

1. Bai, J., et al.: A3T-GCN: attention temporal graph convolutional network for traffic forecasting. ISPRS Int. J. Geo Inf. **10**(7), 485 (2021)
2. Bai, L., Yao, L., Li, C., Wang, X., Wang, C.: Adaptive graph convolutional recurrent network for traffic forecasting. Adv. Neural. Inf. Process. Syst. **33**, 17804–17815 (2020)
3. Cai, L., et al.: Structural temporal graph neural networks for anomaly detection in dynamic graphs. In: Proceedings of the 30th ACM International Conference on Information & Knowledge Management, Changsha, pp. 3747–3756. ACM (2021)
4. Chen, J., Wang, X., Xu, X.: GC-LSTM: graph convolution embedded LSTM for dynamic network link prediction. Appl. Intell., 1–16 (2022)
5. Grattarola, D., Alippi, C.: Graph neural networks in TensorFlow and keras with spektral. IEEE Comput. Intell. Mag. **16**(1), 99–106 (2021)
6. Hochreiter, S., Schmidhuber, J.: Long short-term memory. Neural Comput. **9**(8), 1735–1780 (1997)
7. Javaid, S., Sufian, A., Pervaiz, S., Tanveer, M.: Smart traffic management system using internet of things. In: Proceedings of the 20th International Conference on Advanced Communication Technology, Wonju, pp. 393–398. Springer (2018)
8. Karimi, M., Jannach, D., Jugovac, M.: News recommender systems-survey and roads ahead. Inf. Process. Manage. **54**(6), 1203–1227 (2018)
9. Kipf, T.N., Welling, M.: Semi-supervised classification with graph convolutional networks. arXiv preprint arXiv:1609.02907 (2017)
10. Li, M., Ma, Z., Wang, Y.G., Zhuang, X.: Fast Haar transforms for graph neural networks. Neural Netw. **128**, 188–198 (2020)
11. Li, M., Sonoda, S., Cao, F., Wang, Y.G., Liang, J.: How powerful are shallow neural networks with bandlimited random weights? In: International Conference on Machine Learning, pp. 19960–19981. PMLR (2023)
12. Li, M., Wang, D.: 2-d stochastic configuration networks for image data analytics. IEEE Trans. Cybern. **51**(1), 359–372 (2021)
13. Li, M., Zhang, L., Cui, L., Bai, L., Li, Z., Wu, X.: BLoG: bootstrapped graph representation learning with local and global regularization for recommendation. Pattern Recogn. **144**, 109874 (2023)
14. Li, S., Xu, L.D., Zhao, S.: The internet of things: a survey. Inf. Syst. Front. **17**, 243–259 (2015)
15. Li, Y., Yu, R., Shahabi, C., Liu, Y.: Diffusion convolutional recurrent neural network: Data-driven traffic forecasting. In: Proceedings of the 6th International Conference on Learning Representations. OpenReview.net, Vancouver (2018)

16. Liu, J., Xu, C., Yin, C., Wu, W., Song, Y.: K-core based temporal graph convolutional network for dynamic graphs. IEEE Trans. Knowl. Data Eng. **34**(8), 3841–3853 (2020)

17. Liu, Y., et al.: Anomaly detection in dynamic graphs via transformer. IEEE Trans. Knowl. Data Eng. **01**, 1 (2021)

18. Panagopoulos, G., Nikolentzos, G., Vazirgiannis, M.: Transfer graph neural networks for pandemic forecasting. In: Proceedings of the 35th AAAI Conference on Artificial Intelligence, California, pp. 4838–4845. AAAI Press (2021)

19. Pareja, A., et al.: EvolveGCN: evolving graph convolutional networks for dynamic graphs. In: Proceedings of the 34th AAAI Conference on Artificial Intelligence, New York, pp. 5363–5370. AAAI Press (2020)

20. Rozemberczki, B., et al.: Pytorch geometric temporal: Spatiotemporal signal processing with neural machine learning models. In: Proceedings of the 30th ACM International Conference on Information & Knowledge Management, Changsha, pp. 4564–4573. ACM (2021)

21. Sankar, A., Wu, Y., Gou, L., Zhang, W., Yang, H.: DySAT: deep neural representation learning on dynamic graphs via self-attention networks. In: Proceedings of the 13th International Conference on Web Search and Data Mining, Houston, pp. 519–527. ACM (2020)

22. Scarselli, F., Gori, M., Tsoi, A.C., Hagenbuchner, M., Monfardini, G.: The graph neural network model. IEEE Trans. Neural Networks **20**(1), 61–80 (2008)

23. Seo, Y., Defferrard, M., Vandergheynst, P., Bresson, X.: Structured sequence modeling with graph convolutional recurrent networks. In: Cheng, L., Leung, A.C.S., Ozawa, S. (eds.) ICONIP 2018. LNCS, vol. 11301, pp. 362–373. Springer, Cham (2018). https://doi.org/10.1007/978-3-030-04167-0_33

24. Taheri, A., Berger-Wolf, T.: Predictive temporal embedding of dynamic graphs. In: Proceedings of the 9th IEEE/ACM International Conference on Advances in Social Networks Analysis and Mining, Vancouver, pp. 57–64. IEEE (2019)

25. Taheri, A., Gimpel, K., Berger-Wolf, T.: Learning to represent the evolution of dynamic graphs with recurrent models. In: Proceedings of the 28th World Wide Web Conference, Portland, pp. 301–307. ACM (2019)

26. Velickovic, P., et al.: Graph attention networks. Stat **1050**(20), 10–48550 (2017)

27. Wu, Z., Pan, S., Chen, F., Long, G., Zhang, C., Philip, S.Y.: A comprehensive survey on graph neural networks. IEEE Trans. Neural Netw. Learning Syst. **32**(1), 4–24 (2020)

28. Yu, W., Cheng, W., Aggarwal, C.C., Zhang, K., Chen, H., Wang, W.: NetWalk: a flexible deep embedding approach for anomaly detection in dynamic networks. In: Proceedings of the 24th ACM SIGKDD International Conference on Knowledge Discovery & Data Mining, London, pp. 2672–2681. ACM (2018)

29. Zhao, L., et al.: T-GCN: a temporal graph convolutional network for traffic prediction. IEEE Trans. Intell. Transp. Syst. **21**(9), 3848–3858 (2019)

30. Zheng, X., et al.: How framelets enhance graph neural networks. In: Proceedings of the 38th International Conference on Machine Learning, Graz, pp. 12761–12771. PMLR (2021)

31. Zhou, H., She, C., Deng, Y., Dohler, M., Nallanathan, A.: Machine learning for massive industrial internet of things. IEEE Wirel. Commun. **28**(4), 81–87 (2021)

32. Zhou, J., et al.: Graph neural networks: a review of methods and applications. AI Open **1**, 57–81 (2020)

Advancing Multi-actor Graph Convolutions for Skeleton-Based Action Recognition

Yiqun Zhang[1]([✉]), Zhenyu Qin[2], Yang Liu[2], Tom Gedeon[3], and Wu Song[4]

[1] Australian National University, Canberra, Australia
admin@yiqun.io
[2] Seeing Machines, Canberra, Australia
[3] Curtin University, Perth, Australia
Tom.Gedeon@curtin.edu.au
[4] Rongcheng Cloud-Intelligence Co., Ltd., Rongcheng, China

Abstract. Human skeleton motion recognition, notable for its lightweight, interference-resistant, and resource-saving properties, plays a crucial role in human motion recognition and has found widespread applications. The common approach to capture motion features from human skeleton videos involves extracting skeleton features temporally or spatially using Graph Convolution Networks (GCN) or their improved variants. Nevertheless, existing extraction methods encounter two primary limitations: variability in the number of actors involved in an action and disconnected subgraphs representing multiple actors' actions, resulting in a loss of inter-subgraph features. To overcome these challenges, we propose Human Mirror and Human Link strategies, which replicate diverse human data to fill and interlink multiple subgraphs. Empirically, our proposed methods applied to the NTU RGB+D 120 dataset significantly enhanced the performance of the base model MSG3D, demonstrating the effectiveness of our approach in handling multi-actor scenarios.

Keywords: Skeleton-Based Action Recognition · Graph Convolution Networks · Human Link · Human Mirror · Multi-Actor Interaction · Subgraph Unification

1 Introduction

It is a long-standing problem of computer vision to accurately and promptly recognize human actions [1]. Advances of this problem can lead to improvements in many applications such as human-robot interaction [2], sports analysis [3], and smart health-care services [4]. We study skeleton-based action recognition, a subfield of action recognition emerged recently thanks to the ready availability of human pose estimation algorithms and devices [5–7]. Currently, skeleton-based action recognition is swiftly accumulating attention due to numerous advantages

M. Clayton et al. (Eds.): INTETAIN 2023, LNICST 560, pp. 76–95, 2024.
https://doi.org/10.1007/978-3-031-55722-4_7

of skeletonized human representations such as being concise and free from environmental noises [7]. Taking conciseness as an example, it consumes more than 1 GB to store a minute's RGB videos, whereas it merely costs 100 KB to store the skeleton sequence of the same length according to our empirical studies.

Many skeleton sequences involve more than one participant for displaying interactive actions such as *shaking hands* and *punching others* [8]. When tackling these multi-participant skeletonized representations, a common algorithmic pattern is described as follows [9–12]. (1) Each person's skeleton representation is separately processed to extract spatial and temporal patterns; (2) the extracted features of different participants are fused (such as addition or concatenation) to form the overall representation of the action; (3) the fused feature is further transformed to recognize the interactive action. That is, the action's interactive clues are not taken into consideration until the end of the processing pipeline. On the other hand, interactions between the participants contain abundant informative cues for accurately classifying the actions.

Recognizing human actions, especially involving multiple participants, remains a challenging endeavor in computer vision. While skeleton-based action recognition offers a streamlined approach, many algorithms overlook the rich interplay between participants. This oversight can lead to missed nuances crucial for accurate categorization. Our work introduces mechanisms to bridge this gap, harnessing the potential of interpersonal relationships.

We aim to facilitate existing skeleton-based action recognizers to explicitly exploit the interactive relationships between participants. To this end, we propose the **human link** mechanism. Specifically, instead of processing each person's skeleton individually, we create a giant skeleton containing multiple participants' skeletons. Within this giant skeleton, we link together the joints that correspond to the same body part (such as head and left/right hand). These additional links explicitly enable skeleton-based action recognizers to capture the interactive patterns between participants.

To extend human link to be also applicable to the actions that involve only a single participant, we further propose the **human mirror** mechanism. Specifically, human mirror creates a copy of the person's skeletonized representation and treats the copied skeleton as performing the interactive action with the original skeleton. This newly generated skeleton copy grants the feasibility of human link. Additionally, our experimental results also reveal accuracy improvement when merely implementing human mirror to skeleton-based action recognizers. Our further studies imply that the enhanced performance is due to the reduction of distribution shift between the input skeletons of single and multiple participants.

We summarize our contributions as follows:

1. We propose the **human link** method that facilitates existing skeleton-based action recognizers to explicitly capture the interactive relationships between participants as cues for more accurate action recognition.
2. We present the **human mirror** approach that can not only improve action recognition accuracy for single-participant actions, but also enables human link to be applicable for the non-interactive actions.

3. Both the proposed human link and human mirror are widely compatible with existing skeleton-based action recognizers. Human mirror can independently enhance a recognizer's accuracy. Moreover, applying the two methods in conjunction can further improve the performance. We experimentally demonstrate that both human link and mirror consistently boost the accuracy of numerous recent models.
4. Equipped with the conjunction of human link and mirror, a simple model is competitive with more complex models in accuracy and consumes substantially fewer parameters and less inference time. When combining the two components with a more complicated network, we achieve new state-of-the-art accuracy.

After this introduction, we delve into the relevant literature, discussing *Skeleton-Based Action Recognition*, *Neural Nets on Graphs*, and *Multi-Scale Graph Convolutions* in Sect. 2. Section 3 introduces our proposed methods, where we detail the notations used and provide in-depth discussions on **Human Mirror** and **Human Link**. In Sect. 4, we detail our experimental setups, describe the datasets, preprocessing techniques, and present a thorough evaluation of our methods, including component studies to dissect their individual contributions. We conclude the paper in Sect. 5 with our concluding remarks and directions for future work.

2   Related Work

2.1   Skeleton-Based Action Recognition

In the early time, the features of the entire sequence were encoded into a metric space for skeleton-based action recognition [13]. Since these pioneering models did not explicitly leverage the co-occurrences between frames, they insufficiently extract patterns along the action trajectories, producing low recognizing accuracy. Subsequently, convolutional neural networks (CNNs) were revived and soon applied to skeleton-based action recognition. CNNs bolster capturing dynamical clues by convolving along the temporal direction, prompting higher accuracy for recognizing skeleton-based actions [6,14,15]. However, CNNs are not designed to specifically model a skeleton's structural information, thus leaving rich topological features of a skeleton under-exploited.

Graph convolutional networks (GCNs) were later introduced to model the internal topological interconnections by representing a skeleton as a graph, where nodes and edges represent joints and bones respectively. Spatial Temporal Graph Convolutional Networks (ST-GCN) integrated hierarchical spatial features with multiple graph convolutional layers and obtained temporal patterns with convolution [9]. Then, Li et al. designed AS-GCN [16] to supplant the fixed skeleton graph with a learnable adjacency matrix, improving the flexibility of extracting structural information and delivering a boost to the recognition accuracy. In later work, Si et al. proposed An Attention Enhanced Graph Convolutional LSTM (AGC-LSTM) to aggregate graph convolutional operations into Long

Short Term Memory (LSTM)'s internal gate operations for extracting long-range temporal cues of the skeleton motion trajectories [17]. Subsequently, the Two-Stream Adaptive Graph Convolutional Networks (2 s-AGCN) model additionally utilized bone features apart from joint features and was equipped with learnable residual masks to improve the flexibility of aggregating topological features [18]. Recently, many novel techniques, such as graph-based dropout [10], 3D graph convolutions [19], and shift-convolutions [7], have been incorporated into graph networks for skeleton-based action recognition.

2.2 Neural Nets on Graphs

In order to extract information and features from graph structure, many studies have explored graph structure through neural networks [20–23]. With the introduction of Graph Neural Networks (GNNs) [24, 25], researchers have applied the convolution method of pictures to graph structures, and the extraction efficiency of individual graph structures has been greatly increased. GNNs incorporate the graph structure into a neural network, allowing the network to process and exchange information between nodes based on the graph topology to accomplish information fusion and information extraction. The nodes in the graph are updated layer by layer through a multilayer GNN network. Each node will fuse and exchange its own data with neighboring nodes after convolution operation, so that different nodes can obtain global information to a little extent. The GNN network is then pooled by an aggregation function such as Average Pooling, and finally by an activation function, which greatly facilitates the study of graph structure.

2.3 Multi-scale Graph Convolutions

However, the skeleton structure is a more complex graph structure, the skeleton structure is generally larger and longer distance, the general way of exchanging information with neighboring nodes can not meet the needs of the skeleton graph structure. At the same time, human action is an overall behavior, local information exchange and feature fusion are not enough to judge human action. Therefore, in order to meet the needs of human skeleton action recognition, researchers have proposed many methods to solve this problem [19,26,27]. Firstly, we can cross the simple neighbor relationship to exchange the data with the nodes at a longer distance, and we can capture the information at a longer distance through a higher order polynomial of the adjacency matrix, and give the larger weight to the nodes at a closer distance. In this way, we can learn the information at a closer distance as well as at a longer distance, and fuse the features of the whole human skeleton graph structure.

3   Method

3.1   Baseline Model

The foundation of our work is built upon the MS-G3D model introduced in [19]. MS-G3D stands out for its ability to effectively handle spatial-temporal graphs in skeleton-based action recognition, particularly excelling in unbiased long-range joint relationship modeling under multi-scale operators and ensuring seamless cross-spacetime information flow. The modifications and enhancements we propose in the subsequent sections are specifically tailored for this baseline. Apart from the alterations and improvements we introduce, all other components and configurations of the model remain consistent with their original design as delineated in the baseline. This approach ensures a transparent assessment, enabling any observed performance variation to be directly linked to our introduced methods, facilitating a precise comparison between the original MS-G3D and its modified counterpart.

3.2   Notations

We use graphs to represent the human skeleton. The graph is denoted as $\mathcal{G}$. There are a set of vertices $\mathcal{V}$, a set of edges $\mathcal{E}$. The set of vertices, $\mathcal{V}$, represents the various joints in the human skeleton, such as the elbows, knees, hips, and so on. Each vertex, therefore, corresponds to a specific joint location at a given frame in the video or motion capture data. The set of edges, $\mathcal{E}$, captures the anatomical relationships between these joints. Each edge in $\mathcal{E}$ denotes a physical connection or bond between two joints, resembling the skeletal structure of the human body. For instance, an edge might exist between the shoulder and elbow joints, representing the upper arm bone. It is worth noting that the configuration of $\mathcal{E}$ is based on the natural topology of the human skeleton, ensuring that our graph representation, $\mathcal{G}$, is anatomically consistent. So we know:

$$\mathcal{G} = (\mathcal{V}, \mathcal{E})$$

$\mathcal{V}$ is a vertices set. There are N vertices in $\mathcal{V}$. We use v_i to represent the i-th vertex. So we know:

$$\mathcal{V} = \{v_1, v_2, \ldots, v_N\}$$

$\mathcal{E}$ is a edge set. We use adjacency matrices $\mathbf{A}$ to represent these edges. This matrix is $N \times N$, so we know $\mathbf{A} \in \mathbb{R}^{N \times N}$. We use $a_{i,j}$ to represent the elements of row i and column j in the adjacency matrix. In addition, $a_{i,j}$ indicates the connection state between v_i and v_j. If $a_{i,j}$ is 1, it indicates that there is a connection between v_i and v_j in $\mathcal{G}$; if $a_{i,j}$ is 0, it indicates that there is no connection.

In the graph, there are some vertices around any vertices v_i, which we call neighbors whose set is denoted by $\mathcal{N}(v_i)$. We use $\mathcal{N}_1(v_i)$ to represent the first-order neighbor, $\mathcal{N}_1(v_i)$, $\mathcal{N}_1(v_i) = \{v_j | a_{i,j} \neq 0\}$. For k-order neighbor $\mathcal{N}_k(v_i)$, we can know $\mathcal{N}_k(v_i) = \{v_j | \exists v_h \in \mathcal{N}_{k-1}(v_i), a_{h,j} \neq 0 \ and \ v_j \notin \mathcal{N}_1(v_i) \cup \mathcal{N}_2(v_i) \cup \cdots \cup \mathcal{N}_{k-1}(v_i)\}$.

$\mathcal{X}$ is a feature set of a action. We use a tensor $\mathbf{X}$ to represent it. Each action consists of T frames. Each frame consists of M human skeleton graphs. Each graph has V vertices and each vertice has C features. This tensor is $T \times M \times V \times C$, so we know

$$\mathbf{X} \in \mathbb{R}^{T \times M \times V \times C}$$

The i-th frame in an action is represented by f_i, and the i-th graph in a frame is represented by g_i. x_i represents the set of features of f_i. So we know $f_i \in \mathbb{R}^{M \times V \times C}$. $x_{i,j}$ represents the set of features of g_j in t_i. So we know $x_{i,j} \in \mathbb{R}^{V \times C}$. $x_{i,j,k}$ represents the set of features of v_k in g_j and t_i. So we know $x_{i,j,k} \in \mathbb{R}^C$.

3.3   Human Mirror

In the skeleton data, for different actions, the number of people completing the action is also different. Some actions can be completed by only one person. Such as *Eat Meal*, *Brushing Teeth* and *Brushing Hair*. So for any frame f_i, $x_{i,0}$ represents the data of the first actor and $x_{i,1}$ represents the data of the second actor. In this action, $x_{i,1}$ is all 0. For this type of data, we call it *Single Person Action*.

But some actions need two people to complete. Such as *Hugging Other Person*, *Handshaking* and *Walking Towards Each Other*. In such data, both $x_{i,0}$ and $x_{i,1}$ are not all 0. For this type of data, we call it *Double Person Action*.

This way different data types are involved in the neural network as training data. For *Single Person Action*, the neural network only needs to learn the features of one person in space. But for *Double Person Action*, the neural network not only needs to learn the features of each person in space, but also needs to learn the relationship between two people. For *Single Person Action*, $x_{i,1}$ is blank, so the neural network will receive the influence of these data and it is difficult to balance between the two data.

To solve this problem, we use **Human Mirror** to solve the impact of different types of data on neural networks. **Human Mirror** is a processing method for *Single Person Action*, which aims to eliminate the unbalanced gap between *Single Person Action* and *Double Person Action*. **Human Mirror** is to check whether the action is *Single Person Action* by $x_{i,1}$. If $x_{i,1}$ is blank, we copy the action of the $x_{i,0}$ to $x_{i,1}$. In this way, both $x_{i,0}$ and $x_{i,1}$ are not blank. The neural network surface will train two different data in the same way to avoid the negative impact of blank data.

For a tensor $\mathbf{T}$, we define a function $B(\mathbf{T})$. This function checks if all the values in the tensor $\mathbf{T}$ are 0, if they are 0, then the result is 0, otherwise the result is 1.

$$B(\mathbf{T}) = \begin{cases} 0 & \textit{all values are 0} \\ 1 & \textit{otherwise} \end{cases} \tag{1}$$

Based on this function, we can calculate if a graph is empty. In this way, we can determine whether a action is *Single Person Action* or *Double Person Action*. We calculate $B(x_{i,1})$, if the result is 0, we can know this action is *Single Person Action*, otherwise *Double Person Action*. We check each $B(x_{i,1}), 1 <= i <= N$. When $B(x_{i,1}) = 0$, we assign a new value to $B(x_{i,1})$ so that let $B(x_{i,1}) :=$ $B(x_{i,0})$, otherwise it remains unchanged (Fig. 1).

$$B(x_{i,1}) = \begin{cases} B(x_{i,1}) & B(x_{i,1}) = 1 \\ B(x_{i,0}) & B(x_{i,1}) = 0 \end{cases} \tag{2}$$

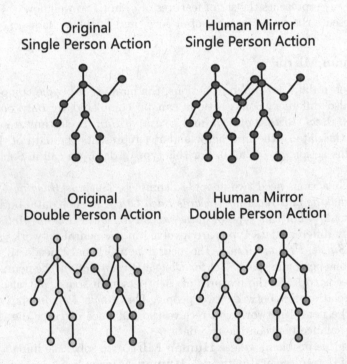

Fig. 1. For *Single Person Action* and *Double Person Action*, Skeleton without **Human Mirror** and with **Human Mirror**

3.4   Human Link

In each frame f_i, g_0 and g_1 are two independent subgraphs without connection. In the traditional strategy [17–19,28], two subgraphs are input into neural network independently, and the temporal and spatial features of the graph are extracted through GCN [29] and other networks. In this way, $x_{i,0}$ and $x_{i,1}$ obtain a feature respectively. Traditional strategy takes the average value of them, and then input the results into the classification neural network for classification.

In this strategy, although the neural network can extract enough features from spatial and temporal scales, the features cannot be exchanged between two individuals. Some actions are performed by two people together, so fusing the features of two people can help the neural network to learn the features better. Also, averaging the features of $x_{i,0}$ and $x_{i,1}$ causes loss of information, which is not a good feature fusion method. These two problems of traditional methods result in inadequate extraction of human features between two individuals.

To solve this problem, we use **Human Link**. **Human Link** optimizes the graph structure by stitching two human skeleton graphs together to form a large human skeleton graph. In this way, two subgraphs consisting of N nodes each are transformed into a super human graph with $2N$ nodes. By connecting two characters together through edges, the GCN [29] network can fuse and extract the features of different characters through the edges, solving the drawback that two people cannot communicate with each other. In addition, by fusing two subgraphs into one, the extracted features are the whole contents of the graph, which avoids the information loss caused by averaging.

The way we connect two people is to connect the corresponding points of two graphs. There are graph g_1 and g_2 in each frame f_i, we replace them with a larger graph g'. To represent this new graph, we need to use the adjacency matrix $\mathbf{A}'$. The larger graph is a splice of g_1 and g_2, so it has $2N$ vertices. So we know

$$\mathbf{A}' \in \mathbb{R}^{2N \times 2N}$$

For g_1 and g_2, their adjacency matrices are $\mathbb{A}_1$ and $\mathbb{A}_2$. In addition, we define the identity matrix $\mathbf{I}_N \in \mathbb{R}^{N \times N}$. So we know:

$$\mathbf{A}' = \begin{bmatrix} \mathbf{A}_1 \ \mathbf{I}_N \\ \mathbf{I}_N \ \mathbf{A}_2 \end{bmatrix} \tag{3}$$

For the large graph g', tensor $\mathbf{X}'$ is its feature tensor. There is only 1 human large skeleton graph in each frame. So this tensor is $T \times 2V \times C$, so we know

$$\mathbf{X}' \in \mathbb{R}^{T \times 2V \times C}$$

We use the larger graph g' obtained by **Human Link** to input it into the neural network for learning. The neural network can learn not only the temporal and spatial features, but also the relationship features between two people, and can input it into the classifier to get the results without taking the average value (Fig. 2 and 3).

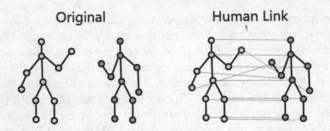

Fig. 2. Skeleton without **Human Link** and with **Human Link**

4   Experiments

4.1   Datasets

NTU RGB+D 60 and NTU RGB+D 120
NTU RGB+D 60 [30] is the skeleton action recognition data set, with a total
of 60 different actions (such as drinking water, brushing hair, drop, etc.). The
movements were performed by 40 actors between the ages of 10 and 35, with
a total of 56880 movement samples recorded. Dataset captured by Microsoft
Kinect 2.0 camera, each with RGB video, depth map sequences, 3D skeleton
data and infrared video. In order to obtain more adequate data, three different
cameras were used for the dataset, all three with the same height and horizontal
angles of 0, −45 and +45°, and each actor had to perform the action twice
(once facing the left camera, then once facing the right camera). In addition, our
cameras will have different setups, which differ in terms of height and distance
from the actor. The dataset use 17 different setups depending on the height and
distance.

We used the 3D skeleton data from the dataset, the node information of the
skeleton was obtained by the skeleton tracking technique in the Kinect camera,
25 key nodes were recorded on each human body, and these data could determine
the 3D coordinates of human hands, head, body and legs in space for each frame.
Depending on the action, each action is performed by 1–2 people (50 kinds of
movements for a single person to complete, 10 kinds of movements by a pair to
complete). Therefore, each frame contains 25 or 50 nodes, and an action consists
of many frames, which are combined together in a temporal order to represent
an action (Fig. 4).

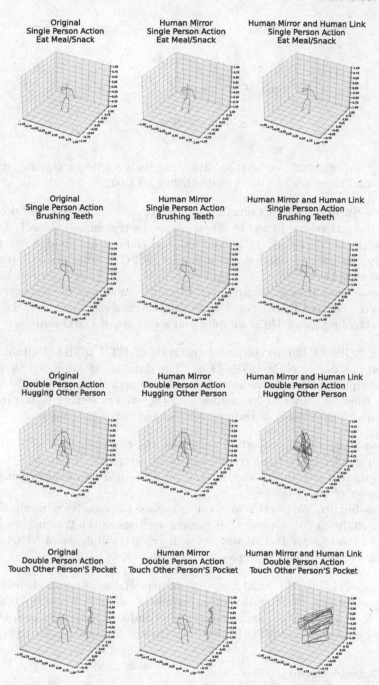

Fig. 3. Comparison figure of different action that original, with **Human Mirror** and **Human Link**. A row represents an action. The left column is without **Human Mirror**, the middle column is with **Human Mirror** and the right column is with **Human Mirror** and **Human Link**. Red represents the coincidence of two blue skeletons. (Color figure online)

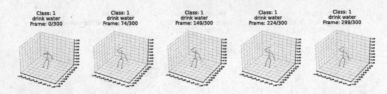

Fig. 4. A skeleton action

In our experiments, we need to divide the data set into a training set and a test set, and there are two ways to do this in NTU60.

– **Cross-Subject.** The actions in the data set are completed by 40 people, we take the actions completed by 20 people as the training set (id is 1, 2, 4, 5, 8, 9, 13–19, 25, 27, 28, 31, 34, 35 and 38), and the rest are divided into the test set. In this way, we will get a training set of 40320 samples and a test set of 16560 samples.
– **Cross-View.** Take the samples collected by camera 1 as the test set, and the samples collected by camera 2 and camera 3 as the training set. So, we will get a training set of 37920 samples and a test set of 18960 samples.

NTU RGB+D 120 [8] continues the style of NTU RGB+D 60 and is the extended content of NTU RGB+D 60. The data set is expanded from 56880 action samples of 60 different actions to 114480 action samples of 120 different actions, from 40 actors to 106 actors, and the camera setting is also increased to 32 kinds. The division of training set and test set is also different.

– **Cross-Subject.** This method continues the method of NTU RGB+D 60, which divides the actions completed by 53 actors into training sets and the rest into test sets. In this way, we will get a training set of 63026 samples and a test set of 59477 50919.
– **Cross-Setup.** We use this method to replace the cross view method used in NTU RGB+D 60. We select 16 camera settings as the training set and the rest as the test set In this way, we will get a training set of 54468 samples and a test set of 59477 samples.

Because NTU RGB+D 120 has more samples and more comprehensive acquisition parameters, the stability of experiments using it is much higher than that of NTU RGB+D 60, and more rigorous and comprehensive results can be obtained, so we will use NTU RGB+D 120 as the data set in our experiments.

4.2 Dataset Setup

– **Dataset Preprocessing.** The data in the dataset needs to be pre-processed in order to be fed into the training program more efficiently. The length of the actions in the dataset is not the same, and in order to be able to input to the neural network for training, we select the first 300 frames for training.

For skeleton sequences beyond 300 frames, we select the first 300 frames and discard the content after that. And for skeleton sequences with less than 300 frames, we use 0 to make up these frames. Making up and discarding are the standard practice in the field. Among the 300 frames selected, one keyframe is selected every three frames, so that we get 100 keyframes. We use these keyframes for training, which greatly accelerates the training speed and memory requirements while extracting sufficient information.

- **Dataset Setup.** In order to experiment, this program adopts the **Cross-Set** setting, in which 54468 data of 16 camera settings are used for training and 59477 data are used for testing. We will get a training set of 37920 samples and a test set of 18960 samples.

4.3 Training and Test Setup

- **Batch Size:** 128
- **Initial Learning Rate:** 0.05
- **Learning Rate Strategy:** Reduce the learning rate to $\frac{1}{10}$ of the original in the 28th, 36th, 44th and 52nd epoch.
- **Epoch:** 60
- **Optimizer:** Adam [31]

4.4 Data Format

For a skeleton action data, we use a graph $\mathcal{G}$ and a feature set $\mathcal{X}$ to represent each action. For all actions, their graph $\mathcal{G}$ are the same, we use adjacency matrix to represent it, which describes the graph structure of human body. For each different action, their feature set $\mathcal{X}$ is different. We use a tensor $\mathbf{X}$ to describe its feature set $\mathcal{X}$. For a skeleton action, it is a graph video, so there are many frames in it, so each frame is represented by a sub-tensor.

For each frame, there are at most 2 people to complete an action, so we need two graphs to represent the action of each frame. For the feature of each graph, we use a sub-tensor.

For each graph, there are 25 vertices, so we need 25 sub-tensor to represent the vertices of each graph.

For each vertex, there are 3 features, each feature represents the coordinates of vertices in space. So we need 3 real numbers to represent the features of each vertex.

So, for an action tensor $\mathbf{X}$, it has four dimensions, namely, the number of frames (T), the number of people (M), vertices (V) and features (C). So we know (Fig. 5):

$$\mathbf{X} \in \mathbb{R}^{T \times M \times V \times C}$$

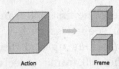
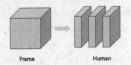

(a) An action consists of many frames, each of which is a sub tensor.

(b) A frame consists of many graph, each of which is a sub tensor.

(c) An graph consists of many vertices, each of which is a sub tensor.

(d) An vertex consists of many features, each of which is a real number.

Fig. 5. .

4.5 Data Preprocessing

In order to improve the training efficiency, [32] method is used to preprocess the data. After pretreatment, the method can save training time and GPU memory grately while keeping the accuracy almost unchanged.

Random Choose. By selectively reducing the frame count, the computational load diminishes, subsequently improving training efficiency. Such reduction, while ensuring that the major patterns are retained, ensures that the model doesn't get overburdened with excessive information. Assume there are T frames in a skeleton action feature tensor x, so we know:

$$x = \{f_1, f_2, \ldots, f_T\}$$

First we have to get the random integer T', which is $0.5T <= T' <= T$. We get a new skeleton action feature tensor x' that x' is the first T' frames of x.

$$x' = \{f_1, f_2, \ldots, f_{T'}\}$$

Then we get a integer T'' and $T'' = \lceil 0.2T \rceil$. We use interpolate to map T' frames in x' to T'' frames:

$$\{f'_1, f'_2, \ldots, f'_{T''}\} = interpolate(\{f_1, f_2, \ldots, f_{T'}\})$$

So we get x'' and

$$x'' = \{f'_1, f'_2, \ldots, f'_{T''}\}$$

We use x'' instead of x as the feature tensor.

Rotation. The introduction of random rotations seeks to enhance the model's generalization capabilities. Real-world data often comes with variability in orientations. By training the model with data in diverse angles, we aim to make the model more robust and adaptive to varied real-world scenarios, thereby improving its predictive capabilities across multiple angles. We randomly rotate all skeletons by an angle θ.

We first get three random values x, y, z while $-0.3 < x, y, z < 0.3$. This represents the rotation angle of the three dimensions. So we can get tensor $\mathbf{r}_x$, $\mathbf{r}_y$, $\mathbf{r}_z$:

$$\mathbf{r}_x = \begin{bmatrix} 1 & 0 & 0 \\ 0 & cos(x) & sin(x) \\ 0 & -sin(x) & cos(x) \end{bmatrix} \tag{4}$$

$$\mathbf{r}_y = \begin{bmatrix} cos(y) & 0 & -sin(y) \\ 0 & 1 & 0 \\ sin(y) & 0 & cos(x) \end{bmatrix} \tag{5}$$

$$\mathbf{r}_z = \begin{bmatrix} 1 & sin(z) & 0 \\ -sin(z) & 1 & 0 \\ 0 & 0 & 1 \end{bmatrix} \tag{6}$$

We can get tensor $\mathbf{r}$.

$$\mathbf{r} = \mathbf{r}_x \times \mathbf{r}_y \times \mathbf{r}_z$$

For a frame i, a graph j, we have $x_{i,j}$. For rotation, we use $x'_{i,j}$ instead of $x_{i,j}$:

$$x'_{i,j} = \mathbf{r} \times x_{i,j}$$

Result. We can see the comparison results with and without data preprocessing in Table 1.

Table 1. Experimental results of training time and GPU memory on Dual NVIDIA RTX 3090 while keeping the accuracy almost unchanged.

Use data preprocessing	Batch Size	GPU Memory	Training Time per Epoch
No	32	45 GiB	24 min 30 s
Yes	32	13 GiB	5 min 40 s
Yes	128	44 GiB	5 min 20 s

4.6   MS-G3D

The method we proposed has the goal to improve the relationship between human graph in the human skeleton based human action recognition, so we need a model to experiment. MS-G3D [19] is a skeleton based human action recognition model.

The most important thing of the human skeleton graph is to fuse the skeleton features, so that the neural network can make classification according to the overall features. In the traditional human skeleton action recognition model, there are two problems:

– The existence of cyclic walks on undirected graphs means that edge weights will be biased towards closer nodes against further nodes.
– Traditional methods hinder the exchange of skeleton models in time and space, and can not capture the complex regional space.

Aiming at these two problems, the author of [19] puts forward **MS-G3D** model, which solves the above problems from two aspects.

– A new multi-scale aggregation scheme is proposed to solve the biased weighting problem.
– The author of [19] proposes **G3D**, a new unified convolution model of Spatial-Temporal graph.

Thanks to the above two contributions, **MS-G3D** model surpasses the traditional graph convolution neural network and performs well in the skeleton based human action behavior recognition model. We experimented with our contribution based on this model.

Overall Architecture. At the high level, **MS-G3D** is composed of many stacked Spatial-Temporal graph convolution (**STGC**) blocks, which can extract features from the skeleton. Then the feature is input into a global average pooling layer, and finally passes through the full connection layer and softmax classifier.

STGC Block. **STGC** block is the main extractor of the model, and the skeleton features first pass through two paths.

– G3D
– GCN, TCN, TCN

After feature extraction of different paths, the features of the two paths are fused, and then input through TCN.

Simplified STGC Block and MS-G3D-Simplified. In order to test our method from multiple dimensions, we propose simplified block based on **STGC** block. Simplified **STGC** block does not go through **G3D**. The **MS-G3D** model composed of simplified stgc block is called **MS-G3D-simplified**.

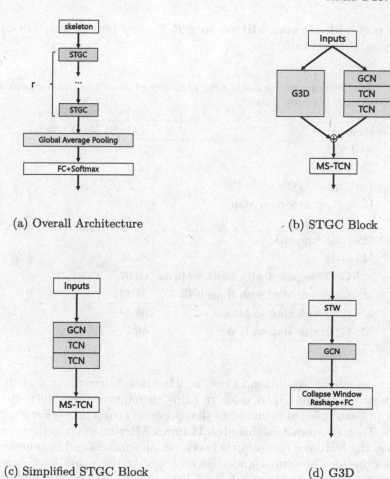

(a) Overall Architecture

(b) STGC Block

(c) Simplified STGC Block

(d) G3D

Fig. 6. .

G3D. This model is to solve the problem that local aggregators (such as GCN and TCN) are weakened in spatiotemporal propagation. The author of [19] uses the method of allowing cross Spatial-Temporal connections to make time and space converge uniformly. The skeleton features are processed by **Sliding Temporal Window, GCN** and **Collapse Window Reshape + FC**, and finally the features of cross Spatial-Temporal aggregation are obtained (Fig. 6).

4.7 Component Studies

To investigate the effectiveness of **Human Mirror** and **Human Link**, we analyze the individual components in the above dataset and data set settings. Performance is reported as Top 1 classification accuracy on the Cross-Set setting of NTU RGB+D 120 using only the joint data. In all experiments, **Human Link** must be used with **Human Mirror**, so *with Human Link* is *with Human Link and Human Mirror* (Table 2).

Table 2. Classification accuracy comparison against state-of-the- art methods on the NTU RGB+D 120 Skeleton dataset.

Method	NTU RGB+D 120(%)
ST-LSTM	57.9
GCA-LSTM	63.3
RotClips+MTCNN	61.8
Body Pose Evolution Map	66.9
2s-AGCN	84.9
MS-G3D-Simplified	85.89
MS-G3D	86.46
MS-G3D-Simplified with Human Mirror	86.07
MS-G3D-Simplified with Human Link	86.13
MS-G3D with Human Mirror	86.69
MS-G3D with Human Link	86.75

From the above experimental results, **Human Mirror** can contribute to neural network learning, and using it helps to improve the ability of neural network to learn in balance, an ability that previous neural network strategies do not have. Then **Human Link** based on **Human Mirror**, can help the neural net to process the feature relationship between action emitters and thus understand the action better. The two approaches proposed in the paper have significant improvement on the accuracy rate and help the neural network performance significantly.

5   Concluding Remarks

5.1   Conclusion

In this study, we propose two optimization strategies: **Human Mirror** and **Human Link**.

Human Mirror eliminates the negative impact of a single person on the neural network in the data set. Under the different data of one action sender and two action senders, the neural network can not use the same strategy to process the data of the two modes, which has a negative impact on the accuracy.

Human Link solves that the neural network can only extract the features of spatial scale and time scale and loss of information caused by averaging in the traditional way. Through the feature extraction of human body scale, the understanding of action by neural network is strengthened.

5.2 Future Work

For **Human Mirror**, the current method is to copy the data from $x_{i,0}$ to $x_{i,1}$, so that the coordinates of the two are exactly the same, but the positions of the two people are not the same for the action performed by the two people, if we can translate the copied $x_{i,1}$ by learning the position interval of the two people, it may be more beneficial for the neural network to learn the two cases in unison.

For **Human Link**, the current method is to connect all the corresponding points of $x_{i,0}$ to $x_{i,1}$, which may not be the best method, we can use other connection methods, such as connecting only a few key nodes instead of all the nodes, or adding some buffer nodes to the connected nodes to increase the connection distance between two people, so that GCN [29] can give priority to extracting features within its own range instead of over-fusing the features between two people.

References

1. Li, Y., et al.: TEA: temporal excitation and aggregation for action recognition. In: Proceedings of the IEEE/CVF Conference on Computer Vision and Pattern Recognition, pp. 909–918 (2020)
2. Fanello, S.R., et al.: Keep it simple and sparse: real-time action recognition. J. Mach. Learn. Res. **14**, 2617–2640 (2013)
3. Tran, D., et al.: A closer look at spatiotemporal convolutions for action recognition. In: Proceedings of the IEEE Conference on Computer Vision and Pattern Recognition, pp. 6450–6459 (2018)
4. Saggese, A., et al.: Learning skeleton representations for human action recognition. Pattern Recogn. Lett. **118**, 23–31 (2019)
5. Du, Y., Wang, W., Wang, L.: Hierarchical recurrent neural network for skeleton based action recognition. In: Proceedings of the IEEE Conference on Computer Vision and Pattern Recognition, pp. 1110–1118 (2015)
6. Ke, Q., et al.: A new representation of skeleton sequences for 3d action recognition. In: IEEE/CVF Conference on Computer Vision and Pattern Recognition (CVPR), pp. 3288–3297 (2017)
7. Cheng, K., et al.: Extremely lightweight skeleton-based action recognition with ShiftGCN++. IEEE Trans. Image Process. **30**, 7333–7348 (2021)
8. Liu, J., et al.: NTU RGB+ D 120: a large-scale benchmark for 3d human activity understanding. IEEE Tran. Pattern Anal. Mach. Intell. **42**(10), 2684–2701 (2019)
9. Yan, S., Xiong, Y., Lin, D.: Spatial temporal graph convolutional networks for skeleton-based action recognition. In: Thirty-Second AAAI Conference on Artificial Intelligence (2018)
10. Cheng, K., et al.: Decoupling GCN with DropGraph module for skeleton-based action recognition. In: Vedaldi, A., Bischof, H., Brox, T., Frahm, J.-M. (eds.) ECCV 2020, Part XXIV. LNCS, vol. 12369, pp. 536–553. Springer, Cham (2020). https://doi.org/10.1007/978-3-030-58586-0_32
11. Zhang, P., et al.: Semantics-guided neural networks for efficient skeleton based human action recognition. In: Proceedings of the IEEE/CVF Conference on Computer Vision and Pattern Recognition, pp. 1112–1121 (2020)

12. Shi, L., et al.: Skeleton-based action recognition with directed graph neural networks. In: Proceedings of the IEEE/CVF Conference on Computer Vision and Pattern Recognition, pp. 7912–7921 (2019)
13. Vemulapalli, R., Arrate, F., Chellappa, R.: Human action recognition by representing 3d skeletons as points in a lie group. In: Proceedings of the IEEE Conference on Computer Vision and Pattern Recognition, pp. 588–595 (2014)
14. Wang, L., Koniusz, P., Huynh, D.: Hallucinating IDT descriptors and I3D optical flow features for action recognition with CNNs. In: Proceedings of the IEEE/CVF International Conference on Computer Vision (ICCV) (2019). https://doi.org/10.1109/ICCV.2019.00879
15. Liu, M., Liu, H., Chen, C.: Enhanced skeleton visualization for view invariant human action recognition. Pattern Recogn. **68**, 346–362 (2017)
16. Li, M., et al.: Actional-structural graph convolutional networks for skeleton-based action recognition. In: Conference on Computer Vision and Pattern Recognition (CVPR), pp. 3595–3603 (2019)
17. Si, C., et al.: An attention enhanced graph convolutional LSTM network for skeleton-based action recognition. In: Proceedings of the IEEE/CVF Conference on Computer Vision and Pattern Recognition, pp. 1227–1236 (2019)
18. Shi, L., et al.: Two-stream adaptive graph convolutional networks for skeleton-based action recognition. In: Proceedings of the IEEE/CVF Conference on Computer Vision and Pattern Recognition, pp. 12026–12035 (2019)
19. Liu, Z., et al.: Disentangling and unifying graph convolutions for skeleton based action recognition. In: Proceedings of the IEEE/CVF Conference on Computer Vision and Pattern Recognition, pp. 143–152 (2020)
20. Hamilton, W., Ying, Z., Leskovec, J.: Inductive representation learning on large graphs. In: Advances in Neural Information Processing Systems, vol. 30 (2017)
21. Cortes, C., et al.: Advances in neural information processing systems 28. In: NIPS 2015 (2015)
22. Bruna, J., et al.: Spectral networks and locally connected networks on graphs. In: arXiv preprint arXiv:1312.6203 (2013)
23. Defferrard, M., Bresson, X., Vandergheynst, P.: Convolutional neural networks on graphs with fast localized spectral filtering. In: Advances in Neural Information Processing Systems, vol. 29 (2016)
24. Kipf, T.N., Welling, M.: Semi-supervised classification with graph convolutional networks. In: arXiv preprint arXiv:1609.02907 (2016)
25. Hammond, D.K., Vandergheynst, P., Gribonval, R.: Wavelets on graphs via spectral graph theory. Appl. Comput. Harmon. Anal. **30**(2), 129–150 (2011)
26. Wan, S., et al.: Multiscale dynamic graph convolutional network for hyperspectral image classification. IEEE Trans. Geosci. Remote Sens. **58**(5), 3162–3177 (2019)
27. Dang, L., et al.: MSR-GCN: multi-scale residual graph convolution networks for human motion prediction. In: Proceedings of the IEEE/CVF International Conference on Computer Vision, pp. 11467–11476 (2021)
28. Zhang, Y., et al.: STST: spatial-temporal specialized transformer for skeleton-based action recognition. In: Proceedings of the 29th ACM International Conference on Multimedia, pp. 3229–3237 (2021)
29. Veličković, P., et al.: Graph attention networks. In: arXiv preprint arXiv:1710.10903 (2017)
30. Shahroudy, A., et al.: NTU RGB+ D: a large scale dataset for 3d human activity analysis. In: Proceedings of the IEEE Conference on Computer Vision and Pattern Recognition, pp. 1010–1019 (2016)

31. Kingma, D.P., Ba, J.: Adam: a method for stochastic optimization. In: arXiv preprint arXiv:1412.6980 (2014)
32. Chen, Y., et al.: Channel-wise topology refinement graph convolution for skeleton-based action recognition. In: Proceedings of the IEEE/CVF International Conference on Computer Vision, pp. 13359–13368 (2021)

Improving Output Visualization of an Algorithm for the Automated Detection of the Perceived Origin of Movement

Giorgio Gnecco[1]([✉]), Martina Fausto[2], Gabriele Romano[2], Gualtiero Volpe[2], and Antonio Camurri[2]

[1] AXES Research Unit, IMT School for Advanced Studies, Lucca, Italy
giorgio.gnecco@imtlucca.it
[2] DIBRIS Department, University of Genoa, Genoa, Italy
{gualtiero.volpe,antonio.camurri}@unige.it

Abstract. The perceived Origin of full-body human Movement (OoM), i.e., the part of the body that is perceived by an external observer as the joint from which movement originates, represents a relevant topic for movement analysis. Indeed, its automated detection is important to contribute to the automated analysis of full-body emotions and of non-verbal social signals, and has potential applications, among others, in dance and music teaching, cognitive and motor rehabilitation, sport, and entertainment. In this work, we further develop a recently proposed algorithm for the automated detection of the perceived OoM, by improving the visualization of its output. Specifically, the core of that algorithm relies on clustering a skeletal representation of the human body based on the values assumed by a movement-related feature on all its vertices, then finding those vertices that are at the boundary between any two resulting clusters. In the work, we improve the visualization of the clusters generated by that algorithm in successive frames, by "colouring" them by means of the resolution of a sequence of minimum cost bipartite matching subproblems. Finally, based on a real-world dataset, we show that the proposed modification of the algorithm provides, indeed, a better visualization of the clusters than its original version.

Keywords: Non-Verbal Full-Body Expressive Interactive Systems · Automated Detection of the Perceived Origin of Human Movement · Clustering · Colouring · Minimum Cost Bipartite Matching Problem

1 Introduction

The automated measurement of movement qualities revealing expressive intentions, emotions, and non-verbal social signals (e.g., leadership and entrainment) is of paramount importance in many applications (Argyle [1], Bieńkiewicz et al. [7], Camurri et al. [9], Karg et al. [18], Meeren et al. [23]). An important role in understanding human movement is played by the so-called perceived Origin of Movement (OoM), i.e., the part of the body perceived by an external observer as the joint from which movement

© The Author(s) 2024
M. Clayton et al. (Eds.): INTETAIN 2023, LNICST 560, pp. 96–106, 2024.
https://doi.org/10.1007/978-3-031-55722-4_8

originates (Kolykhalova et al. [19], Matthiopoulou et al. [21, 22]). In cognitive/motor rehabilitation, the detection and tracking of the (perceived) OoM can help support a patient in learning how to correctly perform a specific movement (e.g., how to get up safely from a chair), reducing the risk of incurring injuries. Moreover, the diagnosis of the origin of a reaching movement is very useful for an individualized rehabilitation of a person with a stroke (Bakhti et al. [4, 5]). In dance and music teaching, the awareness and discovery of the OoM can contribute to increased effectiveness of expressivity and repeatability of a technical gesture. In sport and entertainment, it can enhance performance.

Research on the OoM is grounded in movement science and biomechanics, particularly in the literature related to the so-called Leading Joint Hypothesis (LJH) on limb motion, according to which "there is one leading joint that creates a dynamic foundation for the motion of the entire limb" (Dounskaia [11])[1]. The basis of the LJH is found in the way according to which the central nervous system exploits the biomechanical properties of the limbs for movement organization. The automated detection of the OoM was recently investigated by Kolykhalova et al. [19], who proposed an algorithm, inspired by the LJH, based on a suitably defined skeletal representation of the human body as a graph. The central idea of that algorithm consists of clustering the graph according to the similarity in the values assumed by a suitable movement-related feature (e.g., speed) on its vertices (which are suitably selected joints of the human body). As the specific clustering technique, spectral clustering (Shi and Malik [24]) is used. The clusters so found are then exploited to construct a cooperative game model on an auxiliary graph, having the same vertex set as the original graph, and edges connecting vertices at the boundary between any two different clusters in the original graph. Then, the Shapley value (a measure of the importance of players in a suitable class of cooperative games, see Maschler et al. [20]) is used to find the most relevant vertex, deemed to be the OoM. In the specific case, the Shapley value coincides with weighted degree centrality (Deng and Papadimitriou [10]) on the auxiliary graph. It is worth noting that both the LJH and the algorithm developed by Kolykhalova et al. [19], based on unsupervised machine learning, appear to be closely connected to the following concept already expressed by Aristotle [2]: "the origin of movement [...] remains at rest when the lower part of a limb is moved; for example, the elbow joint, when the forearm is moved, and the shoulder, when the whole arm; the knee when the tibia is moved, and the hip when the whole leg." In other words, it looks quite natural to search for the OoM within a subset of joints that connect clusters with different motor behaviour, i.e., joints belonging to the boundary between any two such clusters.

---

[1] This actually refers to the physical OoM, which is often close to the perceived OoM.

In the algorithm developed by Kolykhalova et al. [19], the clustering step is performed frame-by-frame, imposing no relationships on the clusters found in successive frames[2]. So, in case one wanted to label (or "colour") the clusters in order to visualize their evolution with respect to time, any permutation of the labels in each frame would be admissible (i.e., it would not change the Shapley value). This would make the resulting visualization difficult. In this work, we improve the visualization of the clusters generated by the algorithm in successive frames, by colouring them by means of the resolution of a sequence of minimum cost bipartite matching subproblems. In each subproblem, the labels of the clusters found in one frame are connected in a suitably "smooth" way to the ones of the clusters found in the successive frame, by maximizing the summation of the overlaps of the sets of vertices in common with any two clusters that are coloured in the same way (or equivalently, in order to reformulate this optimization subproblem as a cost minimization subproblem, by minimizing the opposite of such a summation plus a constant). The method is inspired by the curve colouring problem investigated, for a different application to metamaterial analysis, by Bacigalupo et al. [3]. In that problem, a finite set of curves is observed at each time instant, and one has to attribute each observed point to a specific curve, using a different "colour" for each curve, in such a way as to reconstruct the curves in the smoothest possible way. Finally, based on a real-world dataset, we show that the proposed modification of the output visualization of the algorithm developed by Kolykhalova et al. [19] provides, as expected, a better visualization of the clusters than its original version.

The article is structured as follows. Section 2 summarizes the algorithm developed by Kolykhalova et al. [19] for the automated detection of the perceived origin of full-body human movement. Section 3 describes the proposed cluster colouring method, aimed at improving the visualization of the output of that algorithm. Section 4 compares the cluster visualizations obtained, respectively, by the original algorithm and by its proposed modification. Section 5 concludes the work with a discussion, delineating its possible developments.

2   An Algorithm for the Automated Detection of the Perceived Origin of Movement

In this section, we briefly describe the algorithm for the automated detection of the (perceived) OoM, which was developed by Kolykhalova et al. [19]. Its main steps are reported in Fig. 1 and are summarized in the following paragraphs. The reader is referred to that reference and to Matthiopoulou et al. [22] for a more detailed presentation of the algorithm and for a discussion on its implementation details. In the following section, focus is given to the output of Step

---

[2] In the algorithm developed by Kolykhalova et al. [19] to detect the OoM, the clusters are labelled using natural numbers as a by-product of the specific spectral clustering algorithm embedded (Shi and Malik [24]), but their order is not optimized and may depend on implementation details of that spectral clustering algorithm (e.g., rescaling of an eigenvector when computing the spectrum of the graph Laplacian). Indeed, the goal of spectral clustering is just to find suitable clusters (according to a given optimality criterion), but not to label them according to a specific order.

ii) of the algorithm, for which an improved visualization is proposed in the present work.

Fig. 1. Main steps of the algorithm developed by Kolykhalova et al. [19] for the automated detection of the perceived OoM.

i) A weighted undirected graph $G = (V, E, w)$ is built, with the aim of modelling the human body through its suitable skeletal representation. Here, V denotes the vertex set of G, E denotes its edge set, whereas w represents a weight function defined on E, constructed based on data acquired through Motion Capture (MoCap) techniques. The vertices of G form a subset of the set of all body joints. Its edges are further classified into physical/non-physical edges. For each frame, every edge is labelled with a non-negative weight. This is proportional to the current similarity of the values assumed by a given movement-related feature (e.g., speed) at each of the two vertices associated with such an edge. In the case of a non-physical edge, the constant of proportionality is chosen to be much smaller than the one used to define the weight of a physical edge, since the former edge models a more temporary movement-related similarity, originating from the specific movement performed.

ii) For each frame, the weighted undirected graph G is clustered by applying spectral clustering to the set of weights assigned to its edges. The number of clusters is optimized automatically. Labels are assigned automatically to the clusters (but not optimized), as a by-product of the specific spectral clustering algorithm used (Shi and Malik [24]).

iii) For each frame, a suitable weighted auxiliary graph $G^{aux} = (V, E^{aux}, w^{aux})$ is built. Its vertices are the same as the ones of the original graph G. In contrast, its edge set E^{aux} is a subset of the set of physical edges of G, that also connect vertices belonging to different clusters of G. Each edge in G^{aux} is labelled with a weight that is proportional to the dissimilarity (rather than the similarity) of the values assumed by the given movement-related feature on its two associated vertices.

iv) For each frame, a cooperative Transferable Utility (TU) game is constructed, based on the weighted auxiliary graph G^{aux}. The players of this game are the vertices of G (or, which is the same, of G^{aux}). The value $c(V')$ of any coalition $V' \subseteq V$ is defined as the summation of all the weights (in the weighted auxiliary graph G^{aux}) associated with the physical edges belonging to the subgraph of G^{aux} that is induced by V'.

v) For each frame, the Shapley value for the cooperative TU game built in Step 4 is evaluated. For each player, it represents the average marginal contribution of that player when joining a randomly formed coalition. Hence, the Shapley value is used to rank joints according to their "importance" or "centrality" in the weighted auxiliary graph G^{aux}, where the "most important/most central" joint in a frame is one that has the largest Shapley value.

vi) Finally, a filtering step is performed, keeping only the vertices automatically detected
as being the "most important/most central" ones for a given number of successive
frames.

3 Proposed Cluster Colouring Method

The output of Step ii) of the algorithm summarized in Sect. 2 is a set of clusters (subsets
of vertices of the graph G). Visualizing such clusters (by attributing a "colour" to each
of them) can be useful to better understand the output of that algorithm, since the joint
deemed to be the OoM (the one with the largest Shapley value) belongs to the boundary
between two such clusters. However, in the original algorithm, no colour is assigned
explicitly to each such cluster. If colours were assigned based, e.g., on the order of the
clusters produced by the specific spectral clustering algorithm used, it may happen that,
when moving from one frame to the successive one, the clusters did not change, but their
colours were permuted, making the visualization difficult. For instance, in this case a
visual inspection would likely fail to detect a possible relationship between a change of
the OoM and a simultaneous change in the composition of the clusters.

In this section, we propose a method to colour the clusters generated by the algorithm
of Sect. 2 in a "smooth" way, avoiding situations such as the one described above.
For simplicity, we assume that the number of clusters does not change between two
consecutive frames, say, respectively, at times t and $t + 1$. Taking the hint from the
curve colouring problem considered by Bacigalupo et al. [3], starting from the colours
assigned to the clusters at time t, we attribute colours to the clusters at time $t + 1$
by solving a minimum cost bipartite matching subproblem, or assignment subproblem
(Burkard et al. [8]). In other words, first we construct a complete weighted bipartite
graph $G^{bipartite} = (R \cup B, E^{bipartite}, w^{bipartite})$, where R is a set of "red" vertices, B is
a set of "blue" vertices, the two cardinalities $|R|$ and $|B|$ are the same, $E^{bipartite}$ is the
Cartesian product $R \times B$, and $w^{bipartite} : R \times B \to \mathbb{R}$ is a cost function. We recall that
a bipartite matching $M^{bipartite} \subseteq E^{bipartite}$ is a subset of edges such that every vertex in
$R \cup B$ is incident to at most one edge in $M^{bipartite}$. Moreover, the matching is perfect
if every vertex in $R \cup B$ is incident to exactly one edge in $M^{bipartite}$. The cost of the
matching has the expression $C = \sum_{(r,b) \in M^{bipartite}} w^{bipartite}(r, b)$. The objective of the
minimum cost bipartite matching problem is to find a perfect matching in the complete
weighted bipartite graph $G^{bipartite} = (R \cup B, E^{bipartite}, w^{bipartite})$, having minimum cost
C. Various efficient algorithms exist to solve such an optimization problem, e.g., the
Hungarian method (Burkard et al. [5]). For a small cardinality $m := |R| = |B|$ (e.g.,
$m = 4$ or $m = 5$) the problem can be easily solved even by the brute-force method, since
its number of admissible solutions is $m!$.

In our specific case, we choose R as the set of m clusters obtained for the graph
G at time t by means of Step ii) of the algorithm described in Sect. 2[3], B as the set
of clusters obtained for the graph G at time $t + 1$ by means of the same step, whereas

---

[3] As discussed in Kolykhalova et al. [19], the (maximal) number of clusters to be detected in Step
ii) of the algorithm could be chosen as a function of the number of nodes of the adopted skeletal
structure. With 20 nodes, one possible choice is $m = 4$, which makes even the application of
the brute-force approach computationally negligible, since $m! = 24$.

$w^{bipartite}(r, b) := |V| - |r \cap b|$. In other words, the larger the overlap between two clusters r and b at times t and $t + 1$, respectively (in terms of the number of common vertices), the smaller the cost of the weighted edge (r, b) in $G^{bipartite}$. In the particular case in which the two sets of clusters are the same, the optimal bipartite matching preserves the colours of the clusters when moving from time t to time $t + 1$, thus preventing the occurrence of the undesired situation illustrated at the beginning of this section.

4 Results

In this section, we compare the output visualization of the algorithm developed by Kolykhalova et al. [19] and the one obtained by its proposed modification, by considering an illustrative example. The dataset we used was recorded with 13 infrared cameras in March 2016 in the framework of the H2020-ICT-2015 EU Project WhoLoDance. The subjects were two professional dancers, equipped with 64 infrared reflective markers, 5 accelerometers, and 1 microphone, performing contemporary dance movements without music accompaniment, as the latter could have affected the way the dancers performed the movements. The 64 markers' trajectories were tracked by the Qualisys Track Manager (QTM) software and manually interpolated with the same software when markers went missing due to visual occlusion of the minimal set of cameras needed for their tracking. In addition to the video recordings, there were also manual expert annotations regarding which joint was evaluated to be the perceived OoM. Starting from the full marker set, we constructed a smaller set made of 20 joints by means of the reduction of sets of multiple markers into individual joints. The position of each joint was determined by averaging

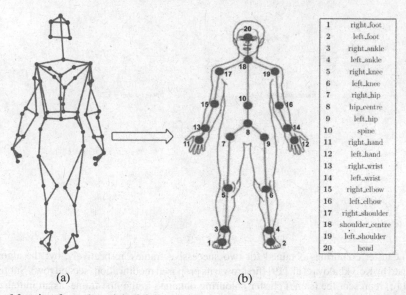

1	right_foot
2	left_foot
3	right_ankle
4	left_ankle
5	right_knee
6	left_knee
7	right_hip
8	hip_centre
9	left_hip
10	spine
11	right_hand
12	left_hand
13	right_wrist
14	left_wrist
15	right_elbow
16	left_elbow
17	right_shoulder
18	shoulder_centre
19	left_shoulder
20	head

(a)   (b)

Fig. 2. Mapping from the original full-body skeletal structure (a) to the reduced one (b). Each marker (joint) in the second subfigure corresponds to a group of markers in the first subfigure. Note: "left" and "right" in the second subfigure refer to the subject's viewpoint.

the positions of the markers belonging to a suitable subset associated with such joint, according to the map reported in Fig. 2. For instance, the positions of the 5 markers on the head in the original full-body skeletal structure were used to determine the position of the joint numbered as 20 (head) in the reduced skeletal structure. Then, in order to find the clusters, the algorithm of Sect. 2 was applied based on this reduced skeletal structure. Specifically, the angular momentum of each joint with respect to the center of mass of the body was selected as the movement-related feature used by that algorithm (see Matthiopoulou et al. [22] for a description of this feature and of the specific measure of similarity adopted).

We considered an example in which the dancer started from a standing position with the right leg raised off the ground and shifted slightly to the left. From this position, the dancer began to rotate the right leg counterclockwise, almost as if attempting a pirouette, which also compelled the torso to rotate. As seen in Fig. 3, we investigated how the cluster colouring changed between two successive frames, first using the algorithm developed by Kolykhalova et al. [19], then using the proposed modification of its output visualization. In order to enhance the visualization, the two frames shown were not consecutive, i.e., there were other frames interposed between them. Moreover, for a fair comparison, the two cluster colourings were initialized in the same way. In the first case, we can clearly observe that some joints initially included in a cluster later belonged to different

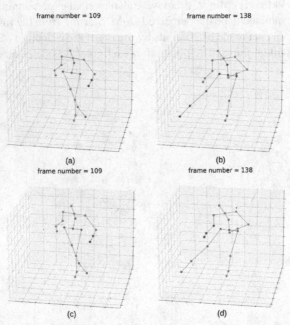

Fig. 3. Cluster colourings obtained for two successive frames, respectively, by: the algorithm developed by Kolykhalova et al. [19] (first row); its proposed modification (second row). Subfigures (a) and (c) represent the (same) cluster colouring obtained in the first frame, as an initialization step; subfigure (b) represents the cluster colouring obtained in the second frame by the first algorithm; subfigure (d) represents the cluster colouring obtained in the second frame by the proposed modification.

clusters. Indeed, most cluster colours were swapped when moving from the first frame to the second frame. In the second frame, only the head and the shoulders maintained the same colour likewise in the first frame, while the set of joints composing the red, blue and green clusters changed completely with respect to the first frame. However, when using the proposed modification, the green and blue clusters remained unchanged compared to the previous frame, and both the head and the shoulders retained their previous colours. Hence, from this simple example, it becomes clear how the proposed modification has the ability to enhance the visualization of the clusters over time, by avoiding continuous occurrence of seemingly random switching.

5 Discussion

In this work, the algorithm for the automated detection of the perceived Origin of full-body human Movement (OoM), proposed by Kolykhalova et al. [19], has been further developed, by improving the visualization of its output through a suitable cluster colouring method. It is worth noting that, differently from the similar curve colouring problem considered by Bacigalupo et al. [3], no further improvement could be obtained by reformulating the cluster colouring problem as a multi-stage optimization problem, in which each frame (stage) is associated with the cost of the bipartite matching between the set of clusters obtained in that frame and the one obtained in the successive frame. This problem could be solved, in principle, by dynamic programming (Bertsekas [6]). However, since the optimization subproblems per stage (i.e., the minimum cost bipartite matching subproblems) are actually decoupled[4] (apart from a permutation of the set of labels), the cluster colouring obtained by solving such a multi-stage optimization problem would be identical (again, apart from a permutation of the set of labels) to the one obtained by the method proposed in this work.

---

[4] In more technical terms, the presence of this decoupling can be easily recognized by investigating the specific form of the optimal cost-to-go function per stage and the associated Bellman's equation (Bertsekas [6]). It is recalled here that the optimal cost-to-go function per stage provides the optimal cost of a multi-stage optimization subproblem (derived from the original multi-stage optimization problem) which starts at that stage, whereas Bellman's equation at that stage allows one to find that optimal cost-to-go function per stage, by solving another optimization subproblem whose cost function is the sum of the cost per stage (at the current stage) and of the optimal cost-to-go function at the next stage (evaluated in correspondence with a suitable choice of its argument). In the specific multi-stage version of the cluster colouring problem, one can easily check that: (i) The optimal cost-to-go function at the final stage is zero, hence it is constant. (ii) The optimal cost-to-go function at any other stage is constant. (iii) To solve Bellman's equation at each stage, one can neglect the (constant) term associated with the optimal cost-to-go function at the next stage, keeping only the cost per stage (at the current stage). In this way, one actually "decouples" Bellman's equations at different stages. Property (i) follows directly from the definition of the optimal cost-to-go function at the final stage, whereas properties (ii) and (iii) are proved by backward induction. In the case of the curve colouring problem investigated by Bacigalupo et al. [3], instead, properties (ii) and (iii) do not hold. This depends on the different structure of its cost per stage with respect to the multi-stage version of the cluster colouring problem.

The proposed cluster colouring method could be used in conjunction with different movement-related features (such as the ones considered by Matthiopoulou et al. [21, 22] in a further alternative extension of the algorithm proposed by Kolykhalova et al. [19] and in its applications) in order to visualize which feature is the best at capturing the OoM. Moreover, the improved visualization could help to identify in which situations (e.g., for which gestures) the algorithm itself performs well or, vice versa, fails to correctly identify the OoM.

It is worth remarking that a limitation of the proposed cluster colouring method is that it can be applied only when the number of clusters does not change with time. This could limit its application to movements characterized by a constant spatial scale. A possible way to overcome this issue could be to use a hierarchical version of spectral clustering, matching the numbers of clusters in any two successive frames. Moreover, instead of performing (spectral) clustering frame-by-frame and solving successively a sequence of cluster colouring problems, one could apply clustering directly to a single "large" graph that represents a set of successive frames, then obtain the clusters per frame simply by "sectioning" the clusters so obtained (Fukumoto et al. [13]). As a successive step, one could make an arbitrary selection for the colours attributed to the clusters of the "large" graph, then make the clusters per frame inherit the colours from the corresponding clusters in the "large" graph. As a by-product of this procedure, also the number of clusters per frame would be chosen automatically (depending on the number of clusters active in each frame). However, this alternative approach could slow down significantly the clustering process, preventing the automated detection of the perceived OoM in real-time.

Finally, it is worth mentioning that other improvements are still possible for the algorithm proposed by Kolykhalova et al. [19] for the automated detection of the OoM. For instance, following the framework of learning with constraints/boundary conditions (Gnecco et al. [14–16]), one could include biomechanical constraints in that algorithm, which could modify the sets of clusters taken as inputs by the cluster colouring method proposed in the present work. Moreover, suitable dimensionality reduction techniques (see, e.g., Fantoni et al. [12] and Gnecco and Sanguineti [17]) could be applied when moving from a skeletal structure characterized by a large number of markers to a reduced skeletal structure (see Sect. 4), used as input for the algorithm for the automated detection of the OoM.

Acknowledgment. The authors were partially supported by the FET PROACTIVE project "En-TimeMent", funded by the European Union (project no. 824160), by the PRIN 2022 project "Multiscale Analysis of Human and Artificial Trajectories: Models and Applications" (CUP: D53D23008790006), funded by the European Union - Next Generation EU program, and by the project "THE – Tuscany Health Ecosystem" (CUP: B83C22003920001), funded by the European Union – Next Generation EU program, in the context of the Italian National Recovery and Resilience Plan, Investment 1.5: Ecosystems of Innovation. Giorgio Gnecco dedicates the work to the memory of his mother Rosanna Merlini.

References

1. Argyle, M.: Bodily Communication, Methuen & Co. (1988)
2. Aristotle: On the Motion of Animals (350 BC). English translation available online at. http://classics.mit.edu/Aristotle/motion_animals.html
3. Bacigalupo, A., De Bellis, M.L., Gnecco, G., Nutarelli, F.: On dispersion curve coloring for mechanical metafilters. Sci. Rep. **12** (2022). Art. no. 20019
4. Bakhti, K.K.A., Mottet, D., Schweighofer, N., Froger, J., Laffont, I.: Proximal arm non-use when reaching after a stroke. Neurosci. Lett. **657**, 91–96 (2017)
5. Bakhti, K.K.A., Laffont, I., Muthalib, M., Froger, J., Mottet, D.: Kinect-based assessment of proximal arm non-use after a stroke. J. NeuroEng. Rehabil. **15** (2018). Art. no. 103
6. Bertsekas, D.P.: Dynamic Programming and Optimal Control, vol. 1. Athena Scientific (2017)
7. Bieńkiewicz, M.M.N., et al.: Bridging the gap between emotion and joint action. Neurosci. Biobehav. Rev. **131**, 806–833 (2021)
8. Burkard, R., Dell'Amico, M., Martello, S.: Assignment Problems. SIAM (2012)
9. Camurri, A., Lagerlöf, I., Volpe, G.: Recognizing emotion from dance movement: comparison of spectator recognition and automated techniques. Int. J. Hum. Comput. Stud. **59**(1–2), 213–225 (2003)
10. Deng, X., Papadimitriou, C.H.: On the complexity of cooperative solution concepts. Math. Oper. Res. **19**(2), 257–266 (1994)
11. Dounskaia, N.: Control of human limb movements: the leading joint hypothesis and its practical applications. Exerc. Sport Sci. Rev. **38**, 201–208 (2010)
12. Fantoni, F., Bacigalupo, A., Gnecco, G., Gambarotta, L.: Multi-objective optimal design of mechanical metafilters via principal component analysis. Int. J. Mech. Sci. **248** (2023). Article no. 108195
13. Fukumoto, K., Yamada, K., Tanaka, Y.: Node clustering of time-varying graphs based on temporal label smoothness. In: Proceedings of APSIPA 2021: The 13th Asia Pacific Signal and Information Processing Association Annual Summit and Conference, pp. 324–329 (2021)
14. Gnecco, G., Gaggero, M., Sanguineti, M.: Suboptimal solutions to team optimization problems with stochastic information structure. SIAM J. Optim. **22**(1), 212–243 (2012)
15. Gnecco, G., Gori, M., Sanguineti, M.: Learning with boundary conditions. Neural Comput. **25**, 1029–1106 (2013)
16. Gnecco, G., Gori, M., Melacci, S., Sanguineti, M.: Learning with mixed hard/soft pointwise constraints. IEEE Trans. Neural Netw. Learn. Syst. **26**, 2019–2032 (2015)
17. Gnecco, G., Sanguineti, M.: Accuracy of suboptimal solutions to kernel principal component analysis. Comput. Optim. Appl. **42**, 197–210 (2010)
18. Karg, M., Samadani, A.-A., Gorbet, R., Kühnlenz, K., Hoey, J., Kulić, D.: Body movements for affective expression: a survey of automatic recognition and generation. IEEE Trans. Affect. Comput. **4**(4), 341–359 (2013)
19. Kolykhalova, K., Gnecco, G., Sanguineti, M., Volpe, G., Camurri, A.: Automated analysis of the origin of movement: an approach based on cooperative games on graphs. IEEE Trans. Hum.-Mach. Syst. **50**(6), 550–560 (2020)
20. Maschler, M., Solan, E., Zamir, S.: Game Theory. Cambridge University Press (2013)
21. Matthiopoulou, O., Bardy, B., Gnecco, G., Mottet, D., Sanguineti, M., Camurri, A.: A computational method to automatically detect the perceived origin of full-body human movement and its propagation. In: Proceedings of ICMI 2020 Companion: Companion Publication of the 2020 International Conference on Multimodal Interaction, pp. 449–453. Association for Computing Machinery (2021)

22. Matthiopoulou, O., Gnecco, G., Sanguineti, M., Mottet, D., Bardy, B., Camurri, A.: Towards the automated analysis of expressive gesture qualities in full-body movement: the perceived origin of movement. Hum.-Centric Comput. Inf. Sci. (2024, forthcoming)
23. Meeren, H.K.M., van Heijnsbergen, C.C.R.J., de Gelder, B.: Rapid perceptual integration of facial expression and emotional body language. Proc. Nat. Acad. Sci. **102**(45), 16518–16523 (2005)
24. Shi, J., Malik, J.: Normalized cuts and image segmentation. IEEE Trans. Pattern Anal. Mach. Intell. **2**(8), 888–905 (2000)

Sports and Competition

Biases in Micro-level Probabilistic Reasoning and Its Impact on the Spectators' Enjoyment of Tennis Games

Stephen Zhu[✉]

Tennis Analyzer App, Atlanta, USA
stephen.zhu6@gmail.com

Abstract. In sports games, the excitement and suspense felt by the spectators are essential to their entertainment experience. The level of excitement and suspense is linked to the spectators' reasoning about the probability of winning or losing. In tennis, as in many other sports, spectators' predictions of winning probabilities largely hinge on the scores. Given tennis's hierarchical scoring system, its probabilistic reasoning is multifaceted and complex. This research examines the winning probabilities across various scoring scenarios, using data from thousands of professional tennis matches and comparing them with theoretical models generally aligned with spectators' common beliefs. The analysis reveals that the theoretical model makes accurate probability predictions at the macro level but inaccurate predictions at the micro level, pointing to possible biases in micro-level probabilistic reasoning. A recent behavioral economic theory may help explain the causes of such biases. Biases are generally seen as undesirable errors, but this study offers a counterargument that biases in micro-level probabilistic reasoning actually enhance the enjoyment of tennis matches by creating expectations, anxiety, and surprises.

Keywords: Sports analytics · entertainment · probabilistic reasoning · bias · behavioral economics

1 Introduction

Why do people enjoy watching sports? Previous research has found suspense to be crucial for the spectators' enjoyment of sports [14, 16, 22, 24, 25, 28, 30, 34, 35]. Suspense, a feeling of excitement or uncertainty about future events, is closely associated with the spectator's reasoning about the probability of winning or losing. Zillmann identified three elements for investigating the connection between suspense in sports and enjoyment: (spectators') dispositions toward participants, (un)certainty about a negative outcome for a favored participant, and repeated opportunities for the favored participant to fall behind and ultimately lose [22, 33]. The second and third elements are directly related to probabilistic reasoning.

A spectator's probabilistic reasoning during a game may be influenced by many factors, such as scores, past performance statistics, the players' physical

© ICST Institute for Computer Sciences, Social Informatics and Telecommunications Engineering 2024
Published by Springer Nature Switzerland AG 2024. All Rights Reserved
M. Clayton et al. (Eds.): INTETAIN 2023, LNICST 560, pp. 109–126, 2024.
https://doi.org/10.1007/978-3-031-55722-4_9

and mental conditions, and the environment, but empirical studies indicated that score difference is a reliable predictor of suspense [16, 22, 30]. The smaller the score difference, the greater the suspense [16, 30], leading to greater enjoyment of the sports game [22]. Thus, it has been empirically established that spectators' enjoyment of sports is closely tied to their probabilistic reasoning about the outcome, especially based on score differences.

Research has shown that probabilistic reasoning is frequently shaped by subconscious biases, such as availability bias, representative heuristics, confirmation bias, etc. [6, 7, 23, 32] Bias in probabilistic reasoning refers to systematic human errors in assessing the probability of future events. Given the close connection between probabilistic reasoning and the enjoyment of sports games, how do probabilistic reasoning biases affect the spectators' entertainment experience? This study seeks to shed light on this rarely explored question in the context of tennis.

Tennis was selected for this study due to its relatively complex scoring system, which leads to more complex probabilistic reasoning about the outcomes. The tennis scoring system is divided into three hierarchical layers: set scores, game scores, and point scores. In this study, the set and game scores are classified as macro-level scores and point scores as micro-level scores. Probabilistic reasoning about the outcome occurs at the macro- and micro-levels, and the predictions are interconnected.

This study makes three main contributions.

– This research analyzes winning probabilities across different tennis scoring scenarios, drawing on data from thousands of professional matches and comparing these to widely accepted theoretical models. The findings show that while the predictions from the theoretical models align well with empirical probabilities at the macro-level of game scores, the model significantly deviates from the empirical probabilities at the micro-level of point scores. Since this theoretical model is considered close to human probabilistic reasoning, these discrepancies point to possible biases in micro-level probabilistic reasoning. Such biases have not been reported before.

– The biases in the micro-level probabilistic reasoning can be explained by recent theories from behavioral economics [7]. It is a type of availability bias because limited human cognitive capacity has difficulty handling the large volume of micro-level data.

– This study suggests that spectators' entertainment experience in tennis is partially based on human errors in probabilistic reasoning. In other words, biases in micro-level probabilistic reasoning actually enhance the entertainment experience of watching tennis matches by creating expectations, anxiety, and surprises. While biases are typically viewed as detrimental due to their role in producing inaccurate predictions, this research presents a counterpoint: these biases can have positive effects on the entertainment experience.

This is the first step toward a comprehensive study of biases in micro-level probabilistic reasoning for tennis spectators.

2 Background and Related Work

2.1 Biases in Probabilistic Reasoning

People often need to make decisions in uncertain circumstances based on sub-jective probabilities of future events. Due to scarcity of data or limited human cognitive capacity, people use certain heuristic principles to simplify their prob-abilistic reasoning [29]. Although these heuristics may work well in many cases, they frequently lead to biases (or errors) that negatively affect people's judg-ments [6,31,32]. Since Tversky and Kahneman's early work [31], researchers have discovered various biases: anchoring effect, framing bias, availability bias, repre-sentative heuristics, recallability trap, survivorship bias, biased beliefs about the random sequence, biased beliefs about sampling distributions, base rate neglect, etc. [6,12,32]

In recent years, some researchers have attempted to uncover the underlying cognitive process associated with such biases. For example, Enke and Graeber [10] argued that cognitive uncertainty might cause systemic biases. Bordalo, et al. [7] proposed a theory that the bias in probabilistic reasoning is related to the similarity and interference in memory retrieval.

2.2 Biases in Sports-Related Probabilistic Reasoning

Bias and heuristics have also been studied in sports [2,9], and one of the most notable examples is the hot-hand bias [6,13]. However, relatively little research has been done on the biases and heuristics in tennis. Most related works in tennis focused on the biases in the tennis betting markets [1,11,18,19]. This work differs from previous works by focusing on the bias in game outcome (micro-level) pre-dictions. In contrast, the previous work on the betting market focused on match outcome (macro-level) predictions. To the best knowledge of this author, the biases in the micro-level probabilistic reasoning have not been reported before.

2.3 Tennis Scoring System

Before getting into the details of predicting winning probabilities in tennis, it is important to understand the basics of the tennis scoring system. A tennis match is divided into three hierarchical layers: match, set, and game. There are three types of scores in tennis: point scores, game scores, and set scores. The two players take turns to server for each game. Each time a player scores in a game, the player's point score increases in the sequence of 0, 15, 30, 40, and Advantage(Ad). To win a game, a player must score higher than 40 and win at least two more points than the opponent. If a player wins a game, the player's game score increases by one. To win a set, a player must score higher than five games and win at least two more games than the opponent or win the tiebreak game after 6–6. If a player wins a set, the player's set score increases by one. To win a match, the player must win the best of three or five sets, depending on the tournament.

In this study, the set scores and game scores are classified as macro-level scores and point scores as micro-level scores.

2.4 Prediction Models for Tennis

There is a large body of work on predicting the winner or calculating the winning probabilities in tennis matches. Kovalchik [17] and Sarcevic, et al. [27] have conducted comprehensive reviews on the subject. The prediction models in tennis can be divided into three categories: point-based models (including regression models), paired comparison models, and machine learning models [27].

Point-based models make predictions based on past performance statistics and the scores. For example, Barnett, et al. [5] developed recursive models for calculating winning probabilities, based on a player's pre-match point-winning statistics and current scores. Based on a similar idea, O'Malley [20] also developed recursive models for calculating the winning probabilities for tennis games, sets, and matches. Sarcevic, et al. [4] developed a combinatorial prediction model that is theoretically identical to the recursive model but more efficient in practice.

Paired comparison models use the players' historical data, such as their rankings and head-to-head records, to make predictions [27]. Previous studies indicate that paired comparison models can better predict match winners than point-based models [17,27]. However, paired comparison models are generally unsuitable for micro-level predictions because there is no tennis ranking data for game-level comparisons.

The benefit of machine learning methods is that they can take in a wide variety of information that is otherwise difficult to integrate into traditional statistical models. Such information may include home-court advantage, player fatigue, court surfaces, weather conditions, player's physical and mental conditions, etc. However, current machine learning models have not generated better results than other types of models [27].

Overall, paired-based and machine-learning models are more suitable for pre-match outcome predictions, but point-based models are more suitable for real-time, in-game outcome predictions.

3 Probabilistic Reasoning and Sports Spectators' Entertainment Experience

The relationship between probabilistic reasoning and sports spectators' entertainment experience can be constructed as follows.

Before and during a sports game, a spectator estimates the probability of a player or team winning or losing, either consciously or subconsciously. This is particularly true if the spectator has a personal affinity for the player or team in question [22,34]. Although the pre-match prediction may involve many factors, such as head-to-head records, ranking differences, home-court advantage, playing venue, and weather conditions, multiple empirical studies have shown that a spectator's subjective probabilistic reasoning during a game is primarily based on the scores, particularly the score differences [16, 22, 30, 34].

The spectator experiences different emotions depending on the winning probability of the player or team. When the spectator believes that a player or team's chance of winning is high or increasing, the spectator feels hopeful. However, if the winning probability is low or decreasing, the spectator fears the negative outcome. During the game, the spectator always has a sense of uncertainty about the game's outcome. However, this feeling of uncertainty intensifies when the probability of winning is perceived to be hovering around 50%.

Based on the OCC theory [8, 21], a combination of hope, fear, and uncertainty generates suspense. Uncertainty is a particularly strong factor in this mix, as it creates a sense of unpredictability and keeps spectators engaged. Empirical studies indicate that the relationship between suspense and probabilistic reasoning can be represented by a bell-shaped curve between suspense and score differences [16, 22, 30, 34]. In such experiments, the subjects usually self-reported the level of suspense they felt. When the score difference decreases, the uncertainty factor is heightened, and so is the suspense. On the other hand, when the score gap increases, the spectators experience hope or fear, but the suspense decreases. However, our research (as discussed below) indicates that the spectators' emotional response to the score differences in tennis matches is likely to be based on accurate predictions on the macro level (set and game scores) but biased predictions on the micro level (point scores).

Psychological studies have established the close correlation between suspense and the spectators' enjoyment of sports games [14, 22, 30, 34]. In other words, the enjoyment would be higher for spectators who viewed a more suspenseful game. Based on Zillman's disposition theory [34], suspense enhances the enjoyment when the spectator's favored player or team wins a close game. Research by Hall [14] indicates that even when the spectator's favored player or team loses, the suspense still enhances the enjoyment by creating a stronger feeling of appreciation.

Therefore, it is reasonable to conclude that a spectator's subjective predictions of the outcome during a sports game generate suspense, which subsequently elevates the entertainment experience. Such assertion is not only supported by scholarly research but also by anecdotal evidence. For example, renowned European football manager Jose Mourinho once said in a press conference: "I think entertaining is emotional until the end, an open result until the end, everybody on their seats until the end, both dug-outs nervous and tense with the unpredictability of the result. For me as a football lover, not as a manager, that's entertaining."

4   Discovering Possible Biases in Probabilistic Reasoning

This part of the research aims to test the following hypothesis.

– H1: Spectators of tennis matches make highly accurate predictions of a player's probability to win a set based on the game scores.

- H2: Spectators of tennis matches make <u>inaccurate predictions</u> of a player's probability to <u>win a game based on the point scores</u>.

The author has developed these hypotheses through personal experience, observations of others, and a study of tennis-related literature.

Predicting match outcomes using the set scores is straightforward because the score scenarios are very limited. For a best-of-three match, the possible set scores are 1–0, 1–1, and 0–1. Because most of the tennis matches are best-of-three matches, analyzing such simple predictions does not offer much insight. Therefore, the focus of this study is on predicting the set winners and game winners.

To test the hypothesis, the spectators' predicted winning probabilities for different tennis score scenarios should be compared with the corresponding empirical (or historical) probabilities for their statistical correlation. The data set from the Match Charting Project [26] is used to calculate the empirical (or historical) probabilities in tennis (see Sect. 4.1). The challenge is to get the spectators' subjective winning probability predictions for different tennis score scenarios.

The ideal approach would be to conduct a controlled experiment where a large number of spectators predict a player's chances of winning under various tennis score scenarios. However, this type of subjective probability prediction data isn't readily available. As an alternative, this study employs a commonly used point-based prediction model [5, 20] to simulate the spectators' subjective probability predictions about the outcomes (see Sect. 2.4).

Is it reasonable to use a point-based, theoretical prediction model to simulate the spectators' subjective predictions? Substantial evidence suggests that it is. As discussed in Sect. 3, several empirical studies have shown that spectators' estimation of winning probability during a game is primarily based on the score differences [16, 22, 30, 34]. As discussed in Sect. 2.4, the point-based prediction models are best suited for real-time, in-game outcome predictions. In addition, anecdotal evidence and individual accounts also support the idea that spectators primarily base their assessment of a player's probability of winning or losing on the score differences. For example, when a player leads by a big game score margin (e.g., 5–1), the commentators would describe the player as "in control." If a returning player leads 40–0 in a tennis game, the commentators often say the player has a "good chance of breaking." In the US Open 2023, BBC reporter Jonathan Jurejko [15] wrote that British tennis player Lily Miyazaki "showed composure to fight back from 0–40 down," implying that the player showed mental toughness and resilience when confronted with significant odds of losing the game.

4.1 Calculating Empirical Winning Probabilities

The data set from the Match Charting Project [26] is used to calculate the empirical winning probabilities for different score scenarios. This data set is a spreadsheet that contains detailed, point-by-point data for over 10K professional tennis matches and over 1.5K male and female players. This data set is used to calculate the comprehensive statistics published on the tennisabstract.com website.

This author developed Python programs to clean and analyze the data set. The data was grouped by players and then by specific score scenarios, such as 30–15, 30–30, and 30–40. Winning probabilities for each player under all possible score combinations are calculated. Based on tennis' hierarchical scoring system, the match-winning probabilities were calculated based on the set scores, the set-winning probabilities were calculated based on the game scores, and the game-winning probabilities were calculated based on the point scores. In this study, the empirical winning probability means the winning probability calculated from the historical data from the Match Charting Project.

4.2 Theoretical Prediction Model

This study adopts a point-based, recursive model very close to the ones developed by Barnett, et al. [5] and O'Malley [20]. This type of model is widely accepted and often used in calculating the winning odds for real-time betting.

Suppose *Player*1 and *Player*2 are playing a tennis match. The point scores are $ps1$ and $ps2$, game scores are $gs1$ and $gs2$, and the set scores are $ss1$ and $ss2$. The probability of *Player*1 winning a service point is $SPWP1$, and the probability of *Player*1 winning a return point is $RPWP1$. In tennis, a service game for *Player*1 is a game where *Player*1 serves for each point. Every point in such a service game is a service point for *Player*1. A return game for *Player*1 is when *Player*2 serves for each point. Every point in such a return game is a return point for *Player*1. The probabilities of a professional player winning a service point ($SPWP1$) and return point ($RPWP1$) can be found on the Association of Tennis Professionals (ATP) and Women's Tennis Association (WTA) websites or tennisabstract.com [26]. In this study, we use the statistics from tennisabstract.com.

To simplify the score calculation, the traditional tennis point scores are converted to a simple incremental score system, where 15 is converted to 1, 30 to 2, 40 to 3, and Advantage to 4. For example, 15–40 is converted to 1–3, and Ad–40 is converted to 4–3. Each time a player wins a point, the player's point score increases by 1.

Thus, the probability of *Player*1 winning a service game is given by the recursive equation below.

$$SGWP1(ps1, ps2) = (SPWP1 * (SGWP1(ps1 + 1, ps2)) + ((1 - SPWP1) * (SGWP1(ps1, ps2 + 1))) \quad (1)$$

The probability of *Player*1 winning a return game is given by the recursive equation below.

$$RGWP1(ps1, ps2) = (RPWP1 * (RGWP1(ps1 + 1, ps2)) + ((1 - RPWP1) * (RGWP1(ps1, ps2 + 1))) \quad (2)$$

The algorithm for calculating *Player*1's probability to win a tiebreak game *TBGWP*1 considers the rule that *Player*1 and *Player*2 take turns to serve.

The probability of *Player*1 winning a set is given by the recursive equation below.

$$SWP1(gs1, gs2) = (NGWP1(0,0) * (SWP1(gs + 1, gs2)) \\ + ((1 - NGP1(0,0)) * SWP1(gs1, gs2 + 1)) \quad (3)$$

where $NGWP1(0,0)$ is either $SGWP1(0,0)$, $RGWP1(0,0)$, or $TBGWP1$, depending on whether the next game is *Player*1's service game, return game, or a tiebreak game.

The probability of *Player*1 winning a match is given by the recursive equation below.

$$MWP1(ss1, ss2) = SWP1(0,0) * MWP1(ss1 + 1, ss2) \\ + (1 - SWP1(0,0)) * MWP2(ss1, ss2 + 1) \quad (4)$$

The model has some limitations, most notably the assumption that each point is independent and identically distributed (IID), meaning that the outcome of one point does not affect the outcome of the next point, and the player's probability of winning each point is constant. The situation is more complicated in real matches. For example, winning a critical point after a long rally or losing a critical point with an unforced error could affect the mental states of both players for the next point. The audience's response at critical points could also affect the players' mental and emotional states.

4.3   Comparing Theoretical Probabilities and Empirical Probabilities at the Macro Level

Table 3 shows *Player*1's theoretical and empirical set-winning probabilities for both male and female professional players under different score scenarios, with *Player*1 serving first in the set. The theoretical probabilities are calculated using the models discussed in Sect. 4.2. The empirical probabilities are calculated using the Match Charting Project data as discussed in Sect. 4.1.

The theoretical probabilities for male players are calculated based on the male players' average service point winning percentage of 66% and average return point winning percentage of 37% [26]. The theoretical probabilities for female players are calculated based on the female players' average service point winning percentage of 59% and average return point winning percentage of 44% [26].

Since the theoretical probabilities are not normally distributed, Spearman's rank correlation coefficient is used to analyze the relationship between the theoretical and empirical probabilities. The result shows that the theoretical set-winning probabilities and empirical probabilities are highly correlated. For both male and female players, $Spearman's\ r = 0.99, p = 0.001$ at the 95% confidence level.

Table 1. Linear regression analysis for the set-winning probabilities and score differences (Player1 serving first). $SWP1$ is Player1's set-winning probability. $gs1$ is Player1's game score. $gs2$ is Player2's game score.

Probability	Linear Regression Line	Standard Error	F Statistics	Coeff. of Determination
Theoretical probability (male players)	$SWP1 = 0.50 + 0.13 * (gs1 - gs2)$	0.007	361.0	0.90
Empirical probability (male players)	$SWP1 = 0.45 + 0.14 * (gs1 - gs2)$	0.007	350.6	0.90
Theoretical probability (female players)	$SWP1 = 0.53 + 0.13 * (gs1 - gs2)$	0.006	501.9	0.93
Empirical probability (female players)	$SWP1 = 0.48 + 0.13 * (gs1 - gs2)$	0.006	562.3	0.93

The data analysis also shows a linear relationship between the game score differences and empirical set-winning probabilities (Table 1).

Table 4 shows $Player1$'s theoretical and empirical set-winning probabilities for both male and female professional players under different score scenarios, with $Player1$ returning first in the set. Spearman's correlation coefficient also indicates a strong correlation between the theoretical and empirical probabilities. For both male and female players, $Spearman's\ r = 0.99, p = 0.001$ at the 95% confidence level. Again, the data analysis also shows a linear relationship between the score differences and probabilities (Table 2).

Table 2. Linear regression analysis for the set-winning probabilities and score differences (Player1 returning first). $SWP1$ is Player1's set-winning probability. $gs1$ is Player1's game score. $gs2$ is Player2's game score.

Probability	Linear Regression Line	Standard Error	F Statistics	Coeff. of Determination
Theoretical probability (male players)	$SWP1 = 0.59 + 0.13 * (gs1 - gs2)$	0.007	342.7	0.90
Empirical probability (male players)	$SWP1 = 0.55 + 0.14 * (gs1 - gs2)$	0.007	350.6	0.90
Theoretical probability (female players)	$SWP1 = 0.58 + 0.13 * (gs1 - gs2)$	0.006	500.0	0.93
Empirical probability (female players)	$SWP1 = 0.52 + 0.13 * (gs1 - gs2)$	0.006	563.0	0.94

The macro-level analysis has shown a straightforward linear relationship between the set outcome and game score differences. **This means that a spectator in tennis can make highly accurate predictions about the outcome of a set based solely on the game score differences.**

118   S. Zhu

Table 3. This table shows *Player*1's theoretical and empirical set-winning probabilities for both male and female professional players under different game score scenarios, with *Player*1 serving first in the set. The theoretical probabilities for male players are calculated based on the male players' average service point won percentage of 66% and average return point won percentage of 37% [26]. The theoretical probabilities for female players are calculated based on the female players' average service point won percentage of 59% and average return point won percentage of 44% [26].

Player1 game score	Player2 game score	Theoretical set-winning probability (male)	Empirical set-winning probability (male)	Theoretical set-winning probability (female)	Empirical set-winning probability (female)
0	0	0.60	0.48	0.60	0.50
0	1	0.33	0.20	0.42	0.28
0	2	0.26	0.15	0.32	0.19
0	3	0.08	0.03	0.15	0.07
0	4	0.04	0.02	0.08	0.03
0	5	0.00	0.00	0.01	0.00
1	0	0.65	0.56	0.68	0.61
1	1	0.59	0.48	0.60	0.51
1	2	0.29	0.18	0.39	0.28
1	3	0.22	0.12	0.28	0.19
1	4	0.05	0.02	0.10	0.06
1	5	0.02	0.01	0.04	0.02
2	0	0.86	0.84	0.83	0.80
2	1	0.65	0.56	0.68	0.62
2	2	0.58	0.49	0.59	0.50
2	3	0.25	0.16	0.35	0.26
2	4	0.17	0.09	0.22	0.15
2	5	0.02	0.01	0.05	0.04
3	0	0.90	0.90	0.89	0.88
3	1	0.88	0.86	0.85	0.82
3	2	0.64	0.57	0.68	0.63
3	3	0.58	0.49	0.58	0.51
3	4	0.19	0.13	0.29	0.22
3	5	0.10	0.06	0.14	0.11
4	0	0.98	0.99	0.97	0.97
4	1	0.93	0.92	0.91	0.89
4	2	0.91	0.88	0.87	0.84
4	3	0.65	0.58	0.69	0.64
4	4	0.57	0.50	0.57	0.50
4	5	0.12	0.08	0.20	0.19
5	0	0.99	1.00	0.99	0.99
5	1	0.99	1.00	0.99	0.98
5	2	0.96	0.95	0.95	0.94
5	3	0.95	0.93	0.92	0.90
5	4	0.65	0.59	0.72	0.67
5	5	0.56	0.50	0.56	0.52
5	6	0.11	0.09	0.19	0.17
6	5	0.64	0.60	0.71	0.70
6	6	0.55	0.51	0.55	0.54

Table 4. This table shows *Player*1's theoretical and empirical set-winning probabilities for both male and female professional players under different game score scenarios, with *Player*1 returning first in the set. The theoretical probabilities for male players are calculated based on the male players' average service point won percentage of 66% and average return point won percentage of 37% [26]. The theoretical probabilities for female players are calculated based on the female players' average service point won percentage of 59% and average return point won percentage of 44% [26].

Player1 game score	Player2 game score	Theoretical set-winning probability (male)	Empirical set-winning probability (male)	Theoretical set-winning probability (female)	Empirical set-winning probability (female)
0	0	0.60	0.52	0.60	0.50
0	1	0.54	0.44	0.52	0.39
0	2	0.26	0.16	0.32	0.20
0	3	0.19	0.10	0.22	0.12
0	4	0.04	0.01	0.08	0.03
0	5	0.01	0.00	0.03	0.01
1	0	0.82	0.80	0.76	0.72
1	1	0.59	0.52	0.60	0.49
1	2	0.53	0.44	0.50	0.38
1	3	0.22	0.14	0.28	0.18
1	4	0.14	0.08	0.17	0.11
1	5	0.02	0.00	0.04	0.02
2	0	0.86	0.85	0.83	0.81
2	1	0.84	0.82	0.77	0.72
2	2	0.58	0.51	0.59	0.50
2	3	0.51	0.43	0.48	0.37
2	4	0.17	0.12	0.22	0.16
2	5	0.08	0.05	0.10	0.06
3	0	0.97	0.97	0.93	0.93
3	1	0.88	0.88	0.85	0.81
3	2	0.86	0.84	0.79	0.74
3	3	0.58	0.51	0.58	0.49
3	4	0.50	0.42	0.45	0.36
3	5	0.10	0.07	0.14	0.10
4	0	0.98	0.98	0.97	0.97
4	1	0.98	0.98	0.95	0.94
4	2	0.91	0.91	0.87	0.85
4	3	0.89	0.87	0.82	0.78
4	4	0.57	0.50	0.57	0.50
4	5	0.47	0.41	0.40	0.33
5	0	1.00	1.00	1.00	1.00
5	1	0.99	0.99	0.99	0.98
5	2	0.99	0.99	0.98	0.96
5	3	0.95	0.94	0.92	0.89
5	4	0.93	0.92	0.87	0.81
5	5	0.56	0.50	0.56	0.48
5	6	0.47	0.40	0.39	0.30
6	5	0.93	0.91	0.87	0.83
6	6	0.55	0.49	0.55	0.46

4.4   Comparing Theoretical Probabilities and Empirical Probabilities at the Micro Level

Table 5 shows *Player*1's theoretical and empirical game-winning probabilities for both male and female professional players under different point score scenarios, with *Player*1 serving in the game. The theoretical probabilities are calculated using the models discussed in Sect. 4.2. The empirical probabilities are calculated using the Match Charting Project data as discussed in Sect. 4.1.

The theoretical probabilities for male players are calculated based on the male players' average service point won percentage of 66% [26]. The theoretical probabilities for female players are calculated based on the female players' average service point won percentage of 59% [26].

Table 5. This table shows *Player*1's theoretical and empirical game-winning probabilities for both male and female professional players under different point score scenarios, with *Player*1 serving in the game. The theoretical probabilities for male players are calculated based on the male players' average service point won percentage of 66% [26]. The theoretical probabilities for female players are calculated based on the female players' average service point won percentage of 59% [26].

Player1 point score	Player2 point score	Theoretical game-winning probability (male)	Empirical game-winning probability (male)	Theoretical game-winning probability (female)	Empirical game-winning probability (female)
0	0	0.85	0.80	0.71	0.66
0	15	0.71	0.79	0.55	0.66
0	30	0.50	0.82	0.35	0.67
0	40	0.23	0.86	0.14	0.70
15	0	0.92	0.80	0.83	0.66
15	15	0.82	0.76	0.69	0.65
15	30	0.64	0.76	0.49	0.64
15	40	0.34	0.79	0.23	0.65
30	0	0.96	0.82	0.92	0.67
30	15	0.91	0.77	0.83	0.65
30	30	0.79	0.74	0.67	0.63
30	40	0.52	0.73	0.40	0.62
40	0	0.99	0.86	0.98	0.71
40	15	0.98	0.79	0.95	0.66
40	30	0.93	0.73	0.87	0.63
40	40	0.79	0.72	0.67	0.62
Ad	40	0.93	0.72	0.87	0.61
40	Ad	0.52	0.72	0.40	0.62
Average		0.74	0.78	0.64	0.65

No statistically significant correlation is found between the theoretical probabilities and empirical probabilities. For male players, $Spearman's\, r = 0.07, p = 0.4$. For female players, $Spearman's\, r = 0.13, p = 0.32$.

No statistically significant correlation is found between the score differences and empirical probabilities. Linear regression can only explain 44% of the data for male players and 42% of the data for female players.

Table 6 shows $Player1$'s theoretical and empirical game-winning probabilities for both male and female professional players under different point score scenarios, with $Player1$ returning in the game.

No statistically significant correlation is found between the theoretical probabilities and empirical probabilities. For male players, $Spearman's\, r = 0.06, p = 0.41$. For female players, $Spearman's\, r = 0.12, p = 0.32$. Again, no statistically significant correlation is found between the score differences and empirical or theoretical probabilities.

Table 6. This table shows $Player1$'s theoretical and empirical game-winning probabilities for both male and female professional players under different point score scenarios, with $Player1$ returning in the game. The theoretical probabilities for male players are calculated based on the male players' average return point won percentage of 37% [26]. The theoretical probabilities for female players are calculated based on the female players' average return point won percentage of 44% [26].

Player1 point score	Player2 point score	Theoretical game-winning probability (male players)	Empirical game-winning probability (male players)	Theoretical game-winning probability (female players)	Empirical game-winning probability (female players)
0	0	0.21	0.20	0.35	0.34
0	15	0.12	0.20	0.22	0.34
0	30	0.05	0.18	0.11	0.33
0	40	0.01	0.14	0.03	0.29
15	0	0.35	0.21	0.52	0.34
15	15	0.23	0.24	0.37	0.35
15	30	0.12	0.23	0.21	0.35
15	40	0.04	0.21	0.07	0.34
30	0	0.57	0.18	0.71	0.33
30	15	0.42	0.24	0.57	0.36
30	30	0.26	0.26	0.38	0.37
30	40	0.09	0.27	0.17	0.37
40	0	0.81	0.14	0.89	0.30
40	15	0.70	0.21	0.81	0.35
40	30	0.53	0.27	0.65	0.38
40	40	0.26	0.28	0.38	0.38
Ad	40	0.53	0.28	0.65	0.38
40	Ad	0.09	0.28	0.17	0.39
Average		0.30	0.22	0.40	0.35

Unlike the macro-level analysis, the micro-level analysis shows significant discrepancies between theoretical and empirical probabilities for different score scenarios. This study is unable to find a statistically significant correlation between the theoretical and empirical probabilities or statistically significant correlations between score differences and empirical game-winning probabilities.

Somewhat surprisingly, the empirical probabilities of a player winning a game are consistent across different score scenarios. For example, a serving male player has, on average, an 87% chance of winning the game even when he is 0–40 down. A female player has a 70% chance of winning the game when she is 0–40 down. In contrast, the theoretical model predicts a 23% winning chance for male and 14% chance for female players if the score is 0–40 (see Table 5).

Similarly, a returning male player has, on average, only 14% chance of winning the game even if he is 40–0 up. A returning female player has only a 30% chance of winning the game if she is 40–0 up. In contrast, the predictions from the theoretical model are 80% chance for male and 89% chance for female players if the score is 40–0 (see Table 6).

This means that if a typical tennis spectator makes similar micro-level predictions as the theoretical model, the spectator will make systematic errors. In other words, there are biases in the spectator's micro-level probabilistic reasoning. The question is whether the theoretical model is consistent with the spectators' beliefs. There is plenty of evidence to support this. First, the micro-level predictions made by the theoretical model make intuitive sense (see Table 5 and Table 6). The theoretical winning probability goes up and down as the score difference goes up and down. This pattern is consistent with findings from the previous empirical studies [22, 30, 34] and anecdotal evidence. The BBC reporter is unlikely to use the word "composure" to describe Lily Miyazaki fighting back from 0–40 down to win the game if the reporter believes Miyazaki has a 70% winning chance at 0–40. It's more likely that the reporter believes Miyazaki only has a 14% chance, as the theoretical model predicts.

Second, as shown in Sect. 4.3, tennis spectators can use the score differences to accurately predict the set outcome at the macro level. It is reasonable to assume that the spectators would subconsciously use the same method to predict the game outcome at the micro level. Besides, very few spectators know the game-level empirical probabilities discussed in Sect. 4.4. Such data is not publicly available. Even tennisabstract.com, which publishes comprehensive and up-to-date statistics about professional tennis players, does not provide winning probabilities for different score scenarios at the micro-level. As behavioral economics theories suggest, when people do not know the true statistics, they are likely to use mental shortcuts (heuristics) to make predictions.

Third, the theoretical model [5, 20] has been around for a long time, and most people have accepted it as statistically reasonable [27]. Many people use the model to make predictions, which may further influence the tennis spectators' beliefs.

This study has shown that the theoretical prediction model is very accurate at the macro level but seriously flawed at the micro level. It is very likely that tennis spectators use the same intuitive model to make predictions at both the macro and micro levels. A possible cause for this phenomenon is discussed in the next section.

5   Possible Causes of the Biases

Herbert Simon [29] proposed that humans have cognitive limitations and must operate within those bounds, leading people to seek "good enough" rather than optimal solutions. When faced with complex or ambiguous situations, people rely on heuristics or shortcuts to make decisions. A possible cause of the biases in tennis in micro-level probabilistic reasoning is its relatively complex scoring system (see Sect. 2.3). The three hierarchical layers of set scores, game scores, and point scores, plus the tiebreak scoring rules, make it harder to retrieve historical information from memory and compare results from the same score scenarios. As a result, tennis spectators are likely to resort to simple heuristics for predicting the outcome.

A recent theory proposed by Bordalo, et al. [7] may explain the biases discussed in this paper. Bordalo, et al. argue that probabilistic reasoning is influenced by the structural similarity between the hypothesis and the information stored in the memory and interference in memory retrieval. If tennis spectators try to predict a player's winning probability at 15–40, they need to recall many cases of 15–40, who scored 15, who was serving, and who eventually won the game. It is difficult to retrieve and classify such information from memory. Instead, it is easier to recall a structurally similar question on the macro level: Who won the set when the game score was 2–4? There are far fewer cases of 2–4, and more importantly, as discussed in Sect. 4.3, their intuitive predictions (based on the score difference) are quite accurate on the macro level. As a result, the spectator is likely to apply the simple and intuitive heuristic to make predictions at both the macro and micro levels. This is likely a type of availability bias.

6   Biases in Probabilistic Reasoning and the Entertainment Experience

Biases in probabilistic reasoning are generally seen as undesirable human errors. But from a tennis spectator's perspective, biased micro-level probabilistic reasoning is actually better for the entertainment experience than the accurate prediction. First, in Table 5 and Table 6, the theoretical probabilities are inaccurate, but they create emotional roller-coasters for the spectators as the probabilities go up and down for different score scenarios. In contrast, the empirical probabilities remain more or less consistent for different scores, arousing no significant emotional change.

Second, discrepancies between theoretical and empirical probabilities create surprises. In the context of sports, surprise can be derived from win probability changes [3]. If a tennis spectator makes systematic errors in micro-level predictions, the spectator is more likely to experience surprises. For instance, a spectator may be surprised when a player wins a game where the perceived winning probability is low, or the reverse. As in films and literature, surprises enhance the entertainment experience and can significantly impact the spectators. In the US Open 2023, Lily Miyazaki fighting back to win the game from 0–40 [15] was objectively not a surprise because she had a 70% empirical (or historical) probability of winning that game at 0–40. However, the BBC reporter Jonathan Jurejko probably thought it was a surprise and highlighted it in the report [15] about Miyazaki's performance. This minor surprise created a strong impression on the reporter.

7   Conclusion and Future Work

This study explores possible biases in probabilistic reasoning for sports and their connections to the sports entertainment experience. It reveals that the well-accepted point-based prediction model for tennis is highly accurate in making predictions at the macro level but inaccurate in making predictions at the micro level. Since evidence suggests that tennis spectators' subjective probability prediction is aligned with the theoretical model, this study reveals likely biases in tennis spectators' micro-level probabilistic reasoning. An explanation for such biases has been offered using a recent behavioral economic theory. Furthermore, this author argues that biases in micro-level probabilistic reasoning are actually beneficial for the sports entertainment experience because they keep the spectators emotionally engaged and create surprises that enhance the enjoyment of the games.

This is the first step toward a comprehensive study of biases in micro-level probabilistic reasoning for tennis. The author plans to carry out user studies to collect subjective probability predictions. The comparison between different theoretical prediction models and empirical probabilities will be explored. It will also be useful to test if similar biases exist in other sports with hierarchical scoring systems, such as volleyball, table tennis, etc.

Acknowledgement. The author is deeply grateful to the anonymous reviewers for their many insightful comments and suggestions.

References

1. Abinzano, I., Muga, L., Santamaria, R.: Game, set and match: the favourite-long shot bias in tennis betting exchanges. Appl. Econ. Lett. **23**, 605–608 (2016). https://doi.org/10.1080/13504851.2015.1093074
2. Altman, H.J.R., Altman, M., Torgler, B.: Behavioural sports economics : a research companion. Routledge (2021)

3. Antony, J.W., Hartshorne, T.H., Pomeroy, K., Gureckis, T.M., Hasson, U., McDougle, S.D., Norman, K.A.: Behavioral, physiological, and neural signatures of surprise during naturalistic sports viewing. Neuron **109**, 377-390.e7 (2021). https://doi.org/10.1016/j.neuron.2020.10.029
4. Šarčević, A., Vranić, M., Pintar, D.: A combinatorial approach in predicting the outcome of tennis matches. Int. J. Appl. Math. Comput. Sci. **31**, 525–538 (2021). https://doi.org/10.34768/amcs-2021-0036
5. Barnett, T., Brown, A., Clarke, S.: Developing a tennis model that reflects outcomes of tennis matches. In: Proceedings of the 8th Australasian Conference on Mathematics and Computers in Sport (2006)
6. Benjamin, D.J.: Errors in probabilistic reasoning and judgment biases. In: Handbook of Behavioral Economics: Applications and Foundations 1, vol. 2, pp. 69–186. North-Holland (2019). https://doi.org/10.1016/BS.HESBE.2018.11.002
7. Bordalo, P., Conlon, J.J., Gennaioli, N., Kwon, S.Y., Shleifer, A.: Memory and probability. Q. J. Econ. **138**, 265–311 (2022). https://doi.org/10.1093/QJE/QJAC031
8. Clore, G.L., Ortony, A.: Psychological construction in the OCC model of emotion. Emot. Rev. **5**, 335 (2013). https://doi.org/10.1177/1754073913489751
9. Coates, D., Humphreys, B.R.: Behavioral and sports economics. Handbook of Behavioral Industrial Organization, pp. 307–342 (2018). https://doi.org/10.4337/9781784718985.00019
10. Enke, B., Graeber, T.: Cognitive uncertainty. Working Paper 26518, National Bureau of Economic Research (2019). https://doi.org/10.3386/w26518
11. Forrest, D., McHale, I.: Anyone for tennis (betting)? Europ. J. Finance **13**, 751–768 (2007). https://doi.org/10.1080/13518470701705736, https://www.tandfonline.com/doi/abs/10.1080/13518470701705736
12. Gilovich, T., Griffin, D., Kahneman, D.: Heuristics and Biases. Cambridge University Press (2002)
13. Gilovich, T., Vallone, R., Tversky, A.: The hot hand in basketball: on the misperception of random sequences. Cogn. Psychol. **17**, 295–314 (1985). https://doi.org/10.1016/0010-0285(85)90010-6
14. Hall, A.E.: Entertainment-oriented gratifications of sports media: contributors to suspense, hedonic enjoyment, and appreciation. J. Broadcast. Electron. Media **59**, 259–277 (2015). https://doi.org/10.1080/08838151.2015.1029124
15. Jurejko, J.: Us open 2023: Lily Miyazaki wins on New York main-draw debut. BBC (8 2023). https://www.bbc.com/sport/tennis/66642122
16. Knobloch-Westerwick, S.S., David, P., Eastin, M.S., Tamborini, R., Greenwood, D.: Sports spectators' suspense: affect and uncertainty in sports entertainment. J. Commun. **59**, 750–767 (2009). https://doi.org/10.1111/j.1460-2466.2009.01456.x
17. Kovalchik, S.A.: Searching for the goat of tennis win prediction. J. Quan. Anal. Sports **12**(3), 127–138 (2016). https://doi.org/10.1515/jqas-2015-0059
18. Lahvička, J.: What causes the favourite-longshot bias? further evidence from tennis. Appl. Econ. Lett. **21**, 90–92 (2014). https://doi.org/10.1080/13504851.2013.842628
19. Štefan Lyócsa, Výrost, T.: To bet or not to bet: a reality check for tennis betting market efficiency. Appl. Econom. **50**, 2251–2272 (2018). https://doi.org/10.1080/00036846.2017.1394973
20. O'Malley, A.J.: Probability formulas and statistical analysis in tennis. J. Quan. Anal. Sports **4** (2008). https://doi.org/10.2202/1559-0410.1100
21. Ortony, A., Clore, G.L., Collins, A.: The Cognitive Structure of Emotions. Cambridge University Press (1988)

22. Peterson, E.M., Raney, A.A.: Reconceptualizing and reexamining suspense as a predictor of mediated sports enjoyment. J. Broadcast. Electron. Media **52**, 544–562 (2008). https://doi.org/10.1080/08838150802437263
23. Pronin, E.: Perception and misperception of bias in human judgment. Trends Cogn. Sci. **11**, 37–43 (2007). https://doi.org/10.1016/j.tics.2006.11.001
24. Raney, A.A.: Why we watch and enjoy mediated sports. In: Handbook of Sports and Media, pp. 313–329. Lawrence Erlbaum (2006)
25. Raney, A.A.: Reflections on communication and sport: on enjoyment and disposition. Commun. Sport **1**(1–2), 164–175 (2013). https://doi.org/10.1177/2167479512467979
26. Sackmann, J.: The match charting project. http://www.tennisabstract.com/ 30 Aug 2023
27. Sarcevic, A., Vranic, M., Pintar, D., Krajna, A.: Predictive modeling of tennis matches: a review. In: Proceedings of the 45th Jubilee International Convention on Information, Communication and Electronic Technology, pp. 1099–1104. IEEE (2022). https://doi.org/10.23919/MIPRO55190.2022.9803645
28. Shafer, D.M.: Investigating suspense as a predictor of enjoyment in sports video games. J. Broadcast. Electron. Media **58**, 272–288 (2014). https://doi.org/10.1080/08838151.2014.906432
29. Simon, H.A.: Models of Man. Wiley (1957)
30. Su-lin, G., Tuggle, C.A., Mitrook, M.A., Coussement, S.H., Zillmann, D.: The thrill of a close game: Who enjoys it and who doesn't? J. Sport Soc. Issues **21**(1), 53–64 (1997). https://doi.org/10.1177/019372397021001004
31. Tversky, A., Kahneman, D.: Judgment under uncertainty: heuristics and biases. Science **185**, 1124–1131 (1974). https://doi.org/10.1126/SCIENCE.185.4157.1124
32. Tversky, A., Kahneman, D.: Probabilistic reasoning. In: Goldman, A. (ed.) Readings in Philosophy and Cognitive Science, pp. 43–68. MIT Press (1993)
33. Zillmann, D.: The psychology of suspense in dramatic exposition. In: Suspense, pp. 199–231. Routledge (1996)
34. Zillmann, D., Bryant, J., Sapolsky, B.S.: Enjoyment from sports spectatorship. In: Sports, Games, and Play. Psychology Press, 2nd edn. (1988)
35. Zillmann, D., Paulus, P.B.: Spectators: reactions to sports events and effects on athletic performance. Handbook of research on sport psychology, pp. 600–619 (1993)

A PLS-SEM Approach for Composite Indicators: An Original Application on the Expected Goal Model

Mattia Cefis[(✉)][iD]

University of Brescia, Contrada Santa Chiara 50, Brescia, Italy
mattia.cefis@unibs.it

Abstract. In the field of football analytics, the goal is to improve (in terms of prediction performance) one of the emerging tools: the expected goal (xG) model. With this final aim, data from different sources have been merged: tracking data, match event data and some players' performance composite indicators obtained using a Partial Least Squares - Structural Equation Model (PLS-SEM) approach. Using a sample of match data relying to season 2019/2020 of the Italian Serie A, composed by 1 outcome variable (i.e. the GOAL) and 22 features, a logistic regression model was applied on different scenarios for sample balanced techniques. Results seem to be interesting in terms of sensitivity, F1 and AUC metrics, compared with a benchmark. In addition, some original performance composites and tracking variables introduced are significant for the classification model.

Keywords: Expected Goal · Logistic Regression · Imbalanced Sample · PLS-SEM

1 Introduction

Football (also called soccer, in North America, Australia and New Zealand) is one of the most popular sports in the world. Due to its appeal, football teams are treated more and more as firms: as a consequence, decisions about their management (coach, technical staff and scouting) are becoming strategic, and, for this reason, in the last few years football has been moving towards a data-driven approach [4]. To predict the final score of a football game is one of the cases where a data driven approach is more adopted. The final score might be predicted by summing the probability of score a goal every time a player shoots the ball. This involves the adoption of many features; this aspect has to do with artificial intelligence, as, by matching a proper method with a set of determinant features, might permit to predict accurately the result of a game. By this work, the idea is to refine and improve, in terms of prediction accuracy, the well-known expected goal (xG, [1]) model that surpasses the most basic and frequently used

Supported by Math&Sport.

M. Clayton et al. (Eds.): INTETAIN 2023, LNICST 560, pp. 127–135, 2024.
https://doi.org/10.1007/978-3-031-55722-4_10

metric in football to summarise the team performance: the shot, which does not consider the quality of the goal-scoring opportunity from which it arises.

2 Literature Overview and Data Employed

The main idea of the xG model is to assign a value between zero and one to each shot; this value represents the probability of a shot resulting in a goal, using a machine learning probabilistic classifier [17]. During the last years, the xG model has become increasingly popular, and it is used more and more in the football world as a proxy for measuring players' finalisation performance and teams' offensive strength during a match [9]. For this reason, some studies and websites have treated this topic: for example, someone [16,19] examined shots, taking in consideration only distance and angle to goal, whereas another one [9] made a spatial analysis of shots of the Mayor League Soccer, using a logistic regression. Another recent work [18] tried to quantify the effectiveness of defensive playing styles in the Chinese Football Super League by using xG. The main deficiency is that current xG models are based just on event data and do not take into account players' features. As an innovation, the objective is to improve the xG model by adding some composite indicators related to the players' performance and obtained by a Partial Least Squares Structural Equation Model (PLS-SEM, [10]), in order to take into account shooters' and goalkeepers' features [5,6] (Fig. 1). These composite indicators have been validated by a Model Invariance COMposite (MICOM) approach [11,12].

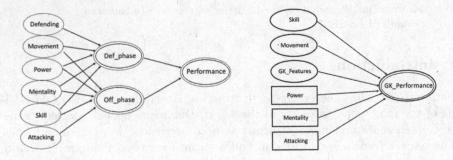

Fig. 1. Players' movement and Goalkeepers models used for the PLS-SEM approach.

In order to reach the aim, a merging between data coming from different sources (e.g. Understat[1] for event data, Math&Sport for tracking data and *Sofifa*[2] for building the players' performance indicators) was done. The final dataset was composed of a sample of 600 shots, 23 variables (e.g. 1 binary outcome and 22 regressors, Table 1) coming from 50 official football matches of the

---

[1] www.understat.com.
[2] www.sofifa.com.

season 2019/2020 (Italian Serie A league). In particular, there are three binary features: GOAL (i.e. the outcome, 1 = goal and 0 = no goal), previous dribbling before the shot (1 = yes, 0 = no) and favourite foot, i.e. if the player shoots on goal with his favourite foot or not: 1 = yes, 0 = no. In addition, the variable that counts the number of opponents around the shooter was converted into two dummies: the first one (i.e. D1.OpponentsPlayer) is equal to 1 when the opponents number is greater than 0, whereas the second one (D2.OpponentsPlayer) is active when that number is greater than 1; the other features are continuous.

Table 1. Statistics of the variables for the sample of 660 shots from the 50 matches of the Italian Serie A 2019/2020.

Variable description	Source Dataset	Mean	Std.	Q1	Q2	Q3
GOAL (Yes/No)	Understat	0.10	0.30	-	-	-
x (shooter coordinate, %)	Understat	83.22	7.64	77.00	83.00	89.00
y (shooter coordinate, %)	Understat	49.98	15.06	37.00	50.00	63.00
Favourite foot (Yes/No)	Understat	0.77	0.42	-	-	-
Previous dribbling (Yes/No)	Understat	0.32	0.47	-	-	-
Angle of shot (degree)	Understat	37.39	20.81	20.22	39.42	52.80
Previous ball distance (%)	Tracking	14.43	8.41	8.60	14.33	17.09
Possession duration (sec.)	Tracking	6.49	4.81	5.68	6.49	6.49
D1.OpponentsPlayer	Tracking	0.13	0.33	-	-	-
D2.OpponentsPlayer	Tracking	0.05	0.21	-	-	-
GK x coordinate (%)	Tracking	96.74	5.25	96.55	97.67	98.41
GK y coordinate (%)	Tracking	50.08	5.06	47.37	50.04	53.07
Defending	Sofifa (PLS-SEM)	0.06	0.99	−0.62	0.14	0.61
Mentality	Sofifa (PLS-SEM)	0.38	1.00	−0.28	0.41	1.17
Movement	Sofifa (PLS-SEM)	0.41	1.03	−0.27	0.32	1.00
Power	Sofifa (PLS-SEM)	0.49	1.06	−0.16	0.53	1.10
Skill	Sofifa (PLS-SEM)	0.47	0.91	−0.15	0.49	1.12
GK Attacking	Sofifa (PLS-SEM)	−0.03	1.01	−0.78	0.2	0.77
GK Features	Sofifa (PLS-SEM)	0.68	0.78	0.32	0.82	1.12
GK Mentality	Sofifa (PLS-SEM)	0.26	0.98	0.08	0.43	0.82
GK Movement	Sofifa (PLS-SEM)	0.55	0.73	0.12	0.53	1.02
GK Power	Sofifa (PLS-SEM)	0.45	0.92	0.10	0.45	1.19
GK Skill	Sofifa (PLS-SEM)	0.06	0.79	−0.51	−0.19	0.52

3   The Frameworks Developed

From a methodological point of view, since the target, namely the Goal, is a rare event [16], a logit model (LM) with parameters estimated by maximum likelihood

[14] was applied on different samples for three situations: the basic Imbalance sample and two machine learning sample-balanced techniques, such as random oversampling examples (ROSE, [15]) and the synthetic minority oversampling technique (SMOTE, [7]). The benchmark adopted was the xG value provided by Understat. From a practical point of view, it was developed a routine in R by using a stratified 3-Fold cross validation for evaluating the model fit and computing the performance measures, with 5,000 replications (R packages *ROSE* and *RSBID*). The LM model was preferred because of its easy interpretation concerning the regressors effects and since the real focus was to introduce new predictors in the xG model, in order to improve the goal probability estimation. In the context of the xG, this model lets to estimate the conditional probability of goal for any shots and their set of features values **X**, and estimate parameters $\hat{\beta}$ in the next Eq. (1). Note that the regression coefficients are estimated by maximum likelihood [14]. Typical classification metrics have been used to assess the models performance [13].

$$xG = P(Goal|\mathbf{X}) = \frac{e^{\mathbf{X}\hat{\beta}}}{1 + e^{\mathbf{X}\hat{\beta}}} \tag{1}$$

In addition, balancing a dataset thanks to some techniques like ROSE or SMOTE, we must take into account the effects of our modifications to the training data [2,8]. Due to the Bayes' Theorem, posterior probabilities are proportional to the prior ones, which can be estimated as the relative frequencies in the respective categories. Therefore, the estimated posterior probability (expected goal) obtained using artificially balanced data set can be corrected (calibrated, xG^*) using the following formula (2):

$$xG^* = \frac{\frac{0.1}{0.5}xG}{\frac{0.1}{0.5}xG + \frac{(1-0.1)}{(1-0.5)}(1 - xG)} \tag{2}$$

Take into account that in this case 10% and 50% are respectively the real and the artificial (balanced) sample proportion of the rare class.

4   Results and Discussion

For what concern the output of the logit, the regression coefficients are presented in Table 2: take in mind that significant coefficients are emphasized by asterisks (e.g. * = 5%, ** = 2.5%, *** = 1%); the main significant estimated regressors (for all the approaches) are the shooter position (in particular, the x coordinate), the Angle of shot, and some new variables introduced: the D2.OpponentsPlayer, the goalkeeper position (GK x coordinate and Gk y coordinate) and some performance features like the shooter Movement ability, GK_mentality and GK_skill related the goalkeeper.

Table 2. The Logistic Regression coefficients estimates after 5,000 replications for the 50 matches of the Italian Serie A 2019/2020.

Regressor	Coeff. ROSE	Coeff. SMOTE	Coeff. Imbl.
x	0.94***	2.09***	1.74***
y	0.02	−0.05	−0.09***
Favourite foot	−0.16	0.10	0.17***
Previous dribbling	0.21*	0.33*	0.46***
Angle of shot	−0.53***	−1.40***	−1.09***
Previous ball distance	−0.09*	−0.22*	−0.06**
Possession duration	−0.18	−0.25*	−0.22***
D1.OpponentsPlayer	−0.74	−1.02*	−0.71
D2. OpponentsPlayer	−5.69***	−6.13***	−5.68***
GK x coordinate	−0.33***	−0.59**	−0.33***
GK y coordinate	0.27***	0.48***	0.46***
Defending	0.14*	0.13	0.16***
Mentality	0.03	−0.23	−0.40***
Movement	0.12*	0.40*	0.27***
Power	−0.01	−0.07	0.14***
Skill	0.08	0.23*	0.21***
GK_Attacking	0.02	0.05	0.03*
GK_features	0.03	0.32*	0.22***
GK_Mentality	−0.15*	−0.44**	−0.33***
GK_Movement	0.10*	0.15	0.07**
GK_Power	−0.17*	−0.20	−0.17**
GK_Skill	0.10*	0.27**	0.20***

The second part of the results is focused on the performance metrics: in order to do this, we must take into account that for binary classification problems usually the probabilistic classifier (xG) is transformed in the categorical one (Goal, NoGoal) using the threshold 0.5. In Table 3 are proposed all the classification performance metrics and their average scores (5,000 replications), comparing them with the benchmark (directly provided from Understat). Take in consideration that asterisks in Table 3 must be interpreted as a value statistically significant different (e.g. * = 5%, ** = 2.5%, *** = 1%) from the benchmark; the metrics that outperform the benchmark are emphasized in bold. Both ROSE and Imbalance significantly outperform in terms of specificity and precision the benchmark (Understat) whereas SMOTE seems able to better detect the goals (sensitivity equals to 0.36 vs 0.16 of the benchmark) and to improve Understat in terms of F1 (the armonic mean between precision and sensitivity) and precision. The Area Under the Receiver Operating Characteristic Curve (AUC) metric is similar for all the situations, except for the Imbalance, that significantly outperforms Understat (0.74 vs 0.72).

Table 3. The performance classification metrics compared with the benchmark (classification threshold = 0.5).

Metric	ROSE	SMOTE	Imbalance	Understat
Accuracy	0.89*	0.86***	0.90	0.91
Sensitivity	0.14*	**0.36***	0.15	0.16
Specificity	**0.98***	0.91***	**0.98***	0.96
Precision	**0.35***	0.32**	**0.51***	0.22
F1	0.16	**0.33***	0.23	0.19
AUC	0.72	0.73	**0.74***	0.72

Now, in order to emphasize the importance of the new regressors introduced in the model, two real situations will be proposed, comparing the expected goal for each framework and introducing some variation, in order to better understand how the xG changes.

In the first real case (Fig. 2) a goal scored from a high distance was proposed, in a situation with a high number of opponents in front of the shooter. Then the expected goal for each situation (xG^* for ROSE and SMOTE) and others two scenarios (Table 5) were proposed: the first one putting a top player as shooter (Ronaldo, Juventus), whereas the second one leaving the same top player as shooter and considering a normal goalkeeper. Let's see how in the real scenario the balanced frameworks increase the estimated goal-scoring probability (higher xG than the benchmark); the xG for the imbalance approach is very similar. It's interesting to note that introducing firstly a top player as shooter (Scenario 1), then a normal goalkeeper (Scenario 2) the expected goal increases in both three situations, emphasizing the importance of introducing players' performance indices in the model, as innovation of this work (Table 4).

Table 4. The expected goal for each situation and different cases

Case	Shooter	GK	xG^* ROSE	xG^* SMOTE	xG Imbalance	xG Understat
Real	Soriano (Bol)	Handanovic (Int)	4.1%	2.3%	2.0%	2.1%
Scenario 1	Roñaldo (Juv)	Handanovic (Int)	5.4%	3.3%	3.1%	2.1%
Scenario 2	Ronaldo (Juv)	Skorupski (Bol)	7.1%	4.4%	4.5%	2.1%

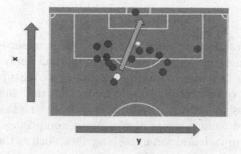

Fig. 2. Real case 1: goal from the distance

In the second real case (Fig. 3a), it has proposed a goal scored from a short distance in a very favourable situation (Atalanta vs Brescia, July 2020). Here, the alternative scenario considers the goalkeeper's position: whereas in the real case he is aligned at his own goal post, in the alternative scenario he is slightly out of the goal (Fig. 3b). Let's see in the real case 2 that the balanced frameworks increase the estimated goal-scoring probability (higher xG than the benchmark), with SMOTE and imbalance having a similar xG. It is interesting to note that moving the goalkeeper position outside the box (Fig. 3b) increases the xG of the shot.

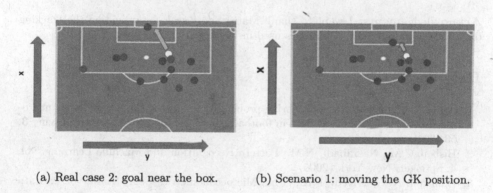

(a) Real case 2: goal near the box.   (b) Scenario 1: moving the GK position.

Fig. 3. The second real case and its alternative scenario on the pitch.

Table 5. The real case 2: expected goal for each framework and its alternative scenario.

Situation	Shooter	GK	xG^* ROSE	xG^* SMOTE	xG Imbl.	xG Understat
Real case 2	Pasalic (Ata)	Andrenacci (Bre)	14.6%	22.1%	21.7%	11.0%
Scenario 1	Pasalic (Ata)	Andrenacci (Bre)	30.0%	58.5%	52.2%	11.0%

5   Conclusion

This contribution proposes an improvement of the current expected goal (xG) model, one of the emerging tools in the field of football analytics. The main idea behind this model is to assign a quality metric (probability) for a goal for each shot. The main lack of the current xG frameworks is that they take into consideration only the classical event data: in order to overcome this weakness, the xG model has integrated some players' performance composite indicators obtained from a PLS-SEM approach and some tracking data, such as the goalkeeper's position and the number of opponents. As summary, the original approach presented in this work seems to suggest that some performance composite indicators and some tracking variables are helpful to detect the goals, refining the benchmark model (in the sense that the prediction in the extended model depends also on such additional features): by replacing a shooter with a better one (or reducing the abilities of the goalkeeper), one increases the estimated goal-scoring probability, which looks quite a reasonable outcome (which is not captured by the baseline model). As future works, it should be interesting to examine in-depth this topic by a larger sample size, and maybe comparing others classification models (for example, Gompit [3] or Classification Trees) performances. Further developments might also regard the generalization of the adopted methodology to other sports, for example in estimating the probability to make a shoot in basketball.

Acknowledgements. I want to thank Math&Sport s.r.l. for providing the tracking data for the Italian Serie A matches used in the statistical analysis.

References

1. Anzer, G., Bauer, P.: A goal scoring probability model for shots based on synchronized positional and event data in football (soccer). Front. Sports Active Living **3**, 53 (2021)
2. Bishop, C.M., Nasrabadi, N.M.: Pattern Recognition and Machine Learning, vol. 4. Springer, New York (2006)
3. Cameron, A.C., Trivedi, P.K., et al.: Microeconometrics Using Stata, vol. 2. Stata Press, College Station (2010)
4. Cefis, M.: Football analytics: a bibliometric study about the last decade contributions. Electron. J. Appl. Stat. Anal. **15**(1), 232–248 (2022)
5. Cefis, M., Brentari, E.: Formative vs reflective constructs: a CTA-PLS approach on a goalkeepers' performance model. Book of the Short Papers, 51st Scientific Meeting of the Italian Statistical Society, pp. 323–328 (2022)
6. Cefis, M., Carpita, M.: The higher-order PLS-SEM confirmatory approach for composite indicators of football performance quality. Comput. Stat. 1–24 (2022)
7. Chawla, N.V., Bowyer, K.W., Hall, L.O., Kegelmeyer, W.P.: SMOTE: synthetic minority over-sampling technique. J. Artif. Intell. Res. **16**, 321–357 (2002)
8. Dal Pozzolo, A., Caelen, O., Johnson, R.A., Bontempi, G.: Calibrating probability with undersampling for unbalanced classification. In: 2015 IEEE Symposium Series on Computational Intelligence, pp. 159–166. IEEE (2015)

9. Fairchild, A., Pelechrinis, K., Kokkodis, M.: Spatial analysis of shots in MLS: a model for expected goals and fractal dimensionality. J. Sports Anal. **4**(3), 165–174 (2018)
10. Hair Jr, J.F., Hult, G.T.M., Ringle, C.M., Sarstedt, M., Danks, N.P., Ray, S.: Partial least squares structural equation modeling (PLS-SEM) using R: a workbook (2021)
11. Hair Jr, J.F., Sarstedt, M., Ringle, C.M., Gudergan, S.P.: Advanced Issues in Partial Least Squares Structural Equation Modeling. Sage Publications, Thousand Oaks (2017)
12. Henseler, J., Ringle, C.M., Sarstedt, M.: Testing measurement invariance of composites using partial least squares. Int. Mark. Rev. **33**(3), 405–431 (2016)
13. Hossin, M., Sulaiman, M.N.: A review on evaluation metrics for data classification evaluations. Int. J. Data Mining Knowl. Manag. Process **5**(2), 1–12 (2015)
14. James, G., Witten, D., Hastie, T., Tibshirani, R.: An Introduction to Statistical Learning, vol. 112. Springer, New York (2013). https://doi.org/10.1007/978-1-4614-7138-7
15. Menardi, G., Torelli, N.: Training and assessing classification rules with imbalanced data. Data Min. Knowl. Disc. **28**(1), 92–122 (2014)
16. Rathke, A.: An examination of expected goals and shot efficiency in soccer. J. Hum. Sport Exerc. **12**(2), 514–529 (2017)
17. Robberechts, P., Davis, J.: How data availability affects the ability to learn good xG models. In: Brefeld, U., Davis, J., Van Haaren, J., Zimmermann, A. (eds.) MLSA 2020. CCIS, vol. 1324, pp. 17–27. Springer, Cham (2020). https://doi.org/10.1007/978-3-030-64912-8_2
18. Ruan, L., Ge, H., Shen, Y., Pu, Z., Zong, S., Cui, Y.: Quantifying the effectiveness of defensive playing styles in the Chinese football super league. Front. Psychol. 1–10 (2022)
19. Umami, I., Gautama, D.H., Hatta, H.R.: implementing the expected goal (xG) model to predict scores in soccer matches. Int. J. Inf. Inf. Syst. **4**(1), 38–54 (2021)

A Comparison of Hosting Techniques for Online Cybersecurity Competitions

Niccolò Maggioni[✉][iD] and Letterio Galletta[iD]

IMT School for Advanced Studies Lucca, Lucca, Italy
{niccolo.maggioni,letterio.galletta}@imtlucca.it

Abstract. Online cybersecurity competitions have gained significant traction in the community for educational and evaluative purposes because they offer dynamic environments for learning intricate technical concepts in an engaging, non-traditional, and interactive manner. While such competitions are increasingly popular and frequently held, organizing them is not straightforward. Developers must design challenges that are both innovative and balanced in difficulty, ensuring an enjoyable learning experience. Concurrently, effective hosting, configuring, and managing the online infrastructure that underpins these games are technical challenges demanding informed decisions. Unfortunately, no comprehensive resource exists to guide organizers in choosing suitable hosting architecture and tools based on their technical proficiency and event scale. This paper contributes to addressing this gap by examining prevalent architectures for hosting Capture The Flag (CTF) competitions and evaluating them using criteria encompassing several factors. These factors include environment setup, deployment, configuration, and updates of vulnerable services, system maintenance, and security mechanisms. Each criterion is qualitatively assessed with an associated numeric score. Finally, the paper puts forward recommendations on architecture and tools based on event size and organizer skills.

Keywords: Cybersecurity games · Capture the Flag · Jeopardy CTF competitions · Hosting architectures · Hosting recommendations

1 Introduction

Recently, cybersecurity games, especially Capture The Flag (CTF) competitions, have gained significant popularity within the computer security community for educational purposes and evaluation objectives. These competitions are widely considered excellent methods for learning deeply technical concepts in a fun, non-traditional, and interactive environment. They cater to a diverse range of skill levels, accommodating beginners, practitioners, and even experts. Participants are usually organized into teams that compete for a prize or recognition. In a typical competition, players face a series of hacking challenges presented as vulnerable remote services. To solve a challenge, players must find an attack to reveal a secret piece of information, which is then submitted to a scoring server.

© ICST Institute for Computer Sciences, Social Informatics and Telecommunications Engineering 2024
Published by Springer Nature Switzerland AG 2024. All Rights Reserved
M. Clayton et al. (Eds.): INTETAIN 2023, LNICST 560, pp. 136–163, 2024.
https://doi.org/10.1007/978-3-031-55722-4_11

These competitions are predominantly hosted online, last a limited period of time, and attract thousands of participants worldwide. The player community is remarkably active, with new competitions occurring on a weekly basis, as documented by the reference portal [6].

However, despite the weekly frequency of new competitions, organizing them is far from a straightforward task. On the one hand, organisers should prioritise participants' game experience: they should design challenges that are both innovative and enjoyable, striking a balance between difficulty and accessibility, and that facilitate players to learn new cybersecurity concepts or subjects. Achieving such an engaging game experience demands considerable dedication from challenge developers. On the other hand, organisers must meticulously handle the design and implementation of the online infrastructure that provides the game environment to participants. A minor mistake in its setup, configuration, or management can lead to malfunctions during the competition, detrimentally affecting players' enjoyment and overall perception of the event. While crafting engaging challenges remains an art honed by experienced developers, effectively hosting, configuring, and managing the game infrastructure is a technical matter that necessitates well-informed decisions during competition design. Although the common choice is to opt for a public cloud environment to host the CTF event, organisers often find themselves overwhelmed by the numerous architectures and tools available. Unfortunately, these options are frequently inadequately documented or are only available as informal articles scattered across the web [13, 14, 23, 44, 48]. To the best of our knowledge, a comprehensive literature that assists organizers in choosing the appropriate architecture and tools according to their technical expertise and the scale of the event is currently missing.

This paper contributes to tackling this issue by examining the prevalent architectures for hosting CTF competitions and conducting a qualitative assessment based on well-defined criteria. These criteria draw inspiration from those typically employed for assessing cloud platforms and encompass diverse facets, including environment setup, packaging, deployment, configuration, and update of vulnerable services, system maintenance, as well as security mechanisms for isolating processes and limiting their resource usage. We furnish a qualitative judgment that elucidates to which extent the architecture meets each criterion alongside a numeric score that synthesizes our evaluation. Additionally, we assign an aggregate score to each architecture, computed as the cumulative sum of criterion scores. The analysis of these scores shows that the architectures providing a certain level of automation in deploying and managing vulnerable services are the most suitable for adoption in a context where CTF organisers have no prior experience or infrastructural preferences. Subsequently, we offer a set of recommendations about the architecture based on the event size and organizers' technical skills. We believe that the outcomes of our analysis can assist CTF organizers in selecting the most appropriate architecture.

In summary, the main contributions of this paper are:

– We examine the prevalent architectures used to host vulnerable applications in the context of CTF competitions.

– We present an evaluation methodology and a set of criteria for assessing different architectures. These criteria encompass various factors, including environment setup, packaging, deployment, configuration, and updating of vulnerable services, system maintenance, as well as security considerations such as isolation capabilities and resource usage limitations.
– We assess each architecture according to the introduced methodology, providing a qualitative judgment alongside a numeric score for each criterion. Our analysis indicates that the architectures providing a certain level of automation in deploying and managing vulnerable services are the most suitable for adoption.
– We provide a list of recommendations to CTF organisers on the architectures to use based on the scale of the event and their technical skills.

The rest of the paper is organised as follows. Section 2 introduces the world of CTF competitions. We present the prevalent architectures to host such competitions in Sect. 3. Section 4 introduces our methodology and the criteria we adopt for the assessment, which is carried out in Sect. 5. We discuss the results of our assessment in Sect. 6, and we furnish recommendations to CTF organisers in Sect. 7. Section 8 compares our work with the relevant literature, while Sect. 9 draws some conclusion and discuss future work.

2   Background

This section introduces CTF competitions and presents the requirements organisers need to meet to host them.

2.1   What CTF Competitions are

CTF events are computer security competitions. Participants engage in a series of hacking challenges consisting of remote services that are designed to contain security flaws and vulnerabilities, e.g., buffer overflow, Cross-Site Scripting (XSS), with the goal of uncovering a concealed piece of information known as the "flag." Flags consist of a string of characters with a known syntax, serve as evidence of successful exploitation, and allow earning a certain amount of points. Typically, participants can either work alone or in teams, and the competition is won by those who accumulate the largest amount of points. At the start of the competition, each challenge is worth a predetermined amount of points by the event organizers. In most competitions, this value decreases exponentially as more and more participants solve the same challenge: this ensures that the most difficult challenges retain a high points value and thus enable stronger players to climb the leaderboards.

There are two types of widely known CTF events: *jeopardy* and *attack-defence*. The first format exposes a list of challenges to the players, who solve them at their own pace and usually without interacting with other players - at least not in a real-time manner. Some challenges may require to be solved in a specific order, but players are generally free to approach them in any order they prefer and to concentrate on those that they feel are the most interesting. Solving all the challenges is considered a noteworthy achievement but not a requirement. Concerning the kind of challenges, jeopardy CTFs follow a standard categorization where the prominent categories include: Binary Exploitation, Cryptography, Forensics, Reverse Engineering, and Web Security. However, the organizers of each event are free to tweak them to their needs and add new - or remove existing - ones if needed. For example, many events propose challenges concerning smart contract technology or hardware. Jeopardy CTFs typically run for two to three days, with some special events lasting up to a few weeks.

The attack-defence format is instead oriented on real-time interactions between teams of players across the network. In this type of competition, each team is either granted access to a remote machine or is assigned the task of hosting it on their premises. These hosts, referred to as "vulnboxes," are connected to the game infrastructure, and operate using pregenerated OS template images that the CTF organizers have equipped with vulnerable software. These applications are the same for all teams and typically range in number from three to six. The competition runs over a series of rounds called "ticks" that typically last from 60 to 180 s. At the start of each round, a central component of the game infrastructure managed by the organizers, the *game server*, interacts with each team's services and verifies that they are working as expected. If the check succeeds, the game server adds new flags to the service. In the meantime, players must exploit the opponent's services to extract the flags using a combination of manual proof-of-concept exploits and, subsequently, automated attacks. The network structure is designed to make it impossible for players to determine whether the network traffic is coming from the game server or another player, forcing them to accurately inspect each packet to identify, block, and eventually replicate malicious exploits.

This paper focuses on requirements for jeopardy CTFs since they are the most common type of event on the scene [6]. Organizers who host attack-defence competitions usually have extensive domain-specific knowledge and build their infrastructure according to their needs, technical preferences, and availability of computational resources.

2.2   Requirements for Jeopardy CTFs

A typical jeopardy CTF needs the following software components to be functional and properly organized:

- A public website that allows players or teams to register, access the various challenges when the competition is running, and see the scoreboard with the scores of the various teams. Currently, CTFd [5] is the most popular choice, followed by the relatively newer rCTF [43]; however, teams are free to adopt custom solutions.
- A real-time messaging platform to let the participants communicate with the organizers; currently, Discord is the most common solution, but other approaches that allow direct communication are fine.

- One or more remote hosts serving the competition website and the challenges. Hosting both on the same host is typically not recommended since possible problems with the challenges could damage the website availability or even the scoring data.
- A set of challenges organized into various categories: each challenge can be either static, such as a file to be downloaded or other static assets served through the Internet, or dynamic, such as an entire application responding to the users' inputs remotely.

There are also other factors to consider when organising a CTF, for example:

- Organisers should adequately balance the difficulty of the challenges. As a practical rule, every participant should solve at least one challenge, but only a small portion of teams should solve the most difficult ones.
- Challenge developers must have a clear and precise understanding of the flaws they introduce and the consequences of possible exploits; failing to do so could pave the way for malicious exploitation of the platform. Examples of issues may include unsafe Inter-Process Communication (IPC), the lack of isolation for expected Remote Command Execution (RCE) attacks, and the absence of Denial of Service (DoS) and scraping filters.
- The available budget for organising the event is usually limited: bigger events can obtain sponsorships from cloud providers or companies active in the cybersecurity field, but most of the time, the events are self-funded by the organizing team. The estimation of the necessary budget must take into account that the environment must be set up ahead of time to allow the participants to register on the website (one month is enough for most events), and that it is customary to leave the website with the scoreboard and challenges online for some time after the end of the competition (typically from one to three weeks) to allow participants to test and document their solutions and improve their skills properly.

3   Hosting Architectures for CTFs

Here, we briefly survey the most common approaches to hosting vulnerable applications in the context of a CTF. We list below the architectures ordered by their level of complexity and required administrative specialization. Their adoption is documented in the literature [22, 40] or in articles that CTF organizers have informally published throughout the years [3, 13, 14, 23, 44, 48].

Dedicated server (legacy deployments). We have a bare metal server or a virtual machine fully dedicated to hosting the CTF challenges. The server must be equipped with the required computational resources from the beginning and must be placed in a securely manageable environment. Services are deployed through a standard pipeline: they are developed on a different machine, and then their code (source or binary), together with the required dependencies, are manually copied into the server; setting the execution environment with all the required configuration parameters is performed manually, as well as restarting the necessary processes. Due to the nature of CTF competitions, the operating system running on this architecture is expected to be a Linux distribution.

Dedicated server (containerized deployments). This is the same physical architecture as above ("Dedicated server (legacy deployments)") but with the key difference that vulnerable services and their dependencies are deployed using application containers. These containers typically run on runtimes and toolchains supported by Docker [10], Podman [36], or equivalent software. A more detailed explanation of this approach has been described by Merkel [31]. Due to the nature of CTF competitions and container runtimes, the operating system running on this architecture is expected to be a Linux distribution.

Hyper-converged infrastructure. In this case, the infrastructure is made of a group of (physical or virtualized) servers that feature virtualization, storage, and advanced networking capabilities and is managed from a single interface. The concept of individual servers is abstracted as much as possible, giving operators the feeling of managing a single piece of hardware equipped with the union of the resources of the involved machines. Here, we consider Proxmox VE [38] as the reference implementation for this category: it is a browser-based environment that enables users to manage QEMU [39] virtual machines, LXC [27] containers, and various types of virtual networks. This solution is based on Debian GNU-Linux [7].

Simple orchestrator or task runner. This architecture consists of software or a combination of applications that assist users in managing the vulnerable services interactively and is characterized by static specifications that describe how to deploy and modify each service. Any changes to the deployment require changes in such specifications. Concretely, these specifications might be configuration files, deployment plans, or other assets similar to human-readable static text files. Here, we consider a combination of HashiCorp Nomad [20] and Consul [17] as a reference implementation for this category: their capabilities allow users to manage and monitor QEMU virtual machines, native Linux containers (LXC and others), application containers (Docker [10], Podman [36]), and standard processes. This architecture is a simple yet powerful starting ground for transitioning to more complex ones.

Complex orchestrator. This architecture typically consists of a tightly coupled suite of components that abstracts away the complexities of deploying, scaling, and managing containerized applications. This kind of orchestrator is usually meant to handle large-scale deployments, but its abstraction capabilities can also help in smaller deployments where it is desirable to define precisely the environment in which each vulnerable piece of software must run. In this paper, the reference implementation for this category is Kubernetes [45]. It can orchestrate different loads, but we focus only on application containers here. Moreover, since many features of this approach are only reliable when used in the Cloud, all the observations in the following sections assume that a public cloud deployment has been chosen and that the best practices recommended by the cloud provider have been followed. If a provide-managed offering is incompatible with the CTF organizers' requirements, it is assumed that they can operate the chosen complex system appropriately.

4   Assessment Methodology

We describe our methodology to assess the various architectures to host CTF competitions. In our evaluation, we neglect the hardware or platforms where the deployment is carried out - such as a public or private cloud provider, on-premises or co-located physical servers, or combinations of the two - since these options are numerous and constantly changing. Their management can be considered unavoidable overhead independently of the goal these resources are used for, and thus, it must not affect the analysis of their characteristics.

We extend the methodology by Maiya et al. [28] on classifying the manageability of cloud platforms. More precisely, we revise the proposed use cases and metrics to fit the organization of CTF competitions. Indeed, these events require managing insecure by-design software and executing exploits crafted by players, with relatively few limitations on what can be done once attackers have taken control of the target service or machine. Running vulnerable software inevitably leads to unexpected behavior of challenges during the competition or unplanned and hard-to-diagnose outages of the game platform. Thus, we introduce security-oriented criteria regarding the isolation of running processes and network activities, mechanisms for limiting computational resources, and tools to quickly servicing internal components when they break. Moreover, we simplify the scoring system where each characteristic receives an absolute rating on a scale from 1 to 3: 1 represents the worst value, while 3 is the best one. Thus, the architecture with the higher score will be considered the most convenient in a generic use case, namely when CTF organisers have no particular prior experience or infrastructural preferences. Later in the paper, we provide recommendations for specific use cases and environments that could slightly change these classifications.

Below, we report the criteria we use to score the various architectures:

Initial setup complexity. The complexity, in terms of required domain-specific knowledge and experience, of the initial bring-up of the whole architecture. A system with few components and self-explanatory configurations will be considered simpler than one with more components or harder-to-understand configurations.

Initial setup duration. An estimate of the time required for the initial bring-up of the whole architecture. Time duration is classified into three segments: *less than an hour*, *multiple hours*, and *multiple days*. A system with a quicker bring-up will be better than one requiring a longer process.

Services packaging. The complexity of packaging software for deployment or for making the code running on the developer's machines ready for deployment on the production infrastructure. A specific differentiation must be made between static assets being served directly, either through a persistent network connection or a single-time download, and dynamic services requiring interaction with players. A system with a streamlined, less error-prone packaging process will be considered better than one with more steps and a higher probability of errors.

Services deployment. The complexity of getting packaged software to run on the production infrastructure through specific protocols or definitions. A system with a streamlined, less error-prone deployment process and more readable deployment specifications will be considered better than one with a more involved, less risk-averse deployment process and less readable deployment specifications.

Services updating. The complexity of updating and applying patches to either the code of deployed vulnerable services or their configuration deployment. A system with a streamlined, less error-prone updating process will be better than one with more steps and a higher probability of errors.

Services configuration. An classification of the capabilities related to adding and editing external configuration parameters for specific services such as environment variables, secret tokens, API keys, passwords, and inter-service dependencies handled separately from the application code. A system that exposes such elements to deployed applications more easily, reliably, and securely will be considered better than one that does so in more complex, unreliable, and insecure ways.

Resources limitation. A classification of the capabilities related to placing, monitoring, and enforcing limits on shared hardware resources like CPU, RAM, disk space, and network bandwidth. A system that enables operators to specify more types of limits in more granular ways will be considered better than one that exposes fewer types of limits in coarser ways.

Isolation & security. A classification of the security capabilities of the platform and their relative complexity. We consider how the solution allows for the management of exposed interfaces and which mechanisms it provides for services isolation (from each other, from the operating system of the hosting machine, and the network), for network filtering and logging, for protection against scrapers and DoS (*Denial of Service*) attacks, and for rate limiting. A system offering more of these capabilities will be considered better than one offering less.

Changes of state. An estimate on the number of ways the solution handles misbehaving services: automatic restarts after crashes, detection and notifications of repeated failures, exponential back-off timers. A system that offers more ways of automatically solving unexpected state discrepancies and more means of notification will be considered better than one that offers less flexibility.

Scaling. A classification of the process of improving a service availability or performance through either vertical (adding more resources to a single instance of the service or its hosting node) or horizontal (adding more copies of the service or more hosting nodes) scaling. A more accessible, faster-to-edit, or more flexible and automated scaling system will be considered better than one with more complex, slower-to-edit, less flexible, and automatic scaling mechanisms.

Introspection and maintenance. A classification of the relative complexity of the system (often referred to as "amount of moving parts") and the required competencies for troubleshooting activities. A critical rating factor will be whether operators can use widely known diagnostic tools or more specialized, domain-specific solutions that need to be installed and configured beforehand. A system that allows easy use of commonly available utilities will be considered better than a more complex one that requires custom diagnostics solutions.

5   Evaluation of the Proposed Solutions

In this section, we provide a qualitative evaluation of the architectures of Sect. 3 according to the methodology of Sect. 4. We make a qualitative judgment for each criterion and assign it a numeric score.

5.1   Dedicated Server (Legacy Deployments)

Below, we report the scores together with a brief qualitative judgment. The scores are summarized in Table 1.

Initial setup complexity (Score: 3). Since the physical hardware or a virtual machine is already provisioned, operators need to set up a customized initialization procedure: they need to install an OS, configure the networking, and audit the overall security of the system, e.g., authentication and authorization parameters, remote access and basic firewall rules. While this process can be tedious to execute on multiple machines, it can be easily automated in a modular way through tools like Ansible [2]. This makes the chain of setup operations declarative, repeatable, and possibly idempotent.

Initial setup duration (Score: 2). Independently from the automation of the setup, the time needed to complete these preliminary operations is measurable in a matter of hours: performing the setup manually is time-consuming and error-prone, but writing a good automated solution takes a comparable amount of time.

Services packaging (Score: 1). While most operating systems use their packaging solutions, such as DEB or RPM archives, the time and effort needed to package software in such formats correctly make them unsuitable in a short-lived and highly dynamic environment required by CTF competitions. Thus, software must be distributed through simpler mechanisms, often using bare source code archives. This makes packaging artifacts difficult to version, organize and transfer reliably.

Services deployment (Score: 1). According to the considerations on services packaging above, the deployment process usually relies on a combination of custom scripts, code launchers, and custom decisions about the structure of the filesystem and the management of background processes. This makes deployments unstable, hardly repeatable, and in need of constant manual interventions.

Services updating (Score: 1). In the context of this architecture, updating services is similar to a new deployment. Thus, the considerations above apply.

Services configuration (Score: 1). Organizing a service's configuration files is a task largely left to its developers: as no standards exist in this context, in the best-case scenario, a group of system operators and service developers might agree on a common configuration format (YAML, TOML, INI, CSV, or other custom syntax) and the path in the file system where files are stored (relative to the application directory, or absolute). Moreover, run-time checks that enforce these informal, internal conventions are often missing.

Resources limitation (Score: 1). With no mechanism that supervises the execution of the services, limiting the resources they have access to can be rather difficult and may lead to hard to troubleshooting issues in seemingly unrelated operations inside the service's logic. Relative scheduling priority and coarse CPU usage percentage can be limited using standard Unix and Linux tools like *nice* and *cpulimit*, but limiting other resources such as RAM and network bandwidth cannot be done reliably without recurring to complex features of modern Linux kernels such as *control groups* [30]. Therefore, limiting the consumption of system resources is a complex task.

Isolation & security (Score: 1). Although organizers might choose to dedicate an entire machine or VM to a single service, this usually never happens due to the enormous amount of resources that would be required for running multiple copies of the same operating system and other low-level resources. Similar to what was said above for resource limitation, isolating processes running on the same host is not an easy task: legacy approaches for this task were based on *chroot* in Linux environments and *jails* in FreeBSD [37], but the modern standards rely on Linux cgroups. Note that these approaches have evolved in the containerization techniques and that applying them manually exposes operators to many nuisances and problems already solved in dedicated tooling.

Changes of state (Score: 2). The operating system processes responsible for starting and upkeeping the system itself (called *init systems* and including *sysvinit, OpenRC, upstart, systemd* as the most historically relevant implementations) can be tweaked and extended to take care of custom services as well. They can be configured to start services on boot, restart them in case of crashes, and redirect their logging to appropriate facilities such as system journals or dedicated log files. While these init systems can be extended to various degrees, they are still limited by their designs, and any additional capabilities such as interactive notifications to operators, checking if the service is replying properly to user requests, or handling misconfigurations must still be implemented manually by the service developers.

Scaling (Score: 2). The aforementioned init systems can be configured to run multiple instances of the same service. But this is an immediate solution only for *stateless* services that either do not hold a state in their memory or rely on

Table 1. Scores assigned to the "Dedicated server (legacy deployments)" architecture.

Criterion	Score
Initial setup complexity	3
Initial setup duration	2
Services packaging	1
Services deployment	1
Services updating	1
Services configuration	1
Resources limitation	1
Isolation & security	1
Changes of state	2
Scaling	2
Introspection and maintenance	3
Total score	18

an external source of data, e.g., a shared database, disk, or memory area, for all their features. *Stateful* services that need keep some context information in the memory, on the other hand, usually need more complex mechanisms to be run in parallel: for example, they might need external *load balancers* that multiplex network connections or other similar devices to operate correctly without providing users with incoherent data. In this kind of architecture, the implementation of such mechanisms is entirely up to the operators of the competition and to the developers of the challenges. This is a burden, however, custom implementations have the advantages that they can be fully inspected, controlled, and understood.

Introspection and maintenance (Score: 3). Although most of the afore-mentioned characteristics require system operators to intervene manually, and challenge developers to know the production system architecture, the barebones dedicated-machine architecture has a great advantage in mainte-nance: since the system is fully custom-built, whoever built it has complete knowledge of its inner workings. Such internal mechanisms can also only reach a certain upper limit of complexity, after which the operators would have already considered adopting other architectural solutions.

5.2 Dedicated Server (Containerized Deployments)

Below, we list the scores (summarized in Table 2) with a brief judgment.

Initial setup complexity (Score: 3). Setting up a container runtime is usually straightforward: installing a package through the system's package manager is typically enough. For the rest, the same observations of the "legacy" version also apply here.

Initial setup duration (Score: 2). Container runtimes do not usually need extensive configuration processes. For the rest, the same observations of the "legacy" version also apply here.

Services packaging (Score: 3). Each container runtime has its own packaging mechanism, but the most common one is using *Dockerfile* [9]. This declarative format originates from Docker but is supported by Podman as well. Independently of the used runtime, the container image built from *Dockerfile* is a portable archive that can be easily versioned, transferred, and archived. Depending on the underlying runtime, each newly built image may reuse cached parts of the previous builds and images so as to reduce disk usage.

Services deployment (Score: 3). Deploying a container image is rarely more complex than transferring the image archive to the target machine - usually either manually or through services called *registries* - and issuing the appropriate shell command to run the image with the needed options (environment variables, network port bindings, storage volumes). These options can be tuned during the first deployment and saved for future reference. If the deployment involves multiple services that interact with each other, tools like Docker Compose [11] can help the operators coordinate multiple containers.

Services updating (Score: 2). Updating an existing containerized deployment consists of transferring the new image, stopping the old container, and starting a new one with the same options. This can lead to short periods of time where services are not reachable or are restarting, but they can usually be timed accurately to minimize the impact on users. However, short and infrequent unavailability bursts are usually not a major concern in CTF competitions. The downside of this approach is that if the new deployment silently fails, e.g., the application runs but cannot interact with users, there are no automated systems to revert the changes, potentially leaving the service in a broken state until the operator realizes the problem.

Services configuration (Score: 2). In this architecture, the configuration files for each service must be either embedded into their respective container images or copied to the host file system and made available inside the containers through the facilities offered by the underlying runtime, such as mount points defined at runtime. Comparing this architecture to the aforementioned legacy one, the usage of containers brings forward a common standard regarding the organization of the configuration files: such files can still end up scattered through the filesystem, but it is always possible to infer their location from the mounts and the other options for running a container. However, this convention is not enforceable, and there could be cases where application configuration files are split into two groups: embedded inside the container and mounted from the outside. This approach improves the coherence, but the problem is not solved.

Resources limitation (Score: 2). Typically, container runtimes allow operators to set specific resource usage limits for core resources: CPU, RAM, and sometimes GPU. These options are exposed to operators as simpler abstractions over the mechanisms provided by the Linux kernel - mainly *cgroups* - and, hence, they inherit the same limitations and complexities. A container runtime is not guaranteed to provide all the options (and their combinations) supported by the kernel, but the main use cases are typically always covered.

Isolation & security (Score: 3). Containerized services run as isolated processes by default: they cannot connect to each other, and their memory and disk spaces are kept separate. Each container can be tied to a specific network interface or virtual bridge if needed, reducing its access to local or remote resources. If a participant of the CTF manages to exploit a containerized service causing an RCE (Remote Command Execution), the scope of that exploit can be limited to the single service's environment. If the targeted service was properly packaged and deployed, the security breach would not easily spread to other components of the competition's architecture.

Changes of state (Score: 1). Container runtimes by themselves have limited capabilities when it comes to detecting faults, restarting crashed applications, and keeping track of these events in general. A typical pitfall of these systems is the handling of fast-failing containers: if a container crashes or stops, the runtime will immediately purge it and start a new one; if this happens immediately after it first gets started, a vicious cycle may start in which the operator does not have enough time to troubleshoot the failing image properly. The operator has then to resort to patching the source code or editing the container's options to override the startup command, usually replacing it with an infinite delay or some sort of *no-op* operation to gain enough time to manually start the service inside the container and investigate the causes of the crash. Some additional tools like Docker Compose introduce health checks, but these mechanisms are often rather limited in their modularity and have their own drawbacks when handling crashes and restarts.

Scaling (Score: 2). Containerizing services make running multiple instances straightforward, but additional tooling is needed to take advantage of the improved load capacity correctly since it still does not follow a standard structure. For the rest, the same observations of the "legacy" version above still apply.

Introspection and maintenance (Score: 2). The complexity of managing a container runtime is usually very low, and standard tools can be installed inside application containers to support troubleshooting. Some peculiarities of the chosen runtime could make troubleshooting certain issues more difficult, typically those related to network and storage resources. For the rest, the same observations of the "legacy" version above still apply.

5.3   Hyper-Converged Infrastructure

Below, we report the scores with a brief qualitative judgment. Our discussion considers Proxmox as the reference implementation of this architecture. The scores are summarized in Table 3.

Initial setup complexity (Score: 3). The setup of a hyper-converged software solution is typically straightforward and not particularly different from a bare

Table 2. Scores assigned to the "Dedicated server (containerized deployments)" architecture.

Criterion	Score
Initial setup complexity	3
Initial setup duration	2
Services packaging	3
Services deployment	3
Services updating	2
Services configuration	2
Resources limitation	2
Isolation & security	3
Changes of state	1
Scaling	2
Introspection and maintenance	2
Total score	**25**

operating system installation. The installation process of Proxmox is simpler than a bare Debian Linux distribution, thanks to its graphical installer, the optimized default configurations, and the selection of preinstalled software packages. In most cases, the system is fully operational and ready to support deployments as soon as the installation process is complete.

Initial setup duration (Score: 3). The time required by the initial setup is comparable to the architectures listed in Sect. 5.1 and Sect. 5.2. The setup can require less than an hour if the CTF organizers have no special requirements regarding network topology, storage technologies, or high-availability capabilities.

Services packaging (Score: 1). Proxmox supports LXC containers and QEMU virtual machines, both of which do not support advanced packaging techniques. Operators can create LXC container templates similar to Docker images: they can start from a blank environment and install all the necessary low-level components of the chosen Linux distribution rather than specify individual libraries and binaries as dependencies required for the services being developed. The same considerations are valid for QEMU virtual machines. These build processes can be automated but are similar to what was reported in Sect. 5.1, thus, the score assigned to this metric.

Services deployment (Score: 1). As explained for the previous criterion, the environment the services will be deployed into is equivalent to the one described in Sect. 5.1. Therefore, the score assigned is the same.

Services updating (Score: 1). In the context of this architecture, updating services can be seen as a new deployment. Thus, the discussion of Sect. 5.1 still applies.

Services configuration (Score: 2). The considerations for this metric presented in Sect. 5.1 apply here because of the nature of LXC containers to behave like "lightweight virtual machines" and QEMU running actual virtual machines. As mentioned in Sect. 5.2, the modularity offered by an arbitrary external filesystem mounted in a LXC container can be seen as a way to keep configuration files close together on the main host's filesystem.

Resources limitation (Score: 3). LXC containers and QEMU virtual machines allow operators to easily limit CPU (sockets, cores, units, and priority), RAM (exclusively pre-allocated, reserved, and maximum amounts), and network (bandwidth and priority) resources available to a given entity. In the case of Proxmox, these limits can be quickly specified through its web interface, and advanced scheduling or limiting algorithms can be chosen. For example, RAM memory can be allocated to virtual machines through *ballooning devices*: these virtual memory spaces can expand and contract at runtime, recovering unused memory from idle VMs and allocating the new ones to those VMs needing resources. Storage limits are set during the creation of the environment and can be extended at will as long as the main host is left with enough storage capacity.

Isolation & security (Score: 3). Since each service runs in its dedicated environment and the resources of the main host are paravirtualized, isolation is guaranteed on every level. Performance is on par with typical virtual machine hypervisors. As reported in Sect. 5.2, malicious exploits can compromise, at most, the environment of a single service. Lateral movement into other environments and services is typically caused by misconfigurations of the main host or failures to keep proper logical bounds between different services.

Changes of state (Score: 1). This architecture typically does not include reactive monitoring solutions: once LXC containers and virtual machines are started, they can only crash due to serious kernel malfunctions - just like a physical machine would. Under very specific circumstances kernel panics or other irrecoverable errors may be triggered and lock up an individual environment instead of crashing it, but nevertheless no native insights are available on the state of the applications running inside those environments. Moreover, in the case of LXC containers, the kernel is shared with the host operating system, and a fault at that level would probably hang or reboot the whole physical machine.

Scaling (Score: 2). Scaling on hyper-converged architectures like Proxmox can be seen as a combination of the observations reported in Sect. 5.1 and Sect. 5.2: running multiple copies of a given service is a simple task, but coordinating them to effectively act as a single unit and share the computational load is a complex effort. The considerations mentioned in the paragraphs referenced above are also valid for this architecture.

Introspection and maintenance (Score: 2). Maintenance of hyper-converged architectures can be quite low, especially given the short period of time that CTF competitions run for. Once the system is set up with the preferred kernel version and system tools, there are few reasons to update or reboot the system if its expected lifetime is less than a month. Introspection, on the other hand, suffers from the multiple layers of abstraction that a single service may be hidden behind: to troubleshoot a problem within an application, an operator might have to delve through all abstraction layers in reverse, starting from the service's shared libraries and ending up tracing the host's kernel behavior.

Table 3. Scores assigned to the "Hyper-converged infrastructure" architecture.

Criterion	Score
Initial setup complexity	3
Initial setup duration	3
Services packaging	1
Services deployment	1
Services updating	1
Services configuration	2
Resources limitation	3
Isolation & security	3
Changes of state	1
Scaling	2
Introspection and maintenance	2
Total score	22

5.4   Simple Orchestrator or Task Runner

Below, we report the scores with a brief qualitative judgment. In our discussion, we consider Nomad and Consul as the reference implementations of this architecture. The scores are summarized in Table 4.

Initial setup complexity (Score: 2). At the time of writing, both Nomad and Consul are distributed as self-contained binaries that run on top of a preinstalled operating system. For this reason, all the assumptions regarding the initial setup reported in Sect. 5.1 are still valid. The setup process of a single-node Nomad cluster is fairly simple and well-documented in the official developer resources. If additional features, e.g., advanced service discovery and health checks, are required, Nomad can be complemented with a basic single-node Consul deployment on the same host. Again, this procedure is fairly well documented and with some experience, it can be deployed inside Nomad itself instead as a separate service for increased coherence and modularity.

Initial setup duration (Score: 2). Due to their binary distributions, both Nomad and Consul are considerably quick to deploy on top of an existing operating system. The initial setup can be completed and tested in a matter of hours, even by those operators who never worked with them. This is because complex features are often optional and can be enabled incrementally when needed.

Services packaging (Score: 3). Typically, in a CTF competition, developers will probably use a container-based packaging system. What was reported about packaging in Sect. 5.2 therefore also applies to this architecture. However, the execution of packaging software in Nomad can also be done in other ways: the platform officially supports *task drivers* for single binaries, Docker and Podman containers, Java JAR files, QEMU VMs, and optionally LXC containers and *systemd-nspawn* namespaces. These last two options are currently maintained by the community but endorsed by HashiCorp. All in all, the reference implementations support enough packaging styles to accommodate the needs of most developers.

Services deployment (Score: 3). Similarly to what is described in Sect. 5.2 about Dockerfiles, Nomad has its own format for a deployment. This file is called *Job Specification* [19] and is written in *HashiCorp configuration language* [18], or HCL for short, which is a purpose-specific JSON [12] notation. Deploying a *Job* is done through the *application* of this file: the main Nomad server parses its contents and proactively creates the environment needed to run the given software package with the specified requirements and limitations. In the case of containers, this specification includes all the options, storage mounts, and other flags that would have been specified manually through the Docker command line interface. The Job Specification format must cover a wide variety of use cases and is thus intrinsically complex, but in the context of CTFs it can have a quite readable and maintainable text structure due to the low amount of functionalities usually needed: once a container has been defined by its basic characteristics, resource limits have been put in place, healthchecks and other minor management policies have been set, it is rare to see other substantial additions to the specification.

Services updating (Score: 3). Updating a deployment can be done by editing its Job Specification and re-applying it. To assist operators in avoiding critical mistakes, the Nomad command line interface supports a special "plan" mode, which does not directly apply the requested changes, but shows a graphical difference between the current and the new specification, highlighting the sections that would change. The plan is assigned a progressive id, which operators can use during re-deployment to ensure that only the previewed changes will be applied. If the context on the server has changed - for example another operator has modified the Job or the server was forced to reschedule it in favor of higher priority tasks - the new deployment will not be accepted, and the operator will be warned of the discrepancies.

Services configuration (Score: 3). As already mentioned in Sect. 5.2 and Sect. 5.3, configuration files for a service can always be mounted from external storage into the target container. The Job Specification format introduces another way of further improving the placement of such files: embedding them directly into the deployment specifications. With some experience, operators can statically define the contents of configuration files and other secret values along the main deployment's options. This enables developers and operators to better use versioning tools without manually cross-referencing different software states with their respective settings.

Resources limitation (Score: 2). While the Nomad orchestrator can technically limit the resources available to a given deployment, it cannot do so through its own mechanisms. It depends on the packaging format used by the developer of a service. The Job Specification file gives operators an abstract way of specifying such limits, which then get re-implemented by the internal driver of each packaging format. For example, raw processes will be directly encapsulated in Linux control groups, containers will have the relevant options passed through to their runtime, and so on. It is not guaranteed that all the task drivers will be able to enforce all the available resource limits.

Isolation & security (Score: 3). Since the underlying technologies typically used in a CTF competition (containers and VMs) are the same as the ones analyzed in Sect. 5.2 and Sect. 5.3, the comments made in those sections are valid for this architecture as well.

Changes of state (Score: 2). Simple orchestrators like Nomad often lack advanced state management capabilities. While they usually implement simple techniques for handling application crashes, such as delayed retries and exponential back-offs, they do not guarantee to react to the changes of the application state themselves. For example, Nomad must be complemented with another HashiCorp product, Consul, to provide proper health checking and interactive service discovery mechanisms. This can greatly enhance the state management capabilities of this orchestrator at the expense of additional architectural complexities and increased maintenance costs (both in terms of time and resources).

Scaling (Score: 2). The number of instances of a single service can be easily adjusted by changing the *count* field of its Job Specification, but no additional networking structures are automatically put in place to distribute the users' requests. The effort required to put these extra components in place is comparable to what was described in Sect. 5.3. A substantial feature of Nomad over other solutions is the embedded Autoscaler [16] that can handle the automated scaling of deployments based on resource usage.

Introspection and maintenance (Score: 2). The level of introspectability of this architecture is comparable to what was analyzed in Sect. 5.3 and is subject to the same observations. However, an aspect favoring this solution is the centralized logging of the most relevant low-level events generated by Nomad. Maintainability can be considered straightforward: Nomad and Consul versions can be easily upgraded and rolled back by replacing their main binary and restarting the corresponding process manually or through the operating system's init facilities.

5.5   Complex Orchestrator

Below, we report the scores with a brief qualitative judgment. In our discussion, we consider Kubernetes as the reference implementation of this architecture. The scores are summarized in Table 5.

Initial setup complexity (Score: 2). Kubernetes heavily relies on cloud-only technology to operate at maximum efficiency. However, two fundamental functionalities, *Load Balancers*, and dynamic *Persistent Volumes*, that can be replicated on on-premises, self-managed hardware with considerable effort and prior knowledge of the inner workings of this solution include. For completeness, we mention two projects that can be used in self-managed environments to regain some of such functionalities: MetalLB [32] and Rancher Longhorn [42]. Deploying Kubernetes on cloud platforms can be done manually, but in the context of CTF competitions, it is more convenient and

Table 4. Scores assigned to the "Simple orchestrator or task runner" architecture.

Criterion	Score
Initial setup complexity	2
Initial setup duration	2
Services packaging	3
Services deployment	3
Services updating	3
Services configuration	3
Resources limitation	2
Isolation & security	3
Changes of state	2
Scaling	2
Introspection and maintenance	2
Total score	27

less expensive to use a minimal provider-managed cluster. Most medium to large-scale providers offer support for Kubernetes clusters at the moment of writing [1,8,15,33,35], and some of them are available to sponsor CTF events. The initial setup complexity of this architecture is very low, although it does require a considerable amount of preparation and documentation by the operators.

Initial setup duration (Score: 3). The initial setup of a provider-managed Kubernetes cluster can be done in a few minutes. Given that a valid account is already registered with the chosen cloud provider, in some cases, it is even possible to complete the setup process through a web browser.

Services packaging (Score: 3). Kubernetes is an orchestrator explicitly designed to manage application containers, hence, the considerations on packaging done in Sect. 5.2 still apply. This orchestrator supports different container runtimes [24] - newer versions comply with the *Container Runtime Interface* (CRI) standard - and consequently, it does not enforce a specific packaging process: as long as the final result adheres to the Docker image specifications, the processes or tools employed by developers are immaterial.

Services deployment (Score: 3). In addition to what was reported in Sect. 5.2 and Sect. 5.4, Kubernetes relies on a custom set of YAML [47] documents, called *manifests*, to define and organize its resources. Writing and understanding manifests can be quite complex: their syntax is not always obvious, many nested fields have repeated or similar names, and the resources' specifications are subject to frequent changes. However, the advantage of using these documents is that all the specifications for the software components required by a particular service can be contained in a single text file. This satisfies the requirement of keeping logically separate services in different images, files, or assets found in all the previously analyzed architectures.

Services updating (Score: 2). Updating a service managed by Kubernetes works similarly as described in Sect. 5.4, except for the absence of the "plan" mode: when a manifest file is modified, the new state is applied with no checks. This approach has the disadvantage of not automatically deleting old resources: if a specific resource is removed from the manifest and the new version is applied, it is up to the operator to manually delete the unreferenced elements from the cluster.

Services configuration (Score: 3). Manifests support the definition of textual key-value pairs to be used as environment variables or mounted as raw files inside the application containers via through the usage of entities called *ConfigMaps* and *Secrets*. This feature allows keeping all the resources to run a service close to its source code and packaging assets. Developers do not need to worry about where to store configuration files; operators are only concerned with properly applying a single specification.

Resources limitation (Score: 3). The approach that Kubernetes takes to resource limitation is similar to the one that was described in Sect. 5.4: CPU, RAM, and storage space limits are defined in the manifest, and the underlying container runtime is in charge of applying the proper *cgroups* configurations to enforce them. Special types of limitations, such as the ones on network bandwidth, can be enforced through purpose-specific overlays and external plugins.

Isolation & security (Score: 2). The perceived security of a container orchestrator is often inversely related to its complexity: due to the large number of separate components and specifications that make up Kubernetes, operators need to pay special attention to each of them to ensure that no misconfigurations occur in the services publicly exposed and their environments. Experienced operators can reach a satisfying level of isolation between services and overall security - both from the outside world and from the inside of the cluster - in a matter of hours, but for CTF events a more thorough, multi-day analysis is suggested. Specialized literature [21,29,34] provides many insights into the key points to be covered during analyses of this kind.

Changes of state (Score: 3). Complex orchestrators, and Kubernetes in particular, handle state changes very well: thanks to their modular nature, it is usually possible to develop custom plugins to react to deployments' state changes in arbitrary ways. Kubernetes itself handles restarts and exponential back-offs natively, as well as proper *healthchecks* for containerized applications: it can interact with them in various ways to determine their status, preventing subtle issues and application lock-ups that simpler orchestrators usually cannot detect. This feature is the cornerstone of the scaling and introspection features analyzed in the following paragraphs.

Scaling (Score: 3). The complexity of scaling workloads is comparable to what was described in Sect. 5.4, with the addition of more advanced techniques revolving around the management of stateful and stateless applications. Once the state issue is solved, most applications can be scaled automatically through Kubernetes' facilities (*load balancers*, *ingresses*, etc.). These components provide a set of strategies for distributing network traffic to

Table 5. Summary of the scores assigned to the "Complex orchestrator" architecture.

Criterion	Score
Initial setup complexity	2
Initial setup duration	3
Services packaging	3
Services deployment	3
Services updating	2
Services configuration	3
Resources limitation	3
Isolation & security	2
Changes of state	3
Scaling	3
Introspection and maintenance	1
Total score	28

the various instances of an application container, relieving operators from the burden of manually setting up such mechanisms and reconfiguring them every time the scaling needs to be adjusted.

Introspection and maintenance (Score: 1). The complexity of these kinds of orchestrators is both their strength and their weakness: since they consist of many components, operators need a great deal of experience to recognize problematic situations and to determine where to intervene, and which tools fit the situation at hand. For the same reason, it is common for an initially simple problem to spread across multiple subsystems and become more complex, creating deadlock situations in which an operator must identify the first component to troubleshoot and follow the chain of events.

6   Discussion of the Results

Figure 1 shows the cumulative scores of the considered architectures in a generic use case when CTF organisers have no particular prior experience or infrastructural preferences. By the discussion of Sect. 5 and the chart in the figure, we conclude that the architectures providing a certain level of automation in deploying and managing services obtain higher scores. Moreover, we can observe that the complexity of the chosen architecture plays a limited role. This is clear when we compare "Dedicated server (legacy deployments)" and "Dedicated server (containerized deployments)" with "Complex orchestrator". In the first case, there is a 10-point difference between the architectures, which highlights a large margin of operational improvement at the cost of the greater complexity of the chosen solution. In the second case, there is only a 3-point difference between the two architectures, which remarks a less relevant difference between environments

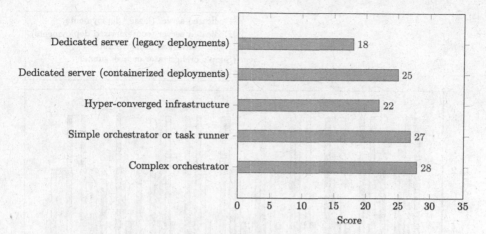

Fig. 1. The cumulative scores of each analyzed architecture.

based on application containers. Similarly, the single-point difference between "Simple orchestrator or task runner" and "Complex orchestrator" shows that once a certain level of abstraction over the physical hardware and automation is reached, the exact technology used has a minor impact in organizing CTF events.

The above observations are strengthened by Fig. 2 showing the scores of the various criteria of Sect. 4 grouped by architectural solution. The chart supports the hypothesis that the most complex solutions have similar characteristics because their scores differ little. For example, the score difference between the criteria of the "Simple orchestrator or task runner" and the "Complex orchestrator" architectures is never greater than 1. This difference grows to 2 when considering the "Dedicated server (containerized deployments)" architecture. Again, this small difference can be explained by the fact that it is sufficient to reach a certain level of abstraction and to ensure a certain amount of fundamental functionalities to reduce the operational burden of the platform.

Finally, it is interesting to consider the case of the "Hyper-converged infrastructure". This solution comes out as a mid-range choice that would present no real advantages over the alternatives, encouraging organizers to either lower their operational complexity and go for one of the simpler solutions or raise it by choosing a more complex but more performant architecture.

7 Recommendations for Specific Use Cases

The previous sections analyzed the various architectures in a generic context where CTF organisers have no prior experience or infrastructural preferences. However, these elements are key factors when the organizers are already experienced with automated, large-scale cloud deployments or have essential technical competencies to carry out such tasks. Below, we provide some recommendations

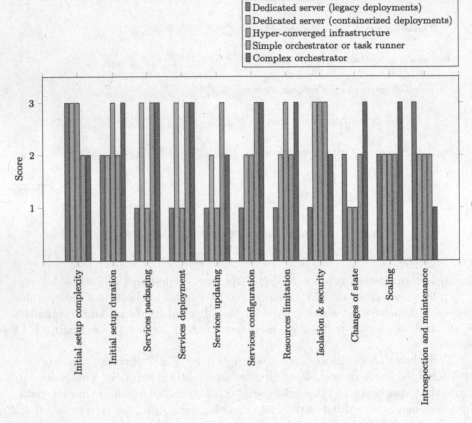

Fig. 2. The cumulative scores of the analyzed architectures, grouped by criterion.

on the architectures to use based on the scale of the event and the technical skills of the organisers.

Small scale. If an event is restricted to a small (<100), selected group of participants and is intended to run for a very limited time (<24 h), it may not be worth it to deploy complex technologies if the organizers have no prior experience with them. Such an event would probably run with acceptable results even with the "Dedicated server (legacy deployments)" architecture because the manual burden of setting up and managing the event is tolerable. However, application containers are strongly suggested to ensure a certain isolation level among the challenges and limit the scope of eventual dangerous operations initiated by participants.

Mid-size CTFs. When the number of participants (>100, <2000) grows, organizers may face challenges related to, e.g., heavier concurrency and resource allocation. Complex architectures may be justified if the organizers have at least some prior experience with such technologies. Still, the downside of this choice is the organizational burden of correctly setting up a complex environment and the number of people who can work on such a process. Application containers are usually a hard requirement at this size since the number of developers involved in the event organization needs a robust development and deployment pipeline with as many automated steps and validations as possible. A simple orchestrator or task runner could be useful in managing the deployment process, but it is still possible for competent operators to carefully manage services manually if desired.

Mid-to-Large size CTFs. An event with >2000 registered participants is usually well-known in the field and probably not run for the first time. At this size, organizers are expected to be already competent with the process of managing and, more importantly, troubleshooting CTF events: it can be supposed that their past experiences have given them enough confidence in their architectural choice that only minimal improvements would need each time a new event is hosted. When it is not ensured that the team who manages the event is the same each time, a leaner, simpler, well-documented approach could be preferred over a more optimized, complex, and less documented one. Operators should prioritize stability and developer experience when choosing an architectural solution, possibly avoiding approaches that rely on a single team member being able to complete certain tasks at any given time.

Large-size CTFs or teams with multiple experienced operators. Advising on how to run large-scale CTFs is beyond the scope of this paper since the organizers of such events already possess enough domain-specific knowledge and have gained enough experience with the past editions of their events to have a clear picture of how the whole infrastructure should look and work. This is especially true for teams that include multiple operators skilled in the same technologies, as this enables them to split their work and avoid cognitive stress in the most intense phases of the event. Such teams would probably favor the progressive introduction of new and potentially unstable technologies not yet widely used in the CTF field to foster innovation and push the limits of the typical challenges offered in smaller competitions.

Finally, note that unforeseen complications are common during CTF events: participants forge more powerful exploits than expected, there is too much computational load - or even not enough, misuse of internal APIs, intentional Denial of Service attacks, etc. Due to this fact, the most important recommendation to CTF organizers can be summarized as *"use a technology that you are familiar with."* Time is essential when players flood services with requests and tentative exploits. When something goes wrong, the time it takes to fix the problem and get the experience back to normal is directly proportional to the participants' opinion of the event.

8 Related Work

Most of the literature focuses on using CTF competitions for educational purposes, and only a limited number of papers delve into their organizational aspects and offer guidance for potential organizers. Herein, we survey select papers regarding these two investigation lines.

As regards the organizational aspects, Kucek et al. [25] compare several game portals, such as CTFd, following a methodology similar to ours. Their criteria comprehend several factors that must be considered when organizing a competition regarding customization, installation, setup, and reliability, and assess open-source solutions available at the time of writing according to them. In contrast, our work does not consider game portals but focuses on the hosting architectures that can be used in CTFs. Karagiannis et al. [22] compare the usage of virtual machines and container technologies (both Linux and application types) in the context of CTF competitions. Differently, our work does not only analyse how virtual machines and containers can be used to run vulnerable services in the context of CTFs, but also considers further aspects such as service configuration, deployment, and update. Following a similar line of investigation, Raj at al. [40] explored the usage of application containers for attack-defence CTFs. Although they consider a different kind of competition, some of the hosting techniques we considered could also be used for hosting attack-defence CTFs. Raman at al. [41] proposed a framework to assess the quality of CTF competitions through subjective and objective metrics. Although the world of these competitions has changed since the publication of their work, their framework could prove useful for organisers in evaluating their course of action.

The effectiveness of CTF competitions as introductions to cybersecurity and ethical hacking for high school and university students has been studied in several papers in the literature. Lagorio et al. [26] outlines the advantages and disadvantages of integrating CTFs into higher education courses and the impact on students' performances before and after participating in such events. They point out that this integration requires careful planning for combining theory and practice. Similarly, Cole [4] studied the impact of this kind of competition on students' motivation and exam scores, specifically what happens when classical exam questions are reformulated into more practical and goal-oriented exercises akin to the challenges found in CTFs. The author verified the positive impact of the new learning method on students without prior or advanced technical skills. Vykopal et al. [46] further corroborated these findings of introducing CTF completion inside standard lectures but outlined potential pitfalls that could negatively impact students' learning and evaluation processes.

9   Conclusions and Future Work

This paper has surveyed the prominent architectures used to host CTF competitions and provided a qualitative assessment according to a set of criteria ranging from the complexity of setting up the infrastructures to the security mechanisms for isolating vulnerable services. Our analysis reveals that the architectures providing a certain level of automation in deploying and managing services are the most suitable to be adopted in a generic context where CTF organisers have no prior experience or infrastructural preferences. Finally, we have provided some recommendations for adopting architectures based on the event's size and the organizers' prior experience. In any case, the organizers' judgment of their skills and desire to experiment with new architectures always win on the proposed recommendations, even if these must always be evaluated in the ever-changing and surprising context of CTF competitions.

In future work, we plan to implement an automated tool to calculate the best fit between various architectures, depending on the requirements, the size of an event, and the competencies of the organizing team. The tool will supply a questionnaire asking the key requirements and will provide a generic recommendation as output. The questionnaire could also involve other aspects, such as the size of the organizing team, whether or not the event is new or has had past editions, the historical or expected number of participants, the number of operators with respect to challenge developers, the categories of challenges to be offered, and the technologies most of the team is already acquainted with. Moreover, this approach could be further extended to combine the questionnaire results with a static analysis of the challenges' source code to automatically determine the packaging format used for developing and testing the challenges and to guess the standard category they belong to. Combining these two factors could pre-determine some of the questionnaire's answers and guide the users toward solutions that support the detected technologies with as little manual intervention as possible.

References

1. Amazon Web Services: Managed Kubernetes Service — Amazon EKS — Amazon Web Services — aws.amazon.com. https://aws.amazon.com/eks/. Accessed 20 Aug 2023
2. Ansible, R.H.: Ansible is Simple IT Automation — ansible.com.https://www.ansible.com/. Accessed 15 Aug 2023
3. born2scan Team: born2scan – How we hosted DanteCTF 2021: A brief tour of the infrastructure that supported the first edition of DanteCTF — born2scan.run.https://born2scan.run/articles/2021/06/29/How-we-hosted-Dante-CTF-2021.html. Accessed 12 Aug 2023
4. Cole, S.V.: Impact of capture the flag (CTF)-style vs. traditional exercises in an introductory computer security class. In: Proceedings of the 27th ACM Conference on Innovation and Technology in Computer Science Education, vol. 1. p. 470–476. Association for Computing Machinery (2022). https://doi.org/10.1145/3502718.3524806
5. CTFd LLC: CTFd: The Easiest Capture The Flag Framework — ctfd.io. https://ctfd.io. Accessed 08 Aug 2023
6. CTFtime team: CTFtime.org/All about CTF (Capture The Flag) — ctftime.org. https://ctftime.org/event/list/past. Accessed 08 Aug 2023
7. Debian: Debian – The Universal Operating System — debian.org. https://www.debian.org/. Accessed 15 Aug 2023
8. Digitalocean: DigitalOcean Managed Kubernetes — digitalocean.com. https://www.digitalocean.com/products/kubernetes. Accessed 20 Aug 2023
9. Docker Inc.: Dockerfile reference — docs.docker.com. https://docs.docker.com/engine/reference/builder/. Accessed 16 Aug 2023

10. Docker Inc.: Home — docker.com. https://www.docker.com/. Accessed 10 Aug 2023
11. Docker Inc.: Overview of Docker Compose — docs.docker.com. https://docs.docker.com/compose/. Accessed 16 Aug 2023
12. ECMA: ECMA-404: The JSON data interchange syntax, 2nd edition. ECMA (European Association for Standardizing Information and Communication Systems), Geneva, Switzerland (2017). https://doi.org/10.13140/RG.2.2.28181.14560
13. Extra Good Labs, Inc: How to Run a CTF — jumpwire.io. https://jumpwire.io/blog/how-to-run-a-ctf. Accessed 12 Aug 2023
14. Goedegebure, C.: Hosting a CTF made easy using Docker and DigitalOcean — coengoedegebure.com. https://www.coengoedegebure.com/hosting-a-ctf-made-easy/. Accessed 12 Aug 2023
15. Google: Google Kubernetes Engine (GKE) — Google Cloud — cloud.google.com. https://cloud.google.com/kubernetes-engine. Accessed 20 Aug 2023
16. HashiCorp: Autoscaling — Nomad — HashiCorp Developer — developer.hashicorp.com. https://developer.hashicorp.com/nomad/tools/autoscaling. Accessed 18 Aug 2023
17. HashiCorp: Consul by HashiCorp — consul.io. https://www.consul.io/. Accessed 10 Aug 2023
18. HashiCorp: GitHub - hashicorp/hcl: HCL is the HashiCorp configuration language. — github.com. https://github.com/hashicorp/hcl. Accessed 18 Aug 2023
19. HashiCorp: Job Specification — Nomad — HashiCorp Developer — developer.hashicorp.com. https://developer.hashicorp.com/nomad/docs/job-specification. Accessed 18 Aug 2023
20. HashiCorp: Nomad by HashiCorp — nomadproject.io.https://www.nomad-project.io/. Accessed 10 Aug 2023
21. Hauber, C.: Taking Over A Kubernetes Cluster: Automating An Attack Chain. Bachelor's thesis, Johannes Kepler University Linz (2022). https://www.ssw.uni-linz.ac.at/Teaching/BachelorTheses/2022/Hauber_Carina.pdf
22. Karagiannis, S., Ntantogian, C., Magkos, E., Ribeiro, L.L., Campos, L.: Pocketctf: a fully featured approach for hosting portable attack and defense cybersecurity exercises. Information **12**(8), 318 (2021). https://doi.org/10.3390/info12080318
23. Kimminich, B.: Hosting a CTF event – Pwning OWASP Juice Shop. https://pwning.owasp-juice.shop/part1/ctf.html. Accessed 12 Aug 2023
24. Kubernetes Documentation: Container Runtimes — kubernetes.io. https://kubernetes.io/docs/setup/production-environment/container-runtimes/. Accessed 20 Aug 2023
25. Kucek, S., Leitner, M.: An empirical survey of functions and configurations of open-source capture the flag (CTF) environments. J. Netw. Comput. Appl. **151**, 102470 (2020). https://doi.org/10.1016/j.jnca.2019.102470
26. Lagorio, G., Ribaudo, M., Armando, A.: Capture the flag competitions for higher education. In: ITASEC. CEUR Workshop Proceedings, vol. 2940, pp. 447–460. CEUR-WS.org (2021). https://ceur-ws.org/Vol-2940/paper38.pdf
27. LinuxContainers: Linux Containers — linuxcontainers.org. https://linux-containers.org/. Accessed 10 Aug 2023
28. Maiya, M., Dasari, S., Yadav, R., Shivaprasad, S., Milojicic, D.: Quantifying manageability of cloud platforms. In: 2012 IEEE Fifth International Conference on Cloud Computing, pp. 993–995 (2012). https://doi.org/10.1109/CLOUD.2012.111
29. Martin, A., Hausenblas, M.: Hacking Kubernetes. O'Reilly Media, Incorporated (2021)

30. Menage, P.: Control Groups — The Linux Kernel documentation — docs. kernel.org. https://docs.kernel.org/admin-guide/cgroup-v1/cgroups.html. Accessed 16 Aug 2023
31. Merkel, D.: Docker: lightweight linux containers for consistent development and deployment. Linux J. **2014** (2014)
32. MetalLB: MetalLB, bare metal load-balancer for Kubernetes — metallb. universe.tf. https://metallb.universe.tf/. Accessed 20 Aug 2023
33. Microsoft: Managed Kubernetes Service (AKS) — Microsoft Azure — azure.microsoft.com.   https://azure.microsoft.com/en-us/products/kubernetes-service. Accessed 20 Aug 2023
34. Minna, F., Blaise, A., Rebecchi, F., Chandrasekaran, B., Massacci, F.: Understanding the security implications of kubernetes networking. IEEE Secur. Priv. **19**(5), 46–56 (2021). https://doi.org/10.1109/MSEC.2021.3094726
35. OVH: Managed Kubernetes Service — ovhcloud.com. https://www.ovhcloud.com/en/public-cloud/kubernetes/. Accessed 20 Aug 2023
36. Podman: Podman — podman.io. https://podman.io/. Accessed 10 Aug 2023
37. Project, T.F.: Chapter 17. Jails — docs.freebsd.org. https://docs.freebsd.org/en/books/handbook/jails/. Accessed 16 Aug 2023
38. Proxmox Server Solutions GmbH: Proxmox - Powerful open-source server solutions — proxmox.com. https://www.proxmox.com/. Accessed 10 Aug 2023
39. QEMU: QEMU — qemu.org. https://www.qemu.org/. Accessed 10 Aug 2023
40. Raj, A.S., Alangot, B., Prabhu, S., Achuthan, K.: Scalable and lightweight CTF infrastructures using application containers (pre-recorded presentation). In: 2016 USENIX Workshop on Advances in Security Education (ASE 2016), Austin, TX. USENIX Association (2016). https://www.usenix.org/conference/ase16/workshop-program/presentation/raj
41. Raman, R., Sunny, S., Pavithran, V., Achuthan, K.: Framework for evaluating capture the flag (CTF) security competitions. In: International Conference for Convergence for Technology-2014, pp. 1–5 (2014). https://doi.org/10.1109/I2CT.2014.7092098
42. Rancher: Longhorn — longhorn.io. https://longhorn.io/. Accessed 20 Aug 2023
43. redpwn: rCTF — rctf.redpwn.net. https://rctf.redpwn.net/. Accessed 12 Aug 2023
44. R'orvik, M.: How to host a CTF? — bekk.christmas. https://www.bekk.christmas/post/2020/18/how-to-host-a-ctf. Accessed 12 Aug 2023
45. The Linux Foundation: Production-Grade Container Orchestration — kubernetes.io. https://kubernetes.io/. Accessed 10 Aug 2023
46. Vykopal, J., Švábenský, V., Chang, E.C.: Benefits and pitfalls of using capture the flag games in university courses. In: Proceedings of the 51st ACM Technical Symposium on Computer Science Education, pp. 752–758. Association for Computing Machinery (2020). https://doi.org/10.1145/3328778.3366893
47. YAML: The Official YAML Web Site — yaml.org. https://yaml.org/. Accessed 20 Aug 2023
48. Zeyu's Infosec Blog: Hosting a CTF — SEETF 2022 Organizational and Infrastructure Review — infosec.zeyu2001.com. https://infosec.zeyu2001.com/2022/hosting-a-ctf-seetf-2022-organizational-and-infrastructure-review. Accessed 12 Aug 2023

Interfaces and Applications

Increasing Accessibility of Online Board Games to Visually Impaired People via Machine Learning and Textual/Audio Feedback: The Case of "Quantik"

Giorgio Gnecco[1,2](✉) [ID], Chiara Battaglini[3] [ID], Francesco Biancalani[1],
Davide Bottari[3] [ID], Antonio Camurri[4] [ID], and Barbara Leporini[5] [ID]

[1] AXES Research Unit, IMT School for Advanced Studies, Lucca, Italy
{giorgio.gnecco, francesco.biancalani}@imtlucca.it
[2] Game Science Research Center, IMT School for Advanced Studies, Lucca, Italy
[3] MoMiLab Research Unit, IMT School for Advanced Studies, Lucca, Italy
{chiara.battaglini,davide.bottari}@imtlucca.it
[4] DIBRIS Department, University of Genoa, Genoa, Italy
antonio.camurri@unige.it
[5] ISTI Institute, National Research Council, Pisa, Italy
barbara.leporini@isti.cnr.it

Abstract. Playing board games is commonly recognized as an effective way to promote the integration and socialization of their participants. However, visually impaired people may encounter accessibility issues when playing online versions of board games, for instance, because such versions may have been designed having initially sighted people in mind. Given this premise, the aim of this work is to design an interface aimed to help visually impaired people play board games online, via an improved interaction with a normal or touch screen. This goal is achieved by means of automatic recognition of the portion of the screen one's finger or the cursor is pointing to, its classification via machine learning, and the use of either textual or audio feedback. In this way, a visually impaired person could explore the screen in quite a natural way, obtaining information, e.g., about the positions of the various pieces on the board. As a case study, a preliminary version of the interface is developed to address accessibility of the online version of a carefully selected pure strategy abstract board game, namely "Quantik" from Gigamic.

Keywords: Visual Impairment · Board Games · Accessibility · Machine Learning

1 Introduction

Playing board games is usually recognized as an effective way to improve the integration and socialization of their participants. In particular, for the case of visually impaired people (i.e., persons affected by any functional limitation of their vision, which cannot

M. Clayton et al. (Eds.): INTETAIN 2023, LNICST 560, pp. 167–177, 2024.
https://doi.org/10.1007/978-3-031-55722-4_12

be corrected by means of either corrective glasses or contact lenses, see Bailey et al. [1]), it is well-known that an increase of their autonomy in playing board games has positive effects on their quality of life and in general, on their personal fulfillment (da Rocha Tomé Filho et al. [13]). However, to promote their effective inclusion, it is important that visually impaired people are put in the conditions of playing together with other people, with similar winning chances, notwithstanding their visual abilities.

Unfortunately, on one hand, the recent Covid-19 pandemic has severely limited social interaction in the real world, making it quite difficult for visually impaired people to play board games by sitting together at the same table and interacting with the board, e.g., in a tactile way[1]. On the other hand, the pandemic has also greatly increased online interaction via the Internet.

Nevertheless, online interaction is often designed having sighted people in mind, so it can present severe accessibility issues to visually impaired people and especially to blind people, in case it is mainly based on visual information, and this is not replaced by either textual or audio feedback. Although some systems already exist to increase accessibility to these categories of people of some digital games (Morelli and Folmer [10]) and particularly of a few online board games[2], in general, their possibility to play board games online is still quite limited. This issue is particularly relevant for either less known or recently developed board games.

In this context, the goal of this work is to design an interface aimed to increase the accessibility of online versions of board games to visually impaired people, forming an additional layer between existing screen readers (mostly focused on making textual content accessible) and online board games, via automatic recognition and either textualization or sonification of their main visual elements. As a case study, instead of considering a general-purpose version of the interface, we limit the focus to its preliminary version aimed at addressing the accessibility of the online version of a carefully selected pure strategy abstract board game, namely "Quantik" from Gigamic.

The article is structured as follows. Section 2 describes the game "Quantik", analyzes it, and reports some accessibility issues of its online version, discussing how they could be solved using machine learning and either textualization or sonification techniques. Section 3 outlines the design of the first version of a possible accessible interface for the online version of "Quantik". Section 4 concludes the work with a discussion and delineates its possible future extensions.

---

[1] See the following hyperlink: https://www.youtube.com/watch?v=pT8vZZS7hZo for a demonstration of the relevance of this modality of interaction, with reference to the case of a chess tournament involving blind people.

[2] See, e.g., the case of the chess server Lichess: https://lichess.org/blog/U5AX_DcAADkAz-L5/accessibility-for-blind-players.

2 "Quantik": Description, Analysis, and Accessibility Issues

The two-player board game "Quantik" (https://en.gigamic.com/game/quantik) is a recent pure strategy abstract game, which was published by Gigamic in 2019. It was inserted in the list of Mensa Recommended Games in 2021. Its online version is available on the Board Game Arena gaming platform, at the following hyperlink: https://en.boardgame arena.com/gamepanel?game=quantik. An illustration of its board and pieces is provided in Fig. 1.

Fig. 1. "Quantik" board (image taken from https://en.gigamic.com/game/quantik).

2.1 Description

The following is a description of the game "Quantik". Each of the two players has a set of eight game pieces in the color associated with that player (light for one player, dark for the other player). The pieces have four different shapes (ball, cone, cube, and cylinder), and, for each player, there are two identical pieces for each shape. Players take turns placing one piece per round on an empty space of the board according to the following single rule: a player is not allowed to place a shape in a row, column, or quadrant on which the opponent has already placed a piece of the same shape. The first player to place the fourth different shape in either a row, column, or quadrant wins the game. For this winning condition, it does not matter if the game pieces already present in the specific row, column or quadrant belong to one player or to her/his opponent. A player wins also if she/he can move in the current turn in such a way that the other player has no admissible move at the next turn. Hence, the game never terminates with a draw.

2.2 Analysis

From a theoretical point of view, it is worth highlighting that "Quantik" is a two-person sequential zero-sum finite game with perfect information[3] (Maschler et al. [9]). Interestingly, one can apply Zermelo's theorem[4] (see, e.g., Peters [11]) to analyze any game belonging to this class. In the specific case of "Quantik", one can prove in this way that one of the two players has a winning strategy, i.e., a strategy that enables such player to win no matter which sequence of moves is chosen by her/his opponent. In principle, finding which player has a winning strategy and constructing that winning strategy can be achieved by using backward induction, relying on the so-called extensive form of the game (i.e., its representation based on a game tree and a list of players' payoffs on the terminal nodes), and constructing the so-called value function, which provides, for every node of the tree, the best payoff that can be guaranteed to the player who has to choose a move in that node. In practice, to apply backward induction, one would need to examine all the nodes of the game tree, moving from its terminal nodes (leaves) to its initial node (root), searching each time for an optimal move for the player whose turn is associated with the specific node under examination. Although finding the value function exactly is computationally intractable for many two-person sequential zero-sum finite games with perfect information, in the specific case of "Quantik" there are actually some computational savings, due to the following reasons:

---

[3] Two-person sequential zero-sum finite games with perfect information model a quite broad class of board games characterized by the following issues: there are two players, who move alternatively, and with opposite goals (e.g., when one wins, the other loses, and vice versa); at any turn, each player has a finite number of choices, and any run of the game always terminates after a finite number of turns (finiteness of the game); each player is able to observe all the previous moves (perfect information). A classic example of a game belonging to this class is provided by chess under any finite termination rule. Although several theoretical results are known for this class of games, their application to the analysis of board games is quite limited. This is motivated, e.g., by: a) the bounded rationality of real-world players, which prevents them to apply too complex strategies (i.e., choices of their moves as functions of the currently available information); b) the fact that solving in closed form such games (i.e., finding exactly their so-called subgame-perfect strategies) can be computationally intractable when these games are characterized, e.g., by a too large board, a too large number of different pieces, and/or a too complex set of rules (associated, e.g., with the possibility of moving the pieces on the board after their first positioning). In the case of "Quantik", these issues are likely reduced, for the following reasons: (i) "Quantik" has a 4×4 board, which is much smaller, e.g., than the 8×8 board used in chess. (ii) The game is characterized by a quite small number of pieces for each player (eight), which are indistinguishable in groups of two. (iii) Once positioned on the board, each such piece cannot be moved from its current position. (iv) Positioning each piece on the board restricts – often severely – the set of admissible positions for the next pieces.

[4] Zermelo's theorem states that, for any two-person sequential zero-sum finite game with perfect information, one (and only one) of the following cases occurs: (i) The first player has a winning strategy. (ii) The second player has a winning strategy. (iii) Both players have a drawing strategy. It is recalled here that a winning strategy for a player is a strategy that enables such a player to win no matter which sequence of moves is chosen by her/his opponent, whereas a drawing strategy for a player is a strategy that guarantees that she/he does not lose under that strategy, whatever is the sequence of moves chosen by the other player. In the specific case of "Quantik", only one of the two cases (i) and (ii) occurs, since the game never terminates with a draw.

- Some moves can be seen immediately to be suboptimal for one player because they lead to the other player's win in a few moves. Hence, starting from a specific node in the game tree, some moves could be immediately excluded from the search for optimal moves for that node.
- The game is characterized by some symmetry: e.g., rotating the board by 90 degrees along a vertical axis produces a node in the game tree that is equivalent to the original node, in the sense that the value function assumes the same value on these two nodes. This depends on the fact that the game subtrees originating from those two nodes have the same structure, and each leaf in one of the two subtrees has the same pair of payoffs for the two players as the corresponding leaf in the other subtree.

Nevertheless, in case finding the value function exactly for "Quantik" turned out to remain computationally intractable in spite of the computational savings above, one could apply suitable advanced machine-learning techniques for its approximation, such as approximate dynamic programming/reinforcement learning (Platt [12], Xenou et al. [15]). Finally, starting from such approximation, one could construct an approximation of a winning strategy.

2.3 Accessibility Issues

For what concerns accessibility issues, first, it is important to remark that the presence of a single (and simple) rule in "Quantik" allows the player to understand easily how the game proceeds and makes it unnecessary to resort to a complicated rulebook (e.g., one containing either several images or a single complex image, difficult to be interpreted by standard optical character recognition systems), which would make the game inaccessible to people with visual impairment (Bolesnikov et al. [2]). Second, it is worth observing that "Quantik" belongs to the category of games that, according to Thevin et al. [14], are deemed to be complicated to make accessible by means of hand-crafted adaptation solutions, since its board configuration is extremely relevant to play that game. However, due to the small size of that board and its low number of different pieces, "Quantik" (particularly, its online version) looks particularly suitable for either a textualization or a sonification of its rows, columns, and quadrants, which would provide visually impaired people with precious information to construct a mental map of the content of the game board. It is expected that, in this way, such players could play competitively with sighted people. Indeed, both the single rule of the game and its winning condition depend on information about pieces located in the same rows, columns, or quadrants. Nevertheless, before applying either textualization or sonification, automatic recognition of the pieces is needed, e.g., to associate each piece with a specific text or sound. In the case of online playing of the game, this could be achieved quite easily, when the gaming device has direct access to the internal state of the game. As an alternative, machine learning can be used to identify the pieces. Compared to the previous solution, this has the advantage of not requiring the additional prior knowledge of the internal state of the game, nor the use of possibly advanced computer programming skills to access that state. In this way, the same machine-learning techniques applied for one game are likely to be applicable to other games, by making only minor modifications to the code. Moreover, machine learning could be used to suggest a specific sonification to the user, depending on her/his needs. For instance, distinct users may have different preferences about timber, pitch, and volume. Hence, one could exploit users' similarities to optimize the selection of the sonification for a specific user.

3   Design of the First Version of a Possible Accessible Interface for the Online Version of "Quantik"

Taking into account the issues highlighted in the section above, a first version of an accessible interface for visually impaired people playing the game "Quantik" online was implemented in MATLAB R2023a, then run on a notebook Intel® Core™ i7850U CPU@1.80 GHz–1.99 GHz under the Windows 10 Enterprise LTSC environment. The interface was thought for use in the two following consecutive phases:

- In the first phase, a sighted individual collects a subset of images directly from the web page of the game and labels them according to their shape. Then, a machine-learning model is trained/validated by means of an augmented dataset obtained by random translation and the addition of white Gaussian noise with varying variance to each element of the subset above. More precisely, the union of the training/validation sets is made of 500 images per class (corresponding to 50 corrupted images for each of the 10 images initially collected and labeled per class). Validation is achieved by using the holdout method, giving the same size to the training/validation sets. Then, a convolutional neural network (composed of the following consecutive layers: 2-D convolutional layer; relu layer; max pooling 2-D layer; fully connected layer; softmax layer; classification layer) is trained/validated to classify objects as belonging to one of four classes, each corresponding to one of the four shapes of pieces that are used in the game "Quantik": ball, cone, cube, and cylinder. The choice of a neural network with a feedforward structure is motivated by its excellent approximation capabilities, a property that is valid already in the case of a single hidden layer (Gnecco et al. [4–6], Gnecco and Sanguineti [7]). Being the specific learning task multi-class classification (with the four classes being represented by one-hot encoding), cross-entropy is used as the loss function (Goodfellow et al. [8]). Training is performed based on stochastic gradient descent with momentum. The resulting validation accuracy turns out to be 94.5% (see Fig. 2). Finally, being it easier to distinguish between the two different colors of the pieces used by the two players, color classification of an image is achieved first by finding the color at its center, then attributing it to the nearest of the colors associated with the two players.
- In the second phase, the same individual or another individual (possibly with visual impairment) navigates the web page, then the trained/validated machine-learning model is tested on the images generated in real time by that user.

All the training/validation/test images have the same size (315×317 pixels, reduced to 26×26 pixels before sending them as inputs to the convolutional neural network), and are possibly obtained also by zooming in/out around the current position of the

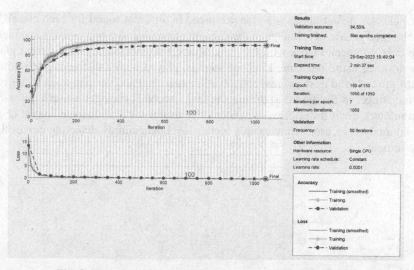

Fig. 2. Details on training/validation of the learning machine.

cursor/finger on the screen. Each image is centered on the position of the cursor/finger on the screen at the time of generation of that image.

Navigation on the screen can be performed in several different ways, all based on the same MATLAB interface: using the mouse, moving a finger on a touch screen, or using Leap Motion (https://www.ultraleap.com), which is an optical hand-tracking device able to capture movements of the hands. The last modality is expected to be more natural for a blind person, who may be not accustomed to the first two modalities.

The screen is split into two equally-sized parts (see Fig. 3):

– In the left part, the user can navigate the online version of "Quantik", which is opened automatically by MATLAB. This is achieved by accessing its associated hyperlink (https://en.boardgamearena.com/gamepanel?game=quantik) with the default web browser.
– The right part shows one figure ('Interface.fig'), which contains several subfigures. Subfigure a) represents a scaled version of the left part of the screen, where the user can move the cursor/place her/his finger. This redundancy is due to the fact that, at least under the operating system used, MATLAB can easily access the content of the whole screen, but it looks that it cannot directly access the content of a window associated with another program (e.g., with the default web browser). Subfigure b) presents a zoom of a rectangular subregion of the image around the current position of the cursor/finger in Subfigure a). Subfigure c) reports the classification of Subfigure b) obtained by the trained/validated machine-learning model, by showing a prototype image corresponding to the recognized class and color[5]. The names of the recognized class and color are also reported at the top of Subfigure c)[6]. For each of the

---

[5] This visual feedback is useful only for sighted people, for a direct evaluation of the accuracy of the classifier. An analogous remark holds for the visual feedback in Subfigures d) and e).

[6] This textual feedback is potentially useful for screen readers, as an alternative to sound feedback.

four classes, a continuous sound is produced (a different sound for each class). This is changed in case of a change in the classification (due to a successive movement of the cursor/finger). Pieces with the same shape but associated with different players are sonified using the same kinds of sounds, played with a different pitch. Finally, Subfigures d) and e) show, respectively, the horizontal and vertical trajectories of the cursor/finger in Subfigure a) during the last s seconds (being s a user-configurable parameter). Such trajectories are potentially useful for a multiscale spatial or temporal analysis of user behavior, at a higher level than simply detecting cursor/finger movement.

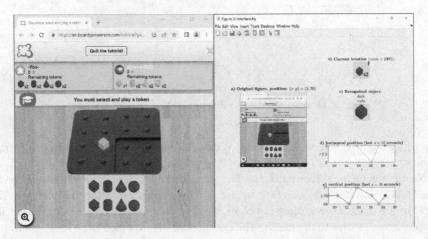

Fig. 3. Screen splitting in the current version of the interface.

The core of the interface relies on event-based MATLAB programming, applied to the figure '*Interface.fig*'. In particular, the occurrence of events associated with three properties ('*WindowButtonMotionFcn*', '*WindowButtonDownFcn*', and '*KeyPressFcn*') of that figure is captured automatically. More specifically, the activation of one of these three properties is associated with the execution of the respective callback function. For instance, in the case of a mouse interface, the first two properties refer, respectively, to mouse movement and mouse clicking. The last property refers to key pressing. The three callback functions are described as follows:

- When the user moves the cursor/finger on the figure '*Interface.fig*', the first callback function is executed. The position of the cursor/finger is detected, and its horizontal/vertical coordinates – expressed as percentages of the total width/height of Subfigure a) – are reported near that subfigure. These coordinates are suitably thresholded when the cursor/finger overcomes one of the horizontal/vertical boundaries of Subfigure a), in such a way as to get always numbers between 0 and 100. Then, the contents of Subfigures b), c), d), and e) are updated accordingly.
- When the user produces a left click, the second callback function is executed. The current image in Subfigure b) is saved in the dataset used for successive training/validation of the machine-learning model (after its suitable data augmentation).

A first persistent variable is used to count the number of figures saved so far, to avoid overwriting. In the current version of the interface, labels for those figures are provided manually by the user.

- When the user presses the left/right arrow key or the '*p*' (play) key, the third callback function is executed. The first two cases correspond with a decrease/increase (by 10%) of the zoom applied to Subfigure b), always remaining in the range [10%, 1000%]. A second persistent variable is used to keep track of the current zoom. The third case corresponds with the activation of the sonification of the currently recognized object, shown in Subfigure c). Persistent variables are used to keep track of the color/shape of that object. According to the current implementation, the sounds used are: '*gong*' (ball), '*splat*' (cone), '*handel*' (cube), '*train*' (cylinder). They are played at two successive octaves (higher for the opponent's pieces, to increase the attention of the player towards those pieces, as their detection is relevant for the application of the single rule of the game).

4 Discussion and Possible Extensions

It is worth comparing the proposed interface with the advanced electronic device designed by Caporusso et al. [3] to provide accessibility to an online version of another board game (specifically, chess). That device was conceived having deaf-blind people in mind. Hence, no sonification is generated by it. Instead, haptic feedback is provided to the player, about both the position of the pointer on the digitalized board and the identity of the object located in that position. However, for people having only visual impairment, a sonification of visual information appears to be a more natural kind of feedback (especially for the case of the game "Quantik", due to the reduced size of its board, compared to that of chess). Moreover, it is worth noting that touch screens were not so widely diffused at the time of publication of Caporusso et al. [3], so an alternative software (rather than hardware) interface seems preferable, being it likely cheaper than the device proposed at the time in that work. Finally, differently from Caporusso et al. [3], the proposed interface makes extensive use of supervised machine learning.

Among possible extensions of this research, we mention:

- *An improvement in the design of the multi-class classifier.* For instance, one could include a fifth class, made of other objects (extracted, for example, from the web page of the specific online board game) not belonging to any of the four main classes. The presence of this fifth class would be motivated by the opportunity of producing no textual/sound output (or, alternatively, producing a low-volume background sound) when the image surrounding the current position of the cursor/finger does not belong to one of the four main classes. This goal could be also achieved by still using only four classes and including an image segmentation step, in such a way as to activate the multi-class classifier in the test phase not for every test image, but only when its segmentation satisfies a suitable constraint (e.g., that the segmented object of interest – the foreground – does not encounter the boundary of the image, or has only a sufficiently small overlap with that boundary).
- *An improvement in the accuracy of the classifier*, achieved, e.g., by using a larger/better-constructed dataset for training/validation, and/or a different architecture for the learning machine.

- *An improvement in the effectiveness of the interface*, motivated by the fact that, in the current implementation, Subfigures a)-e) are updated every time a movement of the cursor/finger is detected, slowing down the execution of the code.
- *An improvement in accessibility of the interface*, motivated by the fact that its current version needs the presence of a sighted individual to generate the dataset used to train/validate the learning machine.
- *An improvement in the choice of the sonification*, possibly based on machine learning and users' feedback. For instance, sonification could be combined with machine learning to suggest/disadvise the choice of specific moves. Moreover, polyphonic/spatialized sonification (using headphones) and/or orchestration techniques could give the user global information about the locations of several pieces on the board, providing her/him additional help to construct a mental map of the content of the game board. Sonification should not require player's learning but provide instead a metaphor that naturally reflects the structure of the board and the single rule of the game. Finally, it should be chosen in such a way as to be pleasant to the player and not to put her/him under stress.
- *The application of the interface to real gaming sessions*, and the collection and analysis of related feedback from users (for instance, initially blindfolded sighted people, then persons really affected by visual impairment).
- *Its extension to the online versions of other board games* (such as "Quarto") *and card games,* based, e.g., on training/validation sets specific for each such game.

Acknowledgment. The authors were partially supported by the Game in Lab 2022 project "Increasing accessibility of online board games to blind and visually impaired people via machine learning", funded by Game in Lab, and by the PRIN 2022 project "Multiscale Analysis of Human and Artificial Trajectories: Models and Applications", funded by the European Union - Next Generation EU program (CUP: D53D23008790006). Giorgio Gnecco dedicates the work to the memory of his mother Rosanna Merlini.

References

1. Bailey, I.L., Hall, A.: Visual impairment: an overview. American Foundation for the Blind (1990)
2. Bolesnikov, A., Kang, J., Girouad, A.: Understanding tabletop games accessibility: exploring board and card gaming experiences of people who are blind and low vision. In: Proceedings of TEI 2022: The 16th International Conference on Tangible, Embedded, and Embodied Interaction, article no. 21, pp. 1–17 (2022)
3. Caporusso, N., Mkrtchyan, L., Badia, L.: A multimodal interface device for online board games designed for sight-impaired people. IEEE Trans. Inf. Technol. Biomed. **14**(2), 248–254 (2010)
4. Gnecco, G., Gaggero, M., Sanguineti, M.: Suboptimal solutions to team optimization problems with stochastic information structure. SIAM J. Optim.Optim. **22**(1), 212–243 (2012)
5. Gnecco, G., Kůrková, V., Sanguineti, M.: Can dictionary-based computational models outperform the best linear ones? Neural Netw.Netw. **24**, 881–887 (2011)

6. Gnecco, G., Kůrková, V., Sanguineti, M.: Some comparisons of complexity in dictionary-based and linear computational models. Neural Netw.Netw. **24**, 171–182 (2011)
7. Gnecco, G., Sanguineti, M.: On a variational norm tailored to variable-basis approximation schemes. IEEE Trans. Inf. Theory **57**, 549–558 (2011)
8. Goodfellow, I., Bengio, Y., Courville, A.: Deep Learning. MIT Press, Cambridge (2016)
9. Maschler, M., Solan, E., Zamir, S.: Game Theory. Cambridge University Press, Cambridge (2013)
10. Morelli, T., Folmer, E.: Real-time sensory substitution to enable players who are blind to play video games using whole body gestures. Entertain. Comput. **5**(1), 83–90 (2014)
11. Peters, H.: Game Theory: A Multi-leveled Approach. Springer Berlin Heidelberg, Berlin, Heidelberg (2015). https://doi.org/10.1007/978-3-540-69291-1
12. Platt, A.: Deep Reinforcement Learning. Springer, Singapore (2019). https://doi.org/10.1007/978-981-13-8285-7
13. da Rocha Tomé Filho, F., Mirza-Babaei, P., Kapralos, B., Moreira Mendonça Junior, G.: Let's play together: adaptation guidelines of board games for players with visual impairment. In Proceedings of CHI 2019: CHI Conference on Human Factors in Computing Systems, article no. 631, pp. 1–14 (2019)
14. Thevin, L., Rodier, N., Oriola, B., Hachet, M., Jouffrais, C., Brock, A.M.: Inclusive adaptation of existing board games for gamers with and without visual impairments using a spatial augmented reality framework for touch detection and audio feedback. In: Proceedings of the ACM on Human-Computer Interaction, vol. 5, no. ISS, article no. 505, pp. 1–33 (2021)
15. Xenou, K., Chalkiadakis, G., Afantenos, S.: Deep reinforcement learning in strategic board game environments. In: Slavkovik, M. (ed.) EUMAS 2018. LNCS (LNAI), vol. 11450, pp. 233–248. Springer, Cham (2019). https://doi.org/10.1007/978-3-030-14174-5_16

A Novel Approach to 3D Storyboarding

Federico Manuri[1]([✉])(iD), Andrea Sanna[1](iD), Marco Scarzello[1],
and Francesco De Pace[2](iD)

[1] DAUIN, Politecnico di Torino, corso Duca degli Abruzzi 24, 10129 Torino, Italy
federico.manuri@polito.it
[2] Institute of Visual Computing and Human-Centered Technology TU Wien, Vienna,
Austria
http://grains.polito.it

Abstract. Creatives in the animation and film industries constantly explore new and innovative tools and methods to enhance their creative process, especially in pre-production. As realistic, real-time rendering techniques have emerged in recent years, 3D game engines, modeling, and animation tools have been exploited to support storyboarding and movie prototyping. This research proposes a 3D storyboarding tool to improve existing storytelling approaches. A novel storyboarding pipeline is proposed, which can automatically generate a storyboard including camera details and a textual description of the events occurring in each scene. Users create storyboards by selecting actors, performing available actions, positioning the camera in the 3D scene, and taking screenshots to save a vignette of the storyboard; the corresponding description is generated based on the actors' actions and their status. A software implementation of the proposed pipeline has also been developed in the guise of a 3D desktop application aimed at expert and novice storyboarders. The system has been tested to evaluate its usability. Preliminary results confirm that the users have appreciated the application.

Keywords: 3D storyboarding · character animation · authoring tool

1 Introduction

Creatives in the animation and film industries constantly explore new and innovative tools and methods to enhance their creative process, especially in pre-production. Traditional approaches rely on hand-drawn storyboards and physical mockups, whereas information technology introduced sketch-based [1] and picture-based 2D [2,3] drawing applications. The production phase of cinematic and computer-generated imagery (CGI) sequences usually includes state-of-the-art technologies. However, the pre-production phase usually relies on more traditional methods. After completing the script, storyboard artists realize 2D panels for each shot, drawing the background, the foreground, and the characters. However, as 3D animation became popular, 3D artists were employed to recreate in

M. Clayton et al. (Eds.): INTETAIN 2023, LNICST 560, pp. 178–192, 2024.
https://doi.org/10.1007/978-3-031-55722-4_13

3D the storyboard drawings. This approach is also helpful in cinematic production to pre-visualize the story before the video shoot phase. Some commercial applications for 3D pre-visualization exist, such as Frameforge 3D [4] or Shot-Pro [5], but these solutions are usually complex to master and present a steep learning curve. Hand-drawn storyboarding has the advantages of an interactive process, as the drawings can be corrected immediately as the lines appear on the paper (or screen). However, the conversion accuracy from 2D images to a 3D scene can only be judged when the 3D artists complete their works: actual production statistics confirm that up to half of the layout shots may need a retake [6], as framing discrepancies occur. Even the best storyboard artist draws only an approximation of a camera shot: it would be challenging to draw a scene as it would look through a specific camera lens with 100% accuracy. Drawing the correct scale of objects without absolute references (for cinematic production) or 3D references (for CGI productions) is another possible mistake. Performing the storyboarding process in 3D can resolve these issues and provide an interactive pre-visualization of the storyboard [7].

This research proposes a 3D storyboarding tool to improve existing storytelling approaches. A novel storyboarding pipeline is proposed, which can automatically generate a storyboard including camera details and a textual description of the actions performed in three-dimensional environments. A software implementation of the proposed pipeline has also been developed in the guise of a 3D desktop application aimed at expert and novice storyboarders. The application enables the user to create a 3D virtual stage starting from an open 3D world: users can add environment tiles to define different locations and populate them with structures, objects, and actors (e.g., humans or animals). Each actor is seen as a state machine: a list of available actions is provided based on the current actor's state and its position in the scene. Once the 3D virtual stage is complete, users can start creating the storyboard, selecting actors, performing actions based on their state, and taking screenshots to save a vignette of the storyboard and the corresponding description. The description is automatically generated based on the actors' actions and their status.

This paper is organized as follows: Sect. 2 provides an overview of the state-of-the-art, whereas Sect. 3 depicts the system design. Section 4 describes in detail the software implementation. Section 5 presents the test performed to evaluate the proposed system and the analysis of the results.

2 Previous Works

As realistic, real-time rendering techniques have emerged in recent years, 3D modeling and animation tools and 3D game engines have been researched and explored to support storyboarding and movie prototyping. A first attempt to automatically generate storyboards was developed by Pizzi et al. [8]: then authors proposed an authoring tool allowing game designers to formalize, visualize, modify, and validate game-level solutions in the form of automatically generated 2D storyboards. The proposed system features planning techniques to plan level solutions, with the main agent corresponding to the player character, game actions to planning operators, and level objectives as goals. The *Director's Lens* instead is a first attempt at exploiting 3D to innovate the shooting process of CGI through assisting filmmakers in camera composition [9]: the proposed system employs an intelligent and automatic cinematography engine that can compute a set of suitable camera placements for starting a shot. The proposed method can potentially simplify the process of shooting CGI, resulting in a novel workflow based on the interactive collaboration of human creativity with automated intelligence. In [7], the authors investigate a novel way to automatically pose 3D models from 2D sketches: the pose inference is formulated as an optimization problem, and a parallel variation of the Particle Swarm Optimisation algorithm has been proposed to search for the minimum of its objective function. The scope of this research was to pose models for pre-visualization, providing a direct link between the storyboarding and the pose layout phases of a 3D animation pipeline. A computer-assisted narrative animation synthesis (CANVAS) authoring tool was proposed by Kapadia et al. in [10] for synthesizing multi-character animations from sparsely specified narrative events. Given the key plot point in a story, the proposed system automatically resolves incomplete story definitions to produce a consistent and complete narrative, filling in the missing details necessary to synthesize a 3D animation that complies with the author's constraints. The proposed system provides an accessible interface for rapidly authoring complex narratives, suitable for pre-visualization or cutscenes. In [11], the authors propose a novel approach for the automated staging of actors and cameras in a virtual 3D environment given a set of constraints specified with a dedicated staging language that extends the Prose Storyboard Language (PSL). The system resolves complex spatial relations such as visibility or character framing, considering the relations that link cameras and entities in the scene to position the characters and the cameras simultaneously. PSL uses a simple syntax and limited vocabulary borrowed from working practices in traditional movie-making, intended to be readable by machines and humans, and has been designed over the last ten years to serve as a high-level user interface for intelligent cinematography and editing systems [12]. Kim et al. [13] developed a tool for Auto-generating Storyboard And Previz (ASAP) for screenwriters and filmmakers: the proposed system enables users to easily simulate stories as 3D animated scenes with virtual characters in a 3D environment. Providing a script that follows the Final Draft screenwriting tool format, the system parses it, identifying actions, characters, and dialogue, using a combination of deep learning, data-driven, and rules-based approaches. The system output consists of automatically generated pre-visualized animations, simulating natural behaviors and realistic dialog scenes. Furthermore, users can create storyboard shots by capturing scenes being played. In [14], the authors propose an open-source, semi-automated cinematography toolset capable of procedurally generating in-game cutscenes in the style of a specific movie director. The system has been developed with the Unity game engine [15]. It combines run-time cinematography automation with a novel timeline and storyboard interface for design-time manipulation, allowing for cutscenes to unfold dynamically based on the game state. Chen et al. [16] proposed a sentiment-aware generative model for visual storytelling based on the sequential vision-to-language approach, which generates coherent and rich image descriptions from a sequence of input images through a multi-layered sentiment extraction module based on deep learning models. Overall, research efforts in recent years are primarily aimed toward automatic generations of storyboards, either in 2D or 3D, starting from the script or other text-based constraints. Some works focus on specific tasks, such as positioning the camera in the 3D scene or providing different camera shot positions. Recent works further exploit artificial intelligence to automatically generate 3D animations or poses from the script or the 2D storyboard as a pre-visualization technique. Others focus on automatically developing the most coherent description of an image through deep learning models. However, artists are still limited to a few options for creating storyboards, including sketch-based or picture-based approaches.

The scope of the proposed system is to investigate a novel approach to storyboarding. The classic process consists of drawing each storyboard shot in 2D: this could be done with either sketch-based or picture-based tools. Users with good drawing skills mostly appreciate sketch-based tools due to the freedom of expression provided by this approach. Instead, those not skilled in drawing generally prefer picture-based tools since they use readily available pictures as building blocks, resulting in less freedom but faster content creation than the previous approach. 3D storyboarding applications usually provide a different paradigm, starting from a set of rigged characters instead of static 2D images and allowing users to pose the characters through their armatures. However, posing a character properly could be difficult and time-consuming, especially for users who are not skilled in 3D animation. The proposed approach lets the user move the character in the scene freely using a video game-based approach, using a combination of keyboard and mouse, likewise first-person and third-person shooter video games. However, instead of posing the character to define their appearance, the user can choose which action the character should perform from a list. The list of available actions depends on the context, the proximity to other objects/characters, and the state of the actors involved; an animation is provided and automatically played upon selection. Actions performed by the user are saved in chronological order as events and are used to generate the descriptions for each vignette of the storyboard automatically. Moreover, the user can move the camera to decide the framing and change the camera's focal length of the lens, which is then reported in the storyboard. Traditional methods require the user to find the best way to convey the script's text in a meaningful, graphical representation enhanced with camera details and additional textual information. The proposed approach lets the user enact the story in a 3D scene, similar to a sandbox video game, shifting the user's attention from the final result to obtain (the storyboard) to the story to play (the script).

The aim of the proposed system is to enable the user to play out the story in a 3D environment, controlling the available characters, trying out different camera views, and automatically obtaining both the camera information and the textual description of the actions happening in each scene. This should help the user focus on the story and define the actions' timing. Thus, the first step should be to enable the user to select the characters available in the scene, change their position, move the camera, and generate a vignette. This can be easily obtained in a 3D game engine such as Unity 3D [15]; however, if the only action available to the characters is to move, obtaining a detailed description of the scene in the storyboard would not be possible. Moreover, there would be no novelty compared to traditional techniques, since the user should focus on the graphical output of the actions without the characters performing them.

3   Proposed System Design

This section describes the design phase of the proposed storyboard pipeline, based on the insight obtained from the analysis of the state-of-the-art.

3.1   3D Virtual Stage

Even if the focus of the research project is to provide a novel approach to storyboarding, the setup of the 3D virtual stage represents a necessary condition. This step should exploit straightforward techniques to create a 3D scene creating locations and adding objects and characters. Based on the state-of-the-art, the system should enable the user to:

- select different kinds of tiles, e.g., stone, wood, and soil, to texture the floors;
- add objects to the scene, either to:
  - define locations, such as rooms, courtyards, streets, etc., through walls, doors, stairs, etc.;
  - furnish existing locations;
- add characters to the scene, defining their starting position.

Once all the elements described in the script are available as 3D assets, the user can start storyboarding.

3.2   Actors' Actions and Animations

The following step is to determine how the user can perform different actions with the actors. This offers two possible options: unconstrained actions versus constrained actions. The first paradigm lets the user perform any possible actions, either selecting them from a list or typing them in a text box; no constraint is applied, neither in terms of environment, objects or characters proximity, or acting character conditions. The most critical problem of this approach regards the consistency of the story since the users may perform actions that make no sense in the given context: performing an action that involves a character or object not available (e.g., closing a door without a door in the scene); performing an action which is inconsistent with the actor status (e.g., swimming while driving a car, going to bed while eating in the kitchen). A secondary problem of an unconstrained approach regards the user interface: to select the proper action, the user should either navigate a long list or complex menu to find the right one or write it down.

On the contrary, a constrained approach means that only the actions available to the characters could be performed based on their status, position in the scene, and proximity to other objects or actors. All the elements in the 3D scene are divided into two groups: invariable elements, whose status is immutable, and variable elements, which may change depending on the actor's actions. Variable elements are either active or passive: active elements (usually characters) can be selected by the user to perform actions, whereas passive elements can only undergo status changes due to active elements' actions. This way, not only the user interface would provide a limited list of available actions, but the actions affecting others, either objects, actors, or the environment, would result in changes in the scene. For example, moving a pot from point A to point B would require the character to move near point A, pick it up, move to point B, and put down the pot. Moreover, since one of the aims of the storyboard is to obtain a graphical representation of the events of a given scene, the user should be able not only to select an action from a list depending on the current character status but also to see a corresponding animation providing a graphical representation of such action. Such transformations to the 3D scene are essential to obtain an accurate visual representation, focusing on the story (what should happen) instead of the storyboard (what should be visible in the storyboard).

3.3 State-Machine Representation

The simplest way to develop a constrained approach involves adopting a finite state machine (FSM) strategy. An FSM is a mathematical model which describes a system with a finite number of states as a graph. Each graph node represents a status, and the arrows connecting the nodes determine the transition between one status and another in response to some inputs. An FSM is denoted by its initial state, the list of its states, and the inputs that trigger each transition. To apply an FSM approach to the proposed scenario, all the elements in the scene should be appropriately classified as invariable, active (variable), or passive (variable). The behavior of each variable element is represented with an FSM (characters and objects). FSMs are frequently used in video games to define playable and non-playable characters. For example, a player may be in the wandering status as long as the enemies are far away and automatically enter the combat status (e.g., drawing weapons) when the enemies are nearby and vice-versa. The mathematical model of a deterministic finite-state machine is a quintuple $(\Sigma, S, s_0, \delta, F)$ where:

- Σ is a finite, non-empty set of symbols, representing the input alphabet;
- S is a finite, non-empty set of state;
- s_0 is the initial state, with $s_0 \in S$;
- δ is the state-transition function $\delta : S \times \Sigma \to S$;
- F is a subset of S, possibly empty, of final states.

FSMs can be described using State Chart XML (SCXML), an XML-based markup language designed for state machine notation. SCXML can simplify the transition between the code used to handle the characters at runtime and a user interface that enables the user to define, change and update the FSM for a character. Figure 1 shows a graphical representation of a simple FSM for a human character.

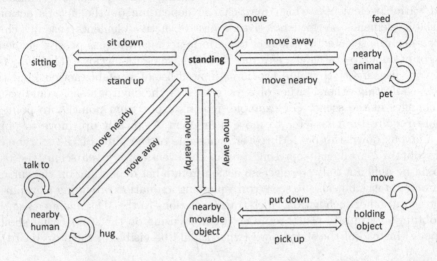

Fig. 1. A graphical representation of a simple FSM for a human character.

Given a 3D asset pertaining to the variable element category, it would be useful to infer its FSM transitions from the available animations list. Moreover, animations could be renamed to incorporate all the information necessary to create the corresponding FSM: every animation can be renamed as a sequence $N; S; E; T$ with N the action's name, S the list of compatible starting status, comma separated, E the list of consistent ending status, comma separated (or $SAME$ if the ending status should be equal to the starting one), and T the target of the action (either self or another variable element, active or passive). For example, $STARTRUNNING; IDLE, WALKING; RUNNING; SELF$, representing the character that may start running from on the three compatible statuses, or $GREET; IDLE, SITTING, WALKING; SAME; CHARACTER$, representing the character that may greet another character, starting from one of the compatible statuses and ending in the same status after the action. Passive elements, such as doors, may have a starting status of *close*, and two animations, *open* and *close*, that should be renamed as $OPEN; CLOSE; OPEN; SELF$ and $CLOSE; OPEN; CLOSE; SELF$, representing the fact that a door can only be open if its starting status is close, and it ends up open, and vice-versa. The element type, passive, should imply that an actor should perform the action. Using this approach, a text parser can be scripted to automatically define the FSM of a variable element (both active and passive) based on the list of available animations.

3.4   3D Storyboarding

Constraining the user choices based on the environment and FSMs of the variable elements available in the scene should simplify transposing the story from the script to the 3D setting. The process of storyboarding in a virtual location would require the user to:

1. select one of the variable active elements (AE);
2. based on the script, choose between:
   - move the AE in the scene;
   - perform one of the available actions;
3. (optional) take a snapshot of the current camera view to generate a vignette of the storyboard;
4. restart from step 1.

Based on the FSM approach described in the previous section, generating a stack of events would be possible, adding one element to the stack each time the user acts. The $SUBJECT$, $ACTION$, $TARGET$, and $FRAME$ values should be saved into the stack for each event. The $SUBJECT$ value corresponds to the currently active actor; the $ACTION$ value is the one chosen by the user, whereas the $TARGET$ is either the active actor or another variable element in the scene; the $FRAME$ value should enable the user to add to the stack multiple events at the same time to describe concurrent events. Thus, the system should provide an interface to edit this value.

The user should be able to undo actions. However, since the system's consistency is essential, the editing of the stack should be handled with extreme care to avoid inconsistent states for one or more elements in the scene. Thus, the system should provide an undo action for the last event in the stack, rolling back to their previous status each element involved by the deleted event. On the other hand, randomly canceling events in the stack should not be possible: a very complex consistency check should be developed to verify the consistency of all the following events unless the system automatically deletes all subsequent actions.

3.5   Camera

In the proposed scenario, the camera would work as a variable active element that can only be moved in the scene. Usually, the storyboard's vignette may contain details on the camera focal lengths or the shot size. The system may provide a menu with camera options (instead of actions), such as a list of camera lens presets or a mechanism to adjust the focal length or the focus. All these camera properties can be easily conveyed in additional info added to the vignette description. On the other hand, the shot size, which depends on the distance between the camera and the subject, would require additional computations to provide an accurate description or labeling in the final storyboard. If necessary, camera movements and variable parameters could be defined as an FSM as well; this could be useful if the user wants to track down in the vignette description not only the events occurring in the 3D scene but also the camera actions (e.g., movements or change of shot size).

3.6   Automatic Vignette Labeling

Once the user wants to save the chain of events in a single vignette of the storyboard, the system would generate a save-point in the stack; then, all the events in the stack following the last save-point should be converted into sentences to automatically label the vignette. A translation script generates a sentence from an event parsing the $SUBJECT$, $ACTION$, $TARGET$, and $FRAME$ variables saved for that element in the stack. The system also takes into account the timing information provided by the timeline to define if multiple actions pertaining to the same vignette occur simultaneously or consequentially and introduce temporal adverbs in the sentence accordingly.

4   Software Implementation

The design requirements described in the previous section guided the development of a prototype that implements the proposed 3D storyboarding methodology. Unity 3D has been chosen to deploy the system since it is a 3D game engine freely available for research. It is highly compatible with various visualization devices like desktop computers, mobile devices, and augmented and virtual reality headsets. WordNet [18] has been used to provide variability in the textual descriptions of the storyboard's vignettes. More specifically, the Syn.WordNet [19] package for Unity has been installed to request sets of synonyms (*synset*) to WordNet from the Unity scripts.

Figure 2 shows the pipeline for the proposed system. When the application starts, it loads both 3D assets and (if available) their FSMs and animations into the system. Then, the starting menu provides three choices to the user to (1) create or edit an existing 3D scene, (2) start storyboarding from an existing 3D scene, or (3) edit or create FSMs for the available 3D assets.

4.1   User Interface

3D Virtual Stage. The system enables users to add, move, or delete 3D assets to the scene. Figure 3 shows the user interface of the virtual staging (on the left). Three dropdown menus let the user choose among environment assets, objects, and characters. Selecting a 3D asset, the user can move, remove or rename it. Whereas move and remove can be obtained through shortcuts, rename is useful for changing characters' names and using them instead of the default value in the automatic text generation for the vignettes' descriptions. Once the 3D scene is ready, the user can save it, move back to the initial menu, or proceed with the storyboarding step.

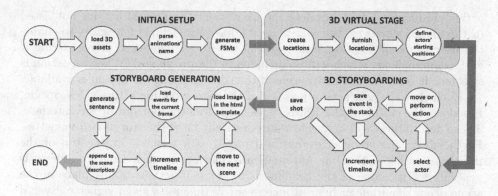

Fig. 2. The pipeline of the proposed 3D storyboarding tool.

Fig. 3. The 3D virtual stage interface (on the left) and the 3D storyboarding interface (on the right).

3D Storyboarding. In the storyboarding phase, the user enacts the story described in the script to automatically generate the corresponding storyboard. Figure 3 shows the corresponding UI for this phase (on the right).

When the user selects a character, the active character label in the bottom right corner of the screen is updated. The user can move the character in the scene using the keyboard through the WASD keys since it is a standard in 3D first and 3rd person videogames. The move action is saved in the event stack, considering the environment the user is moving on, defined by the floor's tiles, and the target the user is moving towards. The target is computed considering the character's forward direction when the movement ends and tracing an orthogonal line that stops at the first 3D assets available in the scene. Then, the user can again select the active character to show the available actions menu. When the character moves inside the range of an interactive element (either active or passive), a light animation is displayed to alert the user that a set of additional actions is available, selecting the given asset, which will be the target of such actions. Clicking on a target, another menu showing other actions available to the active character will be listed, and a button to make the target the active character. A text box lets the user specify additional actions not listed in the menu. Moreover, the *talk to* action has been defined for actors to enable the user to detail a dialog, either typing it with the keyboard or registering it with a microphone, which will be included in the storyboard. When an action is selected, it is played in the 3D scene if the corresponding animation is available.

Each time the user acts, a preview of the corresponding action's description, based on the status of the FSMs, is displayed at the bottom of the interface. These descriptions will be used to automatically label the storyboard vignettes. Furthermore, the stack of events is depicted as a timeline at the top of the interface, with the timeline automatically moving on each time a vignette is generated. The scope of the timeline is to define if actions taking place in the scene occur simultaneously or at a consecutive time for a given vignette. Even if the events are queued in the stack, events with the same frame value are depicted as concurrent in the text description. If the user increments the timeline frame value, actions within the same scene will have different timings and be described sequentially. An undo button/shortcut lets the user undo the last event, resetting the character position if it is movement-related.

The camera can be selected as any other active character in the scene and positioned with a keyboard and mouse interface: the $WASD$ keys are used to pan the camera; the QE keys or the mouse wheel can be used to get closer or far away from the scene; tilting the mouse on its two axes rotate the camera with a standard look-at approach, as usually happen in 3D first-person video games. This approach enables the user to explore different camera angles and shots, even observing the scene from different actors' perspectives, as shown in Fig. 4. A slider on the right of the interface lets the user change the camera's focal distance.

Finally, a button/shortcut lets the user insert a save point in the stack, taking a screenshot of the scene based on the current view, adding a vignette to the storyboard, automatically generating the textual description, and adding the camera focal distance. Each vignette's tuple image/description is saved in an HTML template, and the textual description can be eventually edited.

FSM Editing and Creation. The user can edit or create the FSM of one of the available 3D assets through a 2D interface with two panels. The *status* panel provides a list of all the variable elements. Selecting one, a graphical representation of its FSM is provided in the form of a list, with each line containing: a starting status; an ending status; the action that activates the transition; and the actions available in the end status that do not generate a status change. This view also contains the transitions due to actions done by other actors to the selected one. The *actions* panel provides a list of actors and a list of targets, represented by the variable elements (both active and passive): a list of actions is displayed when selecting an actor and a target. This list represents the actions available to the actors if the target is in range of that action.

Fig. 4. Three different camera views for the same scene.

5 User Test

A 3D scene has been created with the proposed tool to evaluate the system's usability. The 3D models used to furnish the scene are freely available 3D models for non-commercial use downloaded from the Sketchfab website [20]. The 3D characters, with the rigging and animations, have been downloaded from Adobe Mixamo [21] and are also freely available for non-commercial projects.

5.1 Use Case

A script has been written based on the available 3D assets, detailing locations, actions, timing (for concurrent actions), and the camera shot. Eleven students from Politecnico di Torino have been involved in this study: 9 are master's degree students in Cinema and Media Engineering, and 2 are bachelor's degree students in Design and Communication. All the testers were volunteers with previous experience in storyboarding for university projects. The tests have been carried out on one user at a time to avoid learnability effects.

5.2 Test Procedure

Experiments were carried out adopting the following procedure:

1. the user is introduced to the project, the essential concepts, the scope of the tests, and the test procedure;
2. the user is guided through the user interface and the available functionalities;
3. the user is provided with a tutorial scene to freely test the different functionalities for a limited amount of time (10 to 15 min);
4. if the user is satisfied trying out the application, a new scene is loaded, and a paper script is provided to the user; the user starts creating the storyboard, and both times and errors are manually registered;
5. once the users complete the storyboard, they are asked to fill out the SUS questionnaire [22] to measure the system's usability;
6. finally, the user can provide additional feedback on the application usage by answering four open questions.

5.3   Tests' Results

All the users were able to complete the tests, with an average completion time of $7m10s$ and a standard deviation of $2m28s$. On average, one error and a half were committed by each user. Most of the errors involved the concept of simultaneous versus sequential actions, with the user not noticing or forgetting the script's indications when deciding the actions' timing. SUS scores are detailed in Table 1.

Table 1. System Usability Scale questionnaire results for the ten questions ($q_1 - q_{10}$) from eleven testers ($t_1 - t_{11}$) and the average (AVG) score.

	q1	q2	q3	q4	q5	q6	q7	q8	q9	q10	SCORE
t1	3	2	4	2	5	1	5	2	3	2	77.5
t2	3	2	5	2	5	1	4	2	4	1	82.5
t3	4	2	4	2	5	2	5	1	5	1	87.5
t4	2	1	5	2	5	1	3	1	5	2	82.5
t5	2	1	4	2	4	1	5	1	3	2	77.5
t6	3	2	4	1	3	3	5	2	4	1	75.0
t7	5	1	4	1	5	1	4	1	5	2	92.5
t8	5	2	5	2	5	1	5	2	5	1	92.5
t9	4	4	4	1	4	1	4	3	3	2	70.0
t10	4	2	4	2	4	1	4	2	3	1	77.5
t11	4	1	4	1	4	1	4	2	3	1	82.5
AVG											81.6

The open questions aimed at highlighting the most and least appreciated feature or functionality, suggestions for missing functionalities considered helpful by the user, and a personal comment comparing the proposed method with those usually adopted by the users.

5.4   Discussion and Limitations

Based on the feedback provided by the users at the end of the tests, the most appreciated feature was the overall 3D storyboarding approach and its easiness of use, from the scene creation to handling the characters and performing actions (5 out of 11); the automatic text generation and managing the characters actions with an FSM approach have been considered equally relevant (3 out of 11).

On the other hand, the most relevant difficulties involve camera usage and active character selection (6 out of 11). The first problem depends on the user background: those accustomed to video games did not have issues with the proposed interface; the others would have preferred a gimbal or other mechanics available in 3D modeling and 3D animation tools. This alternative commands to handle the camera could be easily added in a future version of the application.

Moreover, the scene view may result in characters obscured by other 3D assets and difficulties in selecting; thus, the user may waste much time changing the camera view to achieve the proper selection. Using the timeline to define the actions' chronological order, combined with the limitations of the undo action, was considered a significant problem by two users out of 11. In contrast, three users could not find any feature to disfavor. The user suggested further enhancing the undo feature, even if there are technical limitations due to the FSM approach, and despite the necessity to maintain overall consistency in the system (3 out of 11). Two users suggested adding more shortcuts to speed up the storyboarding process. Other suggestions comprehend: the automation of the camera shot setup, calculating the zoom level necessary for different shot options based on the camera-target distance; the visibility of the actions/events in the stack; the possibility of changing the duration of each scene at the end of the storyboarding phase; finally, adding more 3D assets to create the scenes. Pertaining a subjective comparison with the testers' traditional techniques previously used for storyboarding, 6 out of 11 users believe that the proposed approach is easier and faster than a sketch-based approach, especially for people not accustomed to drawing. However, two users think drawing is a more flexible and creative approach since the assets' availability does not limit the user. Two users could not choose between the proposed method and the existing ones.

Despite these problems, the questionnaires' results show that the proposed system was highly appreciated by the user. Comparing the results with the SUS chart, five users out of eleven obtained a good score (range $68-80.3$), whereas six users obtained a higher score (≥ 80.3). The average SUS score of 81.6 suggests that the users believe that the proposed system provides excellent usability.

6   Conclusion and Future Work

This research proposes a 3D storyboarding tool to improve existing storytelling approaches. A novel storyboarding pipeline is proposed, which can automatically generate a storyboard including camera details and a textual description of the events occurring in each scene. Users create storyboards by selecting actors, performing available actions, positioning the camera in the 3D scene, and taking screenshots to save a vignette of the storyboard; the corresponding description is generated based on the actors' actions and their status. A software implementation of the proposed pipeline has also been developed in the guise of a 3D desktop application aimed at expert and novice storyboarders. The system has been tested to evaluate its usability. Preliminary results confirm that the users have appreciated the application.

Future works will aim to improve the user interface, exploiting the feedback provided by the testers. Apart from enhancing the camera handling, a further option is to provide a dropdown menu to select a specific character directly and key shortcuts to move to the next/previous actor available in the scene. Despite the necessity to guarantee system consistency, the editing feature could be improved, and the stack of actions could be made visible to the user. The automatic text generation can be further enhanced with an AI approach, such as ChatGPT [17]. The scene creation phase can be enriched with more 3D assets and animations for the variable elements.

References

1. Photoshop homepage. https://www.adobe.com/products/photoshop.html. Accessed 31 Mar 2023
2. Storyboardthat homepage. https://www.storyboardthat.com. Accessed 31 Mar 2023
3. Canva homepage. https://www.canva.com. Accessed 31 Mar 2023
4. FrameForge homepage. https://www.frameforge.com. Accessed 31 Mar 2023
5. ShotPro homepage. https://www.shotprofessional.com. Accessed 31 Mar 2023
6. Gouvatsos, A. 3D storyboarding for modern animation. Doctoral dissertation, Bournemouth University (2018)
7. Gouvatsos, A., Xiao, Z., Marsden, N., Zhang, J.J.: Automatic 3D Posing from 2D Hand-Drawn Sketches. In: PG (2014)
8. Pizzi, D., Lugrin, J.L., Whittaker, A., Cavazza, M.: Automatic generation of game level solutions as storyboards. IEEE Trans. Comput. Intell. AI Games **2**(3), 149–161 (2010)
9. Lino, C., Christie, M., Ranon, R., Bares, W.: The director's lens: an intelligent assistant for virtual cinematography. In: Proceedings of the 19th ACM iNternational Conference on Multimedia, pp. 323–332 (2011)
10. Kapadia, M., Frey, S., Shoulson, A., Sumner, R. W., Gross, M.H.: CANVAS: computer-assisted narrative animation synthesis. In: Symposium on Computer Animation, pp. 199–209 (2016)
11. Louarn, A., Christie, M., Lamarche, F.: Automated staging for virtual cinematography. In: Proceedings of the 11th ACM SIGGRAPH Conference on Motion, Interaction and Games, pp. 1–10, November 2018
12. Ronfard, R., Gandhi, V., Boiron, L., Murukutla, A.: The prose storyboard language: a tool for annotating and directing movies (version 2.0, revised and illustrated edition). In: Eurographics Workshop on Intelligent Cinematography and Editing, vol. 4 (2022)
13. Kim, H., Ali, G., Hwang, J.I.: ASAP: auto-generating storyboard and previz with virtual humans. In: 2021 IEEE International Symposium on Mixed and Augmented Reality Adjunct (ISMAR-Adjunct), pp. 316–320. IEEE, October 2021
14. Evin, I., Hämäläinen, P., Guckelsberger, C.: Cine-AI: Generating Video Game Cutscenes in the Style of Human Directors (2022). arXiv preprint arXiv:2208.05701
15. Unity homepage. https://unity.com. Accessed 31 Mar 2023
16. Chen, W., Liu, X., Niu, J.: SentiStory: a multi-layered sentiment-aware generative model for visual storytelling. IEEE Trans. Circuits Syst. Video Technol. **32**(11), 8051–8064 (2022)
17. ChatGPT homepage. https://openai.com/blog/chatgpt. Accessed 31 Mar 2023
18. WordNet homepage. https://wordnet.princeton.edu. Accessed 31 Mar 2023
19. Syn WordNet homepage. https://developer.syn.co.in/note/wordnet/release-notes.html. Accessed 31 Mar 2023
20. Sketchfab homepage. https://sketchfab.com/feed. Accessed 31 Mar 2023
21. Adobe Mixamo homepage. https://www.mixamo.com/. Accessed 31 Mar 2023
22. Brooke, J.: SUS-a quick and dirty usability scale. Usabil. Eval. Indus. **189**(194), 4–7 (1996)

The WebCrow French Crossword Solver

Giovanni Angelini[1], Marco Ernandes[1], Tommaso Iaquinta[2], Caroline Stehlé[3],
Fanny Simões[4], Kamyar Zeinalipour[2(✉)], Andrea Zugarini[1], and Marco Gori[2]

[1] expert.ai, Via Virgilio, 48/H - Scala 5, 41123 Modena, Italy
`gangelini@expert.ai`
[2] Università degli Studi di Siena, Via Roma, 56, 53100 Siena, Italy
`tommaso.iaquinta@student.unisi.it`,
`{kamyar.zeinalipour2, marco.gori}@unisi.it`
[3] Université Côte d'Azur, INRIA, Institut 3IA Côte d'Azur, Nice, France
`caroline.stehle@inria.fr`
[4] Université Côte d'Azur, Institut 3IA Côte d'Azur, Nice, France
`fanny.simoes@univ-cotedazur.fr`

Abstract. Crossword puzzles are one of the most popular word games,
played in different languages all across the world, where riddle style can
vary significantly from one country to another. Automated crossword
resolution is challenging, and typical solvers rely on large databases of
previously solved crosswords. In this work, we extend WebCrow 2.0, an
automatic crossword solver, to French, making it the first program for
crossword solving in the French language. To cope with the lack of a
large repository of clue-answer crossword data, WebCrow 2.0 exploits
multiple modules, called experts, that retrieve candidate answers from
heterogeneous resources, such as the web, knowledge graphs, and linguistic rules. We compared WebCrow's performance against humans in
two different challenges. Despite the limited amount of past crosswords,
French WebCrow was competitive, actually outperforming humans in
terms of speed and accuracy, thus proving its capabilities to generalize
to new languages.

Keywords: Natural Language Processing · Crossword · Crossword
Solver · Artificial intelligence · Linguistic Puzzles · Probabilistic
Constraint Satisfaction

1 Introduction

Crossword puzzles have gained immense popularity as a widely played language
game on a global scale. Daily, millions of individuals engage in the challenge,
requiring a combination of skills. To solve crosswords effectively, humans need
to possess a broad vocabulary, general knowledge across various subjects, and the
ability to decipher wordplay and puns. Human solvers should master the crossword language, its peculiarities, and specific knowledge belonging to the country

---

Supported by expert.ai, https://www.expert.ai/.

M. Clayton et al. (Eds.): INTETAIN 2023, LNICST 560, pp. 193–209, 2024.
https://doi.org/10.1007/978-3-031-55722-4_14

in which it is spoken. They must also excel in pattern recognition, interpret contextual clues accurately, employ problem-solving strategies, and demonstrate patience and perseverance. Mastering these skills enables individuals to tackle crossword puzzles with efficiency, accuracy, and a higher likelihood of success.

This scientific paper introduces a novel version of WebCrow 2.0, an AI-powered application specifically designed for efficiently solving French crosswords. It represents the first of its kind in the realm of French crosswords, building upon the previous versions developed for Italian and American crosswords. We will discuss the peculiarities of the French version in Sect. 4 and the underlying architecture in Sect. 5.

Solving crosswords based on clues is widely recognized as an AI-complete problem [12], owing to its intricate semantics and the extensive breadth of general knowledge required. Artificial intelligence has recently shown an increasing interest in crossword solving. [21] Through this work we are introducing a notable milestone in the literature, the French WebCrow system, which achieved human-like performance on French crosswords by leveraging numerous knowledge-specific expert modules.

WebCrow 2.0 can rely on a limited amount of previously solved crosswords and clue-answers pairs. In the case of French crosswords, WebCrow 2.0 made use of about 7.000 previously solved crossword puzzles and about 312,000 unique clue-answers pairs. Studies in American crosswords rely on millions of clue-answers pairs, 6.4M [21], and on the fact that almost all of the answers are in previously seen crosswords. This is not the case with French crosswords, for which the availability of a huge collection is limited, thus a more robust approach is required.

The primary objective of French WebCrow is to establish its competitiveness against human crossword solvers by leveraging expert modules, NLP (Natural Language Processing) technologies, web search, and merging techniques to efficiently generate candidate answer lists and fill crossword grids accurately. The goal of the web search source of information is to provide accurate solutions to crossword puzzles without the burden of maintaining an up-to-date multitude of domain-specific modules. By tapping into the web as an extensive source of information, French WebCrow offers the promise of scalability and adaptability.

The upcoming sections provide information on related works and a comprehensive overview of the various components of WebCrow 2.0. Detailed explanations will be given on the French WebCrow version, accompanied by a thorough analysis of the experimental results. Finally, the paper will conclude by summarizing the findings and highlighting the significance of this research in the field of crossword solving.

2   Related Works

In the literature, various attempts have been made to solve crossword puzzles. However, none of these approaches have adequately addressed the specific challenges posed by French crosswords. In the following, we will delve into a review of existing works that have tackled the task of solving crosswords.

One of the first works on crossword solving is Proverb [14], which tackles American crosswords. The system makes use of independent programs that solve specific types of clues, leveraging information retrieval, database searching, and machine learning. During the grid filling phase, it tries to maximize the number of most probable words in the grid, using a loopy belief propagation, combined with A* search [10].

Taking into account the Proverb experience, WebCrow [1,2,7] is the first crossword solving for Italian crosswords. WebCrow introduces the use of a Web Search Module (WSM), that extracts and filters potential answers from the Web, being this an extremely rich and self-updating repository of human knowledge. Additionally, the system retrieves clues from databases of previously solved crossword puzzles (CPs). A merging process aims to consolidate the potential solutions from both web documents and previously solved CPs. Subsequently, the system employs a probabilistic Constraint Satisfaction Problem (CSP) approach, similar to the Proverb system [13], to fill the puzzle grid with the most suitable candidate answers. Both Proverb and WebCrow proved to be better-than-average cruciverbalists (crossword solvers).

Following these experiences, we can find Dr.Fill work [9], a program designed to solve American-style crossword puzzles. Dr.Fill converts crosswords into weighted Constraint Satisfaction Problems (CSPs) and utilizes innovative techniques, including heuristics for variable and value selection, a variant of limited discrepancy search, and postprocessing and partitioning ideas. The program's performance in the American Crossword Puzzle Tournament suggests it ranks among the top fifty crossword solvers globally.

In the field of crossword solving, there is also SACRY [3], introduced in 2015, a system that leverages syntactic structures for clue reranking and answer extraction. The authors build upon the foundation of WebCrow [1,2,7] to develop SACRY. The system utilizes a database of previously solved crossword puzzles (CPs) to generate a list of candidate answers. One of the key contributions of SACRY is its emphasis on exploiting syntactic structures. By incorporating syntactic analysis, SACRY improves the quality of the answer list, enhancing the accuracy of crossword puzzle resolution.

Recently, there is the Berkeley Crossword Solver, a cutting-edge approach that revolutionizes automatic American crossword puzzle solving. The system employs neural question-answering models to generate answer candidates for each crossword clue and combines loopy belief propagation with local search techniques to discover complete puzzle solutions. One of the standout features of the Berkeley Crossword Solver is its use of neural question-answering models, which significantly enhances the accuracy of generating answer candidates.

In the subsequent sections, we will provide a comprehensive and detailed explanation of the various components comprising our system. We aim to delve into each part, elucidating its functionalities and intricacies, to offer a thorough understanding of our system's architecture and its underlying mechanisms.

3   Overview of WebCrow 2.0

WebCrow 2.0 is based on the previous WebCrow project experience [7]. As shown in Fig. 1, WebCrow has a first phase of clue analysis and clue answering. For each clue a list of candidate answers, of the suitable length, is generated by a variable number of experts. Then, all ordered lists are merged into a unique list for each clue. The merging phase takes into account information like the expert module's confidence, the clue type and the answer length. The list merger module and list filtering module, based on morphological information, are both trainable on data. Next comes a belief propagation step [13] which reorders the candidate lists based on the puzzle constraints. Finally, the last step is the real-solving mechanism that actually fills the grid with letters, using a new grid-filling approach, the Char Based Solver algorithm.

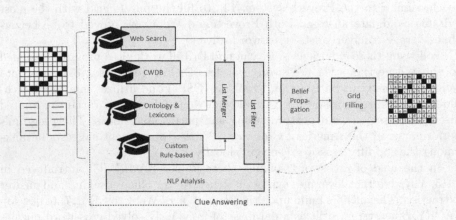

Fig. 1. WebCrow Overview.

3.1   Modularity

WebCrow 2.0 has a modular architecture, based on Redis as a communication backbone. Redis implements a Publish/Subscribe messaging paradigm which allows asynchronous communication between agents of nearly every programming language [19]. The advantage is that with little effort we are able to design expert modules for new languages or based on state-of-the-art natural language processing techniques.

Based on our experience, expert modules should cover these three types of knowledge:

- **Lexical and Ontological Knowledge:** knowledge about the way we use language to represent the world and organize information.
- **Crossword-specific experiential Knowledge:** frequent crossword clue-answer pairs, specific conventions and rules which recur in crossword puzzles.
- **Factual and Common Knowledge:** encyclopedic knowledge, common sayings, facts, and events of a common cultural background. The Web can be viewed as a repository of this kind of knowledge.

In the next section, we are going to analyze in more detail the most crucial expert modules that contribute to the creation of candidate answer lists.

3.2   The Expert Modules

Word Embedding Expert. The Word Embedding expert takes into account the idea that crossword puzzles often contain knowledge that has already been encountered in previously solved crosswords. Word embeddings [5,6,11,16,17] offer a way to map individual words or sequences of words (sentences) to specific vectors within a high-dimensional geometric space. This mapping ensures that similar words or sentences are located in close proximity to each other, while sentences with unrelated meanings are positioned far apart.

Building upon a retrieval and ranking approach for crossword clue answers [22], this expert employs the Google Universal Sentence Encoder (USE) to embed each puzzle clue. It then searches for the most similar clues within the clue-answers dataset, leveraging the capability of word embeddings to discover linguistic connections between clues.

WebSearch Expert. The Web Search Module utilizes web documents and search engines to identify suitable answers for crossword clues. It consists of a web-based list generator, a statistical filter, and an NLP category-based filter. The module excels in handling longer word or compound word targets. It is particularly useful for obtaining up-to-date data that may not be available in other modules. In our current implementation, we have seamlessly integrated the Bing API [15], but it is also feasible to utilize alternative search APIs.

Knowledge Graph Expert. In this paper, we introduce a novel expert that utilizes expert.ai's linguistic knowledge graph [8], which provides a domain-independent representation of the real world through concepts and their related meanings and the different relationships that exist among concepts. Each linguistic concept is explained using its similar meanings, its definition, and its related concepts extracted from the Knowledge Graph. The concept is then mapped using word embedding, which enables a search similar to the Word Embedding expert.

By employing word embedding techniques, the concept can be effectively searched, similar to the functionality of the Word Embedding expert. This new expert has proven to be invaluable in solving clues that require both lexical and ontological knowledge, such as "Sick" [ILL] or "Supportive kind of column"

[SPINAL]. Inside expert.ai Knowledge Graph "sick" and "ill" are two words belonging to the same concept, they are synonyms. As far as "spinal", there is a concept "spinal column" which is a specification (kind of) of the concept "column".

Other Expert Systems for Language-Specific Crosswords. Expert systems for language-specific crosswords are designed to cater to the specific nuances of the language. For example, in Italian crosswords, there are often word plays with 2-letter answers. To address this, a hard-coded expert system has been developed that encodes many of the possible types of word plays, resulting in high-confidence answers. A similar approach has been taken for French solvers, as described in Sect. 5.3. However, such a situation is not present in American-style crosswords, where the minimum number of letters for an answer is 3.

3.3 Merging

Once all the experts have produced their outputs, which are lists of candidate words each one associated with a probability the list is merged together in a unique list. The merging procedure consisted of a weighted average of the experts list based on the length of the answer, the weights are picked based on a specific training phase.

3.4 Grid Filling

For the grid-filling phase, we made use of a Char Base Solver. This approach is more robust in case some candidate lists do not have the correct answers, which is very likely in French crosswords.

For each slot s we cumulate the probability mass $p_d^s(c)$ of a letter c, in a given direction d (Across or Down), adding all the probabilities of words that contain letter c in the slot s with direction d. We compute the probability mass $p^s(c)$ as:

$$p^s(c) = p_A^s(c) \cdot p_D^s(c), \tag{1}$$

This can be seen as the probability of the letter c being correctly inserted in a given cell, considering the constraint network and the answer lists. We then use two criteria to assign to the given box the letter c and in this way constrain the grid filling.

$$(p^s(c) > 99.99\%) \text{ and } (best_A(c) == best_D(c)) \tag{2}$$

$$(p^s(c) > 99.00\%) \text{ and } (best_A(c) == best_D(c)) \text{ and } (p_A^s(c), p_D^s(c) > 90\%) \tag{3}$$

In other terms Eq. 2 states that a letter c is chosen for a cell if the confidence on that letter being in that cell is higher than 99.99% and it is the most likely prediction in both directions. Where $best_A(c)$ is the most likely letter in the across direction and $best_D(c)$ the most likely in down direction. Obviously this two letter must be the same.

Equation 3 instead states that if the confidence on a given letter being in a given cell is only 99.00% then it is not enough to be the most likely for both directions ($best_A(c) == best_D(c)$) but that letter must have more than 90% probability for both directions.

If either of these criteria is met, then the character is assigned to that particular position. Otherwise, it will be filled in a second phase with the most probable word that does not break any other char-based constraint. In the unlikely event that no word satisfies the bond, the cell is left unfilled or could be filled by another post-processing expert, such as an implicit module.

4   The French Crosswords

4.1   Format and Rules

The French crossword format is similar to Italian crosswords. Unlike American crosswords, two-letter words and "Blind cells" (cells that belong to only one word) are allowed. Stacked answers made up of multiple words are less common in French crosswords and generally correspond to expressions.

French crossword puzzles vary greatly in size and in the type of knowledge used. In the next sub-sections, we will describe in more detail these aspects.

4.2   French Crosswords Dataset

For the French dataset, we collected over 300,000 clue-answer pairs, with the answer length distribution shown in Fig. 2. Additionally, we compiled a collection of approximately 7,000 solved crossword puzzles from diverse sources. We owe our success in this endeavor, completed in just a few months, to the invaluable collaboration of two prolific authors, Serge Prasil and Michel Labeaume.

Table 1. Dataset of previously seen clue-answers pairs and crosswords.

Language	unique clue-answers pairs	crosswords
American Crosswords	3,100K	50,000
Italian Crosswords	125K	2,000
French Crosswords	300K	7,000

As we can see in Table 1, the French dataset of previously seen clue-answers pairs and crosswords is comparable to the Italian dataset, while the American dataset is considerably huger. Moreover, American crosswords are more standard. Almost all clue answers are present in previous crosswords, which is not the case with French crosswords.

In Fig. 2 we show the statistics of the answer length present in French crosswords. The majority of the answer's lengths are below 10. Answers with higher lengths are covered by verb inflections, compound words, or linguistic expressions.

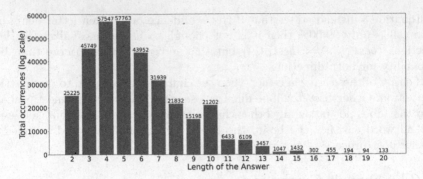

Fig. 2. Statistics on French crosswords dataset.

4.3   Linguistic and Cultural Peculiarities

Unlike Italian and American crosswords, French crosswords use a wide range of verb inflections in their solutions, covering nearly every possible tense and person. However, the definitions provided in the clues often lead to the correct inflection.

Furthermore, we have observed that French crossword authors have distinct individual styles that vary greatly from one another. As in other crossword languages, the aim of a crossword author is to provide clues that are obscure enough while keeping solutions that should appear obvious once found [4]. He must find the right level of difficulty for all the pairs of solutions. When this level is too high, the risk is to discourage people from trying to solve the crossword. On the contrary, if the clues are too simple, it is a memory or patience game, but there is no challenge, and usually, French crossword players prefer tricky enigmas, with few clues, twisted words, or traps.

French crossword authors inherit from the art of conversation in classical French culture, which is well represented by the periphrase "la langue de Molière" to designate French. As a result, French authors take pride in being witty in the definitions they provide. They must be creative in finding jokes that make the solver laugh [4], which leads to the development of distinct individual styles.

4.4   Examples of Clues in French Crosswords

In this section, we categorize the types of clues found in French crosswords and provide illustrative examples. Some of the examples are very specific to the French language, in particular the examples given in sections Inflections or Domain Specific Knowledge, and some other examples related for instance to rare words or word games can be found in other languages as well.

Inflections. French crosswords make extensive use of rare verb tenses and modes, which can make it challenging to find the correct inflection of the word to be guessed through a direct web search. For instance, in the following clue answer pair: *Auraient des soucis excessifs [CAUCHEMARDERAIENT]*, the verb to guess "cauchemarder", which means "having a nightmare", is rarely used at the conditional present, at the third person plural. In another example, *Apitoie [ATTENDRISSE]*, the clue can refer to either the first or third person at the indicative or subjunctive present tense. Depending on the verbal group of the solution, the inflection can vary significantly at these tenses and persons.

Rare Words. Some clues may involve words that are rare in French, either because they are ancient words or foreign words, or these words belong to the literary register or, conversely, to the colloquial or slang register. For instance, the solution of the clue *Dessiner sans soin [STRAPASSER]* is an old verb. As the frequency of these words is low, they may appear with a very low probability, and in some cases, they may not appear at all in the candidate solutions list.

Domain Specific Knowledge. Some puzzles require domain-specific knowledge, such as very specific geographical knowledge. For example, a clue may be: *Elle habite une commune située dans le département de l'Isère [SICCIOLANDE]*, meaning that we need to search for the name of the female inhabitants of a city in a specific French department. There is no generic rule in French for determining the name of the inhabitants from the name of the city, and sometimes the name of the inhabitants (in this case, "SICCIOLANDE") can be very different from the city name; in this example, the city name is "Siccieu-Saint-Julien-et-Carisieu". Therefore, solving this type of riddle requires a combination of encyclopedic knowledge, spelling rules, and potential knowledge of spelling exceptions.

The following example requires specific knowledge of French literature: *Le bleu et le blanc du poète [OE]*. This example pertains to the poem "Voyelles" by the renowned French poet Arthur Rimbaud, where each vowel is linked to a color. In this poem, the vowel "O" is associated with the color blue ("bleu"), and the vowel "E" is associated with the color white ("blanc").

Generic Words with Few Indices. On the other hand, some clues may consist of a few generic words such as color names and adverbs, which can be linked to numerous solutions. In such cases, the definition is not clearly connected to the answers, making automatic graph search more challenging. For instance, consider the following clue: *Pétales de rose [ESE]*. One may be misled by the words "Pétales" and "rose", which could refer to the lexical field of flowers. However, in French crosswords, they refer to the compass rose, and the solution could be of the type ESE ("Est, Sud, Est" meaning direction East, South, East), NN, NSN, and so on.

Word Games. Word games are a type of clue in which the solver must manipulate the multiple meanings of the words in order to arrive at the solution. In crossword puzzles, common word games involve the letters of a single word, which may be either part of the clue or part of another word that must be guessed. For example, consider the clue *A la sortie de Strasbourg [RG]*. The phrase "A la sortie de" translates to "At the exit of" and suggests that the solution is composed of the last letters of the word "Strasbourg". This clue is made more challenging by the fact that "Strasbourg" is a proper noun, and solvers may be tempted to look for a solution that is geographically related to the city.

Two Steps Clues. Some crossword puzzles can be challenging as they require two or more steps to arrive at the solution. For instance, consider the clue *À l'envers : coût [FIRAT]*. To solve this puzzle, one must first identify a synonym for the word "coût" (TARIF) and then invert the letters (FIRAT), as indicated by the phrase "À l'envers :". Similarly, in the clue *Grecque a l'envers [ATE]*, the solver must recognize that "Grecque" refers to a Greek letter before inverting the letters of the word found. In the example *Impro de jazz sans voyelle [SCT]*, while it may seem straightforward to humans, this could prove to be a challenging task for a machine. The solver should find the answer to the definition of "impro de jazz" ("jazz improvisation") without any information about the word length before removing the vowels.

Multiple Categories. Finally, crossword puzzles often combine multiple difficulties. In this example: *Attaquerai les portugaises [ESSORILLERAI]*, the author Serge Prasil used slang expression "les portugaises", to refer to ears. The verb to guess is further an ancient word, a medieval torture that means cutting off the ears, in an unusual form, because it is conjugated at the future.

5   The System Architecture

The recent changes in the architecture allowed for easy incorporation of new agents and modification of existing ones by simply adjusting the parameter configuration. For example, the web-search expert (see Sect. 3.2) was ported to French by modifying the query language in the parameter set.

To update the Word Embedding Expert, we required the French crosswords dataset described in Sect. 4.2. The clues had to be encoded further with the Universal Sentence Encoder, as explained in the Word Embedding expert section (see Sect. 3.2).

After implementing these two expert agents, we analyzed the results to identify the areas where most errors occurred. We discovered that 29% of missing answers were due to missing verb inflections, and 8% were due to adjective or noun inflections. Among all verb forms, the present tense was used only 20% of the time, while the past simple, a tense rarely used in everyday life, was used 40% of the time. Among the inflections of adjectives, the feminine form was used 58% of the time, and the plural form was used 55% of the time.

5.1   Knowledge Graph Expert

As per the analysis of the most common errors, we have enhanced expert.ai's French knowledge graph. The results analysis revealed the need to incorporate inflections of verbs, adjectives, and nouns. To achieve this, we followed the same approach as described in Sect. 3.2. However, in this case, in addition to adding the connected concepts with the same description, we also included the required inflections.

5.2   Lexicon

In addition, we identified a need to enhance the lexicon utilized by WebCrow. To address this, we incorporated Lexique 3.83, a French lexicon database containing approximately 123K distinct entries of at least 2 letters, as described in [18]. We combined this dataset with data from a French dictionary, resulting in a final lexicon comprising approximately 198K words.

5.3   Rule-Based Expert

We have developed a Python-based expert module for French crosswords that can decipher common word games. The module is designed to identify target words in the clues and provide associated lists of solutions. The target words may include Arabic number conversions to words, Roman numerals, chemical elements from Mendeleev's table, French departments, grammar lists (such as personal pronouns, conjunctions, and prepositions), and Greek letters.

Furthermore, the Rule-based expert was designed to decipher clues that indicate the presence of word games in finding the answers, and where the solution involves either the inversion of a word, a reduced set of letters, or a mix of letters. The word on which the word game applies may be included in the clue or not. In the latter case, which we called "two steps clues" in Sect. 4.4, the rule-based expert first searches for a list of possible solutions by calling the Word Embedding expert and then applies the word game to the letters of each word in the list.

6   Experimental Results

In this section, we present the comprehensive results obtained from our experimentation. Following the development of the system, as outlined in the preceding sections, we proceeded to assess its performance on previously unseen crosswords.

Test Dataset

To ensure a robust evaluation, we carefully selected a dataset comprising 62 distinct crosswords that were published subsequent to the crosswords used for constructing the different experts, such as the Word Embedding expert Sect. 3.2.

This selection criterion ensured that there was no overlap between the crosswords utilized for training and those employed for testing purposes.

To evaluate the performance of our proposed solution, we conducted an extensive analysis using a diverse set of crossword puzzles sourced from multiple authors and publications. Our dataset comprises 10 puzzles each from two renowned creators, Michel Labeaume and Serge Prasil. Furthermore, we incorporated 40 additional crosswords from established publishers to facilitate a thorough assessment. Detailed information about the test crossword can be found in Table 2.

Table 2. Test CrossWords.

Source	Number of Puzzles	Dimension
Michel Labeaume	10	10×10
Serge Prasil	10	20×20
Other Sources	42	Variable max 15×15

We used diverse crosswords to test the system's ability to handle different puzzle styles, author preferences, and construction variations. This approach helped us understand the system's performance and adaptability in unseen crosswords.

Results

We evaluated the system's performance using three distinct metrics: percentage of correct words, which measures the accuracy of inserting the correct target answers, percentage of correct letters, which evaluates the accuracy of inserting individual letters, and percentage of inserted letters, which assesses the system's ability to fill crossword slots.

For a comprehensive overview of these metrics across different sources of crosswords, refer to Table 3. It encapsulates the corresponding results obtained from the test sets of various crossword sources, shedding light on the overall performance of our system in solving French Crosswords.

Table 3. Performance of the System on the Test CrossWords.

Source	Words Accuracy	Letters Accuracy	Inserted Letters
Michel Labeaume	92.97%	98%	100%
Serge Prasil	91.82%	96.9%	99.15%
Other Sources	73.86%	81.16%	96.99%

Our crossword solver achieved impressive results in solving French crosswords from Michel Labeaume and Serge Prasil, with some 100% solved crosswords. On the other sources, the performance varied a lot, we had some sources with fully correct solved crosswords, while on other crosswords the system performed poorly. Based on our analysis some authors use very specific styles and knowledge, which demonstrates that solving crosswords is an AI-complete and open-domain problem. In some cases, answers were very domain-specific, see Sect. 4.4.

Overall, these remarkable results demonstrate the robust performance of our system in solving French crosswords. The accuracy rates obtained highlight the system's ability to effectively fill in words and letters, thus confirming its competence in solving French crossword puzzles.

In Table 4, we tested the system by removing some expert modules. These tests show that each module is necessary to obtain the best results, the Full version, and that different source of knowledge is required to solve crosswords. Unlike American crossword studies, there is not a huge dataset of previously solved crosswords. Moreover, French crosswords are not as standard as American ones. Each crossword can vary a lot, influenced by the style and imprint of its author.

Table 4. Ablation test.

Configuration	% of correct words	% of correct letters	% word drop
Full	65.71	75.22	-
No Rule based	65.16	74.79	0.55
No Websearch	61.60	72.68	4.11
No Lexicon	61.36	71.98	4.35
No KG	56.28	68.38	9.43

To gain insights into our system's strengths, limitations, and relative performance compared to human crossword solvers, we conducted challenging competitions. The subsequent section presents a detailed analysis of these comparative evaluations.

6.1 AI vs Human Challenges

We organized an internal challenge at INRIA to evaluate our system's performance in a real-world scenario, putting it against human participants. The challenge included French and American crossword puzzles. Both humans and WebCrow were allowed to utilize web searches during the challenge.

The challenge included three crosswords: an easy-medium-level French crossword with a 10-min time limit (score counted), a medium-hard level French crossword with a 20-min time limit (score counted), and an American crossword with a 10-min time limit (score counted). The experimental results, including the performance of WebCrow (Live and Lab), the average human performance, and the best human performance are presented in Table 5.

Table 5. Results of the Crossword Solving Competition (INRIA).

Player	Score	Time (sec.)
WebCrow Live	296.18	419
WebCrow Lab	313.75	556
AVG Human	50.39	2570
Best Human	104.22	2700

Two modes were implemented: "WebCrow Live" where the system ran in real-time with predetermined configurations, and "WebCrow Lab" where results were computed in advance in the laboratory. It is important to note that variations in web information could lead to discrepancies between the results of the two modes.

We also conducted a public challenge at the World AI Cannes Festival 2023, evaluating the French version of WebCrow. There were three challenges, one for each language: French crosswords, Italian crosswords, and American crosswords. Each challenge had two crosswords valid for the competition with time limits. The two French crosswords were created specifically for the challenge by renowned authors Serge Prasil and Michel Labeaume.

The scoring system gave points from 0 to 100 based on the percentage of correct words (0 to 110 for the second crosswords. Then some additional points (maximum 15) were added based on the percentage of time not used. We had 15 min for the first crossword and 20 min for the second. Finally, in case of a fully correct answer, 15 points were awarded.

Table 6. Results of the French Crossword Solving Competition (WAICF).

Player	Score	Time (sec.)
WebCrow Live	228,90	559
WebCrow Lab	249,86	368
AVG Humans	24.24	2570
Best Human	69,53	1493

The detailed experimental outcomes of the WAICF French crossword-solving challenge can be found in Table 6. This challenge provided insights into WebCrow's performance and its cross-lingual capabilities. Humans cruciverbalist are strong only on one language.

In the French crossword challenge, there was no strong human competitor present. This leaves space for further challenges with French experts in crosswords.

7   Conclusion and Future Works

In conclusion, this work represents a significant advancement in the field of crossword solving. By capitalizing on our previous experience in the field we present a novel version of WebCrow 2.0 and its French WebCrow version, which represents the first French crossword solver.

In this work we collected a dataset of French crosswords, enabling us to make some comparisons with crosswords in other languages, Italian and American. Moreover, we analyzed the peculiarities of French crosswords. French crossword puzzles vary greatly, they are not standard like the American ones, the size, the knowledge, and the language games involved are influenced by the style and imprint of its author.

French WebCrow is an above-human-average crossword solver, but there is still room for improvements. The potential for French WebCrow to achieve competitive performance serves as a strong motivation for further research and development, paving the way for AI-powered crossword solving to reach new heights. There are three main branches for future development. First of all, there is room to improve the performances of both the Italian and French solvers by working on filters and re-ranking based on systems that can predict the grammatical type of the answer. Another improvement can be achieved by leveraging on the output of the Char Based Solver which fills the grid with the most probable letters, leaving empty the cells which have more uncertainty. We would like to implement a system that exploits the letters that are actually fixed to find out the missing ones on the internet or with a Generative Pre-trained Transformer. Another branch of development resides in the intrinsic characteristic of WebCrow 2.0, in which the modularity of its frameworks allows us to add a new language solver with little effort. Of course, as happened for Italian, English, and French, language-specific experts have to be developed to obtain high performances in crossword solving. We are already in touch with German universities to explore this road.

The last branch regards the inverse task, the crossword generation [20]. The experience gained, but even more the data collected during the WebCrow 2.0 experience, could represent a launch pad for the complex task of crossword generation. Consider that, for instance, the New York Times crosswords (one of the biggest collections of crosswords) contains an average of 96% of already seen answers, and only the 4% of the answers, on average, are new [21]. This task is still performed principally through semi-automatic proprietary software. New approaches should take into account Generative Pre-trained Transformers, which, at the moment, represent the most advanced approach for generating text and could be tested on generating crossword clues, which may also be ambiguous or tricky, covering different kinds of human knowledge.

208   G. Angelini et al.

Acknowledgements. This research owes its accomplishment to the generous collaboration of esteemed French crossword authors, Serge Prasil and Michel Labeaume. The University of Siena, expert.ai, and the 3IA Côte d'Azur Investment in the Future projects administered by the National Research Agency (ANR), under the reference number ANR-19-P3IA-0002, provided invaluable support for this endeavor

References

1. Angelini, G., Ernandes, M., Gori, M.: Solving Italian crosswords using the web. In: Bandini, S., Manzoni, S. (eds.) AI*IA 2005. LNCS (LNAI), vol. 3673, pp. 393–405. Springer, Heidelberg (2005). https://doi.org/10.1007/11558590_40
2. Angelini, G., Ernandes, M., Gori, M.: Webcrow: a web-based crosswords solver. In: Maybury, M., Stock, O., Wahlster, W. (eds.) INTETAIN 2005. LNCS (LNAI), vol. 3814, pp. 295–298. Springer, Heidelberg (2005). https://doi.org/10.1007/11590323_37
3. Barlacchi, G., Nicosia, M., Moschitti, A.: SACRY: syntax-based automatic crossword puzzle resolution system. In: Proceedings of 53rd Annual Meeting of the Association for Computational Linguistics: System Demonstrations, Beijing, China, July. Association for Computational Linguistics (2015)
4. Berthelier, V.: L'humour des mots croisés, étude stylistique (2018)
5. Cer, D., et al.: Universal sentence encoder. arXiv preprint arXiv: 1803.11175 (2018)
6. Devlin, J., et al.: BERT: pre-training of deep bidirectional transformers for language understanding. arXiv preprint arXiv:1810.04805 (2018)
7. Ernandes, M., Angelini, G., Gori, M.: Webcrow: a webbased system for crossword solving. In: AAAI, pp. 1412–1417 (2005)
8. Expert.ai: expert.ai Knowledge Graph (2023). https://www.expert.ai/products/expert-ai-platform/knowledge-graph/. Accessed 2023
9. Ginsberg, M.L.: Dr.Fill: crosswords and an implemented solver for singly weighted CSPs. J. Artif. Intell. Rese. **42**, 851–886 (2011)
10. Hart, P., Nilsson, N., Raphael, B.: A formal basis for the heuristic determination of minimum cost paths. IEEE Trans. Syst. Sci. Cybern. **4**(2), 100–107 (1968). https://doi.org/10.1109/tssc.1968.300136
11. Li, Y., Xu, L.: Word embedding revisited: a new representation learning and explicit matrix factorization perspective. In: Join Conference on Artificial Intelligence (IJCAI) (2015)
12. Littman, M.L.: Review: computer language games. In: Marsland, T., Frank, I. (eds.) CG 2000. LNCS, vol. 2063, pp. 396–404. Springer, Heidelberg (2001). https://doi.org/10.1007/3-540-45579-5_26
13. Littman, M.L., Keim, G.A., Shazeer, N.: A probabilistic approach to solving crossword puzzles. Artif. Intell. **134**(1–2), 23–55 (2002)
14. Littman, M.L., Keim, G.A., Shazeer, N.M.: Solving crosswords with Proverb. In: AAAI/IAAI, pp. 914–915 (1999)
15. Microsoft: Bing Web Search API (2023). https://www.microsoft.com/en-us/bing/apis/bing-web-search-api. Accessed 2023
16. Mikolov, T., et al.: Advances in pre-training distributed word representations. In: International Conference on Language Resources and Evaluation (2018)
17. Mikolov, T., et al.: Distributed representations of words and phrases and their compositionality. arXiv preprint arXiv:1310.4546 (2013)
18. Boris Pallier Christophe & New. Openlexicon, GitHub repository (2019). https://github.com/chrplr/openlexicon

19. Redis: Redis Pub/Sub (2022). https://redis.io/docs/manual/pubsub/. 22 agosto 2022
20. Rigutini, L., et al.: Automatic generation of crossword puzzles. Int. J. Artif. Intell. Tools **21**(03), 1250014 (2012)
21. Wallace, E., et al.: Automated crossword solving. arXiv preprint arXiv:2205.09665 (2022)
22. Zugarini, A., Ernandes, M.: A multi-strategy approach to crossword clue answer retrieval and ranking. In: CLiC-iT (2021)

Evaluating Touchless Haptics for Interaction with Virtual Objects

Ana M. Bernardos[✉], Juan A. Besada, Gloria Cobo, and José R. Casar

Information Processing and Telecommunications Center, Universidad Politécnica de Madrid, ETSI Telecomunicación, 28040 Madrid, Spain
anamaria.bernardos@upm.es

Abstract. In recent years, touchless (mid-air, hands-free) haptic interactive concepts with machines have gained popularity due to their health benefits and accessible feedback in everyday items. In particular, touchless haptics are particularly effective in creating realistic virtual environments. This paper examines the performance and user experience of touchless haptics for manipulating virtual objects. A comparative study involving seven participants was conducted to evaluate the efficacy of a touch controller versus a touchless haptic system (Ultraleap). Participants tested three interaction techniques in a virtual environment, performing a range of control actions on various virtual objects, including adjusting the size and spatial position of geometric volumes and manipulating a lever. Results indicate that while the touch controller remains the preferred tool for simpler tasks due to its ease of learning, touchless haptics reveals nearly as effective when a virtual representation of the user's hands, as visual reference, is incorporated into the immersive environment. Under these conditions, both systems demonstrate comparable effectiveness for specific command and resizing tasks.

Keywords: Haptics · Interactive systems · Virtual Reality

1 Introduction

Nowadays, the growing commercial offer of head mounted displays (HMD) enables the consumption of virtual reality services and applications in different domains. Many of the existing HMD proposals are designed to be used as a computer peripheral (e.g. Oculus Rift, HTC Vibe, Play Station VR or PSVR, etc.), while others work standalone or leveraging the computing power and visualization of capabilities of smartphones. HMDs also differ on their capabilities. A relevant aspect is the vision angle (usually, the wider the better), as this factor influences on the immersive perception of the user. Typical values are $100°–110°$; in some cases, the system includes an eye tracker, so it is possible to better focus on specific zones of the image, while others are faded, simulating the focus work performed by the human eye (to achieve a continuous immersive feeling without dizziness, the refresh rate must be above 60 frames per second (fps), being usual values above 90 fps).

M. Clayton et al. (Eds.): INTETAIN 2023, LNICST 560, pp. 210–221, 2024.
https://doi.org/10.1007/978-3-031-55722-4_15

For navigation within the environment, it is usual that virtual reality systems include tracking and navigation features to manage the view in a realistic way. The most basic technique is to track the HMD position with 3 degrees of freedom (3DoF), taking as input the accelerometer, magnetometer and gyroscope inertial sensors. Advanced systems (such as PSVR) rely on 9 LEDs and an external camera to monitor position signals, while others rely on a wireless controller with sensors that are different to those in the smartphone (past Google Daydream, Samsung Gear VR or Google Cardboard). Some other techniques include joysticks, keyboards, voice commands or gloves. In this context, the fields of Virtual Reality (VR) and haptic interaction are obviously strongly related. VR offers to the user the possibility of getting into a realistic virtual environment; thus the user expects to interact in the same way as in the real world (i.e. physically).

In this article, we analyze to which extent touchless haptic interaction, enabled by an ultrasound device (Ultrahaptics Touch Development Kit UHK), may work equivalently to the one provided by a joystick-like controller interface. The UHK device tracks the hand position by using depth sensors and provides haptic feedback as an opposition force, which may implement different feeling patterns. For our tests, the objective would be to be able to provide feedback on the shape of a virtual object (a lever, a cylinder, a sphere, etc.), so the user can feel its boundaries and physically interact over it (to resize it, activate it, etc.).

The paper is structured as follows. Section 2 compiles related work. Section 3 details the implemented system, while Sect. 4 goes over the user study. Discussion and conclusions are presented in Sect. 5.

2 Related Work

The integration of haptic/physical interaction into the VR experience has been widely explored in literature, to enhance the feeling of intensiveness and achieve more realistic experiences and safer user interactions [1, 2]. The haptic component can be delivered by using wearable devices [3–7], such as fingertip tactile devices, soft robotic gloves, Novint Falcon haptic device [8], etc. User studies demonstrate that haptic feedback can improve the user experience, although devices are still bulky, and application targeted.

Contactless/touchless haptic technologies bring the benefit of not requiring instrumenting the user. Different approaches have been considered: fans or pressurized air jets [9, 10], subwoofers in an enclosed space to compress air through a narrow aperture (AIREAL [11] and [12, 13]), lasers [14–17], electric arcs (e.g. Sparklee [18]), and electromagnetic fields [19, 20] in some cases with the help of magnetic gel or wax resulting in perceptible sensations from the hair follicles [21]. But all these solutions have limitations in range or spatial and temporal resolution greater than ultrasound haptics, being this one an outstanding solution within this field.

The main advantages that make this technology stand out are its spatial resolution that allows the simulation of multiple points, a high degree of temporal resolution, thanks to its high sampling frequency and the speed of sound itself, which also allows almost instantaneous and continuous presentation [22].

Thanks to all this, it is recently receiving a great deal of academic and commercial interest, becoming more accessible thanks to commercials such as Ultraleap [23] and open source initiatives such us Ultraino [24] that have allowed its extension into new areas in works such as [25] where it is used an ultrasound phased array to provide haptic feedback in the mouth area, the second most mechano-receptive area after fingertips. Or the Contactless Elevator [26] which allows the creation of an elevator interface for visually impaired people allowing them to read Braille with an accuracy of 88%.

Combining haptic feedback with other types of feedback such as thermal feedback is also experimented with the work [27] by combining the ultrasound haptic display with a hot air source, or auditory feedback with [28] by having the ultrasound device itself generate sounds in addition to haptic sensations.

Although research is growing, it is not known exactly what the most attractive scenario for these technologies is, but for now where they are being used the most are in sterile medical interfaces such as UltraSendo [29] (the first application in the context of medical training simulators) or UltraPulse [30] (which allows trainee doctors to search for a pulse mimicking the pulsation effect), and also most recently [31] that used an AR and haptic feedback teleoperation ultrasound system, automotive applications that typically use ultrasound haptics to deliver feedback for interface control such as [32, 33]; digital advertising adding to visual and auditory modalities the tactile sensations to achieve more informative or entertaining experiences with the marketed products such as [34–36]; VR/AR where ultrasound haptics are unobtrusive maintaining freedom of movement and can represent a wide range of sensations like recreating physical objects using haptics such as HaptoClone [37] or [38]; other more recent applications to create novel entertaining experiences such as [39, 40] and Ultraleap with its "supernatural" feelings [41, 42].

Another line of research for VR interaction explores smart watches. Authors in [43] introduce a combination of smartphone (iPhone 6+ mounted on a Leap HD VR viewer) and smartwatch (Apple Watch Gen. 1) for fully immersive environments. To measure the effectiveness of the system, a second setup was built, consisting in the same VR system and a 3D camera for gesture recognition (Axus Xtion Pro Live). The user study shows that the interaction with the smartwatch obtains similar or better rating or better than the camera.

However, despite the progress in these technologies, ultrasound haptics is still in its infancy and needs more research to achieve both more effective systems and better understanding of perception in order to be able to recreate these sensations. In this work, we analyze to which extent mid-air haptic interaction, enabled by an ultrasound-based device (i.e. UHK), may work equivalently to the one provided by a standard haptic interface (i.e. graspable controller) to manipulate virtual objects.

3   Components and Architecture

Our interactive system is built on two hardware solutions. The first one is a hardware kit composed by a headset and a controller; the latest is equipped with two buttons (APP and HOME), a touchpad and two lateral buttons for volume. The headset is ready to host a smartphone with high-quality graphics and resolution screen.

The second device is UHK, which is a 16×16 ultrasound transductors board that enables to provide contactless haptic feedback to the hands (touchless opposition force).

In practice, this means that a grid of small ultrasound speakers can be configured, in terms of number and height of control points, frequency and emission intensity to generate different feelings. The UHK device integrates the Leap Motion controller to locate the hand and detect gestures. Android, Unity and Unreal SDKs are provided together with the device. In this project, Unity has been our choice.

Additionally, a computer is used to plug UHK controller and to run the software associated to both devices and the interaction manager, which bundles the logic coordinating and sending the interaction commands to the mobile device. The computer is wirelessly connected to the smartphone, which oversees receiving the interaction commands and managing the virtual reality scenario. The graphical interface has been developed using Unity, together with some in-house developments to show the user movement when using the graspable controller.

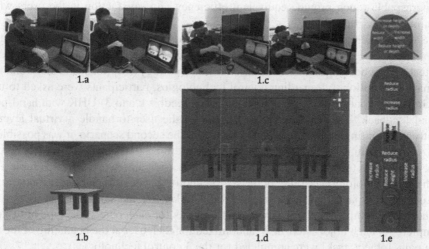

Fig. 1. a) User interacting in the LeverScene; b) Lever scenario; c) User interacting in the ResizingScene; d) Resize object scenario, overall view and prism and sphere manipulation. In the second case, it is also necessary to physically select the target object; e) Controller configuration. (Color figure online)

On this system, two prototypes have been built. The first one, LeverScene, enables to handle a lever in a virtual environment, to control the lighting level of a room. The lever is controlled by pushing or pulling a virtual lever object. The haptic system simulates the lever object by providing column-shaped feedback that varies depending on the user's hand movement. To manipulate it, the user must place her hand on the top of the fictional column, in the same way she would do it with a real object (Fig. 1a). The second one, ResizingScene enables the user to modify the size of different virtual objects (i.e. a prism, a sphere and a cylinder) using both hands. The system provides simulate air volumes consistent with shapes (shaped air columns with specific boundaries and power) that are to be constrained or expanded depending on the hands position (Fig. 1c).

With respect to the interaction handled through the controller, the coordinates transformation applied over the touchpad enables the user to move to all directions depending on the active part of the touchpad. Additionally, by touching the upper part of the touch-pad, the user will always move forwards the direction to which she is looking at. To manipulate the lever with the controller, the user will have to scroll fingers on the touch-pad. To manipulate an object, the user will have to navigate the environment to approach to it until it gets activated (the object will be highlighted in blue). Then, to start inter-action with the object, the user will have to press the standard APP button. After that, the touchpad's sections have been organized to enable every type of resizing for the proposed objects.

4 User Study

4.1 Method

The main hypothesis to verify in the user study is that "H0: Both mid-air haptics (UHK) and graspable touch provide equivalent efficiency and satisfaction to the users when manipulating virtual objects".

Seven participants (volunteers among the research personnel), with ages between 22 and 44 and no previous experience on the use of the technologies in the study, completed the test. Independent variables were the control technology (3 options) and the interactive scenarios (2 options). Regarding control technologies, participants were asked to use: 1) Graspable controller, 2) UHK without visual feedback and 3) UHK with hand-pose visual feedback. The first test scenario required the user to handle a virtual lever to control the lighting in a virtual room (3 tasks). In the second scenario, it was possible to resize some virtual 3D volumes in their different dimensions: cube (4 tasks), sphere (3 tasks) and prism (4 tasks). A total of 27 tasks per participant were evaluated (Table 1), 9 with each technology. The order of the six [technology, scenario] pairs were randomized for each participant, finally getting 189 valid tasks. For the sake of time, users were requested to complete only two manipulation tasks for each object; the type of tasks to complete for each object were also randomized for each user at the beginning of the test (the pairs [object, task] were completed for the 3 control technologies).

Prior to the use of each technology, the participant had a training time, that was concluded when the user explicitly stated to feel ready to start with the test (5 min was the limit). After each technology trial, a SUS (Standard Usability Scale) questionnaire and some extra questions specifically designed were completed; some open additional questions regarding preferences and opinion were posed to conclude the test.

In these conditions, the following *dependent variables* were defined:

- *System performance*, measured by success rate and number and error types, execution time to complete each task and learning time.
- *Usability*, calculated from adapted questions in the System Usability Scale Question-naire.
- *Preference ranking*, the order of technology preference for the user.

Errors were classified into three groups: a) *Timeout*: The user is not able to finish the task in less than the average completion time (calculated over all participants) plus one standard deviation. b) *Task failure*: The user finishes the task, but the result does not lie on the success criteria. c) *System error*: The system is unexpectedly blocked or shut down (the system needs to be restarted).

Table 1. Tasks to perform in each scenario, with the success metrics.

Objects	Task list	Success criteria
Lever	Pull the lever up to the maximum lighting level	$\alpha < -40\degree$
	Bring the lever back to initial position, no light	$\alpha > 40\degree$
	Pull the lever up to the vertical position	$-5\degree < \alpha < 5\degree$
Prism	Min prism size in its 3 dimensions	Min size: $w, d, h < 0.3$ Max size: $w, d > 1$; $h > 1.4$
	Min size in 2 dim. & max in 1 dim.	
	Min size in 1 dim. & max in 2 dim.	
	Max size in 3 dim	
Sphere	Min size	$r < 0.5$
	Max size	$r > 1.9$
	Medium size	$0.8 < r < 1.2$
Cylinder	Min radius and height	$r < 0.2, h < 0.25$
	Min radius and max height	$r < 0.2, h > 0.8$
	Max radius and min height	$r > 0.8, h < 0.25$
	Max radius and height	$r > 0.8, h > 0.8$

4.2 Results

On System Performance. Regarding *success rate*, no technology was able to offer full reliability to complete the proposed tasks for all the participants (Table 2). As expected, the controller was the most efficient solution; around an additional 20% of tasks were completed when using the controller, taking the UHK success rate as a reference. Around 12% of errors were *time out* ones, while the rest were due to not fulfilling the success criteria.

Table 2. Success rate for each scenario-technology combination. The second column indicates, for the tasks that were more difficult to complete (min) and easier (max) how many users were able to successfully finish them.

Scenario-technology	Success rate	Min—Max no of users
Lever-controller	86%	[4..7]
Lever-UHK without visual feedback	67%	[2..6]
Lever-UHK with hand-pose feedback	62%	[3..6]
Objects-controller	88%	[6..7]
Objects-UHK without visual feedback	69%	[3..7]
Objects-UHK with hand-pose feedback	67%	[3..6]

When analyzing the *execution time* (Fig. 2a) by the participants to complete the tasks, a Wilcoxon signed-rank test for paired samples shows that in the Lever Scenario, the median difference between joystick and UHK without visual feedback times is not statistically significant ($p_{lever} = p_l = 0.12$), while it is for the joystick and UHK with hand-pose feedback times ($p_l = 0.05$). In the objects scenario, it is possible to reject the null median time difference hypothesis for both pairs of technologies ($p_{objects} = p_o \ll 0.05$). Regarding the influence of visual feedback when using UHK, no statistical significance is found independently of the scenario ($p_l = 0.476, p_o = 0.759$).

Taking execution time into consideration, a set of Kruskal-Wallis tests show that it is not possible to state that the seven participants are differently skilled in the use of the systems neither as a whole ($\chi^2(6) = 11.76, p = 0.067$) nor when taking into consideration the three-available interaction means separately (controller: $\chi^2(6) = 5.9, p = 0.43$; UHK without visual feedback: $\chi^2(6) = 6.9, p = 0.33$; UHK with visual feedback: $\chi^2(6) = 7.84, p = 0.25$).

Regarding *learning time* (Fig. 2b), a Wilcoxon signed-rank test for paired samples shows that the median difference is not statistically significant in the Lever Scenario when comparing controller and UHK without visual feedback ($p_l = 0.063, \alpha = 0.05$), while it is in the controller and UHK with hand-pose feedback ($p_l = 0.018$). In the Objects Scenario, the difference is not significant neither for the controller-UHK without visual feedback pair ($p_o = 0.31$) nor for the controller-UHK with hand-pose feedback ($p_o = 0.091$). With respect to the comparison between UHK with or without visual feedback, the same test shows that it is not possible to reject the null hypothesis of zero median difference ($p_l = 0.31, p_o = 0.735$) for both scenarios.

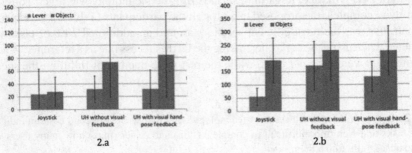

2.a   2.b

Fig. 2. a) Average task execution time (in seconds), for the 3 technology combinations, compared for the 2 testing scenarios. b) Average learning time (in seconds) comparison, for the 2 testing scenarios. Error bars show 1 standard deviation.

On Usability. After finishing each [scenario, technology] test, in order to evaluate *usability*, participants were asked to complete a System Usability Scale questionnaire (SUS), a simple, ten-item scale giving a global view of subjective assessments of usability [14]. Results (Table 3) show that, on average, the controller solution achieves the highest SUS value of 78/100, while the UHK option gets 64/100 when hand-pose feedback is provided and 50/100 when there is no visual feedback. The three technologies were ranked as less usable in the Object Resizing scenario.

Table 3. System Usability Scale rating, with standard deviation and p-value for paired samples Wilcoxon signed-rank test with significance value 0.05.

Scenario-technology	$SUS/100$	std	$p(\alpha = 0.05)$
1. Lever-controller	83	21.2	$p1 - 2 = 0.063$
2. Lever-UHK without visual feedback	54	23.8	$p1 - 3 = 0.351$
3. Lever-UHK with hand-pose feedback	77	13.7	$p2 - 3 = \mathbf{0.028}$
4. Objects-controller	74	17.7	$p4 - 5 = \mathbf{0.027}$
5. Objects-UHK without visual feedback	45	23.3	$p4 - 6 = \mathbf{0.046}$
6. Objects-UHK with hand-pose feedback	52	26.2	$p5 - 6 = 0.051$

In the case of the Lever Scenario, a set of Wilcoxon signed-rank tests show that the difference in the obtained SUS rating comes to be statistically significant only in the case of comparison of UHK-based solutions, when comparing the solution with visual hand feedback against the one with no feedback. In the Objects Resizing Scenario, the null hypothesis of zero median between technology pairs can be rejected for both pairs of controller-haptic solutions.

Interaction conditions the quality of the perceived immersive experience: the controller solution (over 10, mean $\eta = 7.86$; standard deviation $\sigma = 1.68$) and the UHK with hand-pose visual feedback ($\eta = 7.86$; $\sigma = 1.86$) are the ones providing the best immersive experience in the Lever Scenario. In the Objects Resizing one, the controller solution is the best rated ($\eta = 7.57$; $\sigma = 1.61$), followed by the UHK with hand-pose visual feedback ($\eta = 6.29$; $\sigma = 2.14$).

Some questions regarding the easiness of performing resizing over different dimensions of the geometrical figures show that resizing the prism depth is the task showing worst control ($\eta = 4.5$) while controlling its width ($\eta = 6.5$) is easier. The action of modifying radius obtains reasonable evaluations both for sphere ($\eta = 7.5$) and cylinder ($\eta = 7$). Regarding height, it is also efficiently done, both for prism ($\eta = 7.3$) and cylinder ($\eta = 7.3$). Coherently with the previous analysis on technology solutions, the controller is the proposal providing the best control ($\eta = 7.9$; $\sigma = 1.8$), followed by the hands improved UHK ($\eta = 6.5$; $\sigma = 2.4$) and the UHK with no visual feedback ($\eta = 5.5$; $\sigma = 2.8$). For both UHK solutions, the actions to modify prism depth ($\eta_{no\_hands} = 2.5$; $\eta_{hands} = 4$) and width ($\eta_{no\_hands} = 4.7$; $\eta_{hands} = 6.6$) are the worst rated.

On Preferences

Regarding preference, five out of seven participants state that the preferred system is the joystick ($\eta = 6$ in a 1–7 Likert scale of perceived control), followed by the UHK ($\eta = 4.7$ over 7) with hand-pose feedback. When asked about the possibility of building a multimodal interaction system, eye tracking was pointed by five participants, while voice was pointed by three of them. A participant talked about the possibility of building a system using a sensor-equipped bracelet.

With respect to open comments, some interested notes were gathered. While four participants did not mention fatigue, two pointed out that the use of UHK was more tiring than the joystick control, and another one told exactly the opposite. Regarding the

UHK solution, one participant stated he was feeling lost without hands representation, and another one pointed out the (obvious) difficulty of finding the correct position on top of Ultraleap controller when wearing the HMD. A participant complained on the unstable behavior of the systems, while three of them pointed out that they had enjoyed the experience.

5 Discussion and Conclusions

In this paper, we have presented a user study which aims at comparing the performance and usability of a touch graspable interface (controller) vs. a mid-air haptic one (UHK with and without hands representation) to perform tasks within an immersive virtual environment. With the controller, spatial touch movements enable us to manage the dimensions or movements of objects, while the UHK is programmed to generate simulated air volumes (through air flow columns), so the user can manipulate the objects by 'touching' them, through directional hand movements. Even if the user sample is small, the work gives some hints on to which extent both interaction methods may be effective and acceptable for the proposed scenarios (lever and objects).

The first issue to consider is that only two participants (over seven) were able to complete all the proposed tasks by using the controller, even after a learning session. This fact shows that the commercial technology for immersive interaction might still have a learning curve that may be steepest than desired. Participants that obtain higher hits with the controller also do it with the UHK alternatives, although no causality has been proven.

Neither the controller nor the UHK-based system has revealed as a perfect interaction tool for the proposed immersive environments. Both devices (controller and UHK) require that the user gets familiar to them. Actually, the learning time has demonstrated to be equivalent independently of the interaction technology in use. For example, the resizing tasks are more difficult to manage with the controller than the pull-push lever actions (as the touch space has to be divided into smaller sections). The user takes a similar time to learn how to perform the interaction either with the controller or the UHK.

Regarding execution times and tasks hits, the controller is obviously more efficient than the UHK-based proposal. Participants state that it is easier to use the touch controller, although mid-air haptic interaction with hands representation provides a better immersive experience.

No significant difference in terms of execution time has been found between the two UHK options (with/without hands), although the presence of the virtual hands as a reference is highly appreciated by the users. A non-expected effect is that, with the UHK, all the participants have managed to better complete the proposed tasks when they were not able to see their hands in the virtual environment. The learning time was also more reduced in the case of the Lever Scenario. There is not a real improvement in time execution or success rate related to the presence of hands references. This might be since the hands' view may complicate the interactive response, as users are less flexible to accept misalignments that are not relevant to complete the action.

In any case, users have positively assessed the mid-air haptic experience, although most participants prefer this method for simpler tasks (i.e. to control the lever, in this testing space) and specific applications. It is important to note that the mid-air touch system still offers limited capabilities, e.g. technical difficulties related to hands detection in specific hand postures (e.g. when the palm is perpendicular to the surface) makes more challenging some resizing tasks, finger tracking is only correctly done by UHK at a specific height from the device that may not be natural for the user, etc. Thus, depending on the interaction requirements, we feel that replicating the physical interaction model may not be the best option to guarantee the best success rate in terms of task completion. The creation of a proposal of a new vocabulary involving haptic feedback may be something to consider integrating this type of interaction with mid-air tools.

Acknowledgements. Authors thank F. Pedraza for his technical contribution and participants who volunteered in the user study for their time and support. Additionally, authors acknowledge the funding under grant P ID2020-118249RB-C21 funded by the Spanish Ministry of Science and Innovation.

References

1. Inwook, H., Hyungki, S., Ryong, K.J.: Air piano: enhancing music playing experience in virtual reality with mid-air haptic feedback. IEEE (2017). https://ieeexplore.ieee.org/stamp/stamp.jsp?tp=&arnumber=7989903. Accessed 3 Feb 2023
2. Rümelin, S., Gabler, T., Bellenbaum, J.: Clicks are in the air: how to support the interaction with floating objects through ultrasonic feedback. BMW Group (2017). https://doi.org/10.1145/3122986.3123010
3. Chen, F., Lin, Y.-C., Chien, J.-W., Tsai, C.-E.: Virtual reality for digital user experience and interactive learning based on user satisfaction: a pilot study. In: 2016 International Conference on Computational Science and Computational Intelligence (CSCI), pp. 374–377, December 2016. https://doi.org/10.1109/CSCI.2016.0077
4. Ball, C., Johnsen, K.: An accessible platform for everyday educational virtual reality. In: 2016 IEEE 2nd Workshop on Everyday Virtual Reality (WEVR), pp. 26–31, March 2016. https://doi.org/10.1109/WEVR.2016.7859540
5. Ishikawa, R., Inoue, A., Hoshi, T.: Investigating perceived slope gradient in virtual environment with Visuo-Haptic interaction, vol. 18, pp. 559–562 (2018). https://doi.org/10.1145/3292147.3292234
6. Amirkhani, S., Nahvi, A.: Design and implementation of an interactive virtual control laboratory using haptic interface for undergraduate engineering students (2016). https://doi.org/10.1002/cae.21727
7. Manawadu, U.E., Kamezaki, M., Ishikawa, M., Kawano, T., Sugano, S.: A haptic feedback driver-vehicle interface for controlling lateral and longitudinal motions of autonomous vehicles. In: 2016 IEEE International Conference on Advanced Intelligent Mechatronics (AIM) (2016). https://doi.org/10.1109/AIM.2016.7576753
8. Martin, S., Hillier, N.: Characterisation of the Novint falcon haptic device for application as a robot manipulator (2009)
9. Gurocak, H., Jayaram, S., Parrish, B., Jayaram, U.: Weight sensation in virtual environments using a haptic device with air jets. J. Comput. Inf. Sci. Eng. **3**(2), 130–135 (2003). https://doi.org/10.1115/1.1576808
10. Suzuki, Y., Kobayashi, M.: Air jet driven force feedback in virtual reality. IEEE Comput. Graph. Appl. **25**(1), 44–47 (2005). https://doi.org/10.1109/MCG.2005.1

11. Sodhi, R., Poupyrev, I., Glisson, M., Israr, A.: AIREAL: interactive tactile experiences in free air. ACM Trans. Graph. **32**(4), 1 (2013). https://doi.org/10.1145/2461912.2462007
12. Gupta, S., Morris, D., Patel, S.N., Tan, D.: AirWave: non-contact haptic feedback using air vortex rings. In: Proceedings of the 2013 ACM International Joint Conference on Pervasive and Ubiquitous Computing, pp. 419–428, September 2013. https://doi.org/10.1145/2493432.2493463
13. Hashizume, S., Koike, A., Hoshi, T., Ochiai, Y.: Sonovortex: rendering multi-resolution aerial haptics by aerodynamic vortex and focused ultrasound. In: ACM SIGGRAPH 2017 Posters, pp. 1–2, July 2017. https://doi.org/10.1145/3102163.3102178
14. Ochiai, Y., Kumagai, K., Hoshi, T., Hasegawa, S., Hayasaki, Y.: Cross-field aerial haptics: rendering haptic feedback in air with light and acoustic fields. In: Proceedings of the 2016 CHI Conference on Human Factors in Computing Systems, pp. 3238–3247, May 2016. https://doi.org/10.1145/2858036.2858489
15. Cha, H., Lee, H., Park, J., Kim, H.-S., Chung, S.-C., Choi, S.: Mid-air tactile display using indirect laser radiation for contour-following stimulation and assessment of its spatial acuity. In: 2017 IEEE World Haptics Conference (WHC), pp. 136–141, June 2017. https://doi.org/10.1109/WHC.2017.7989890
16. Lee, H., et al.: Mid-air tactile stimulation using laser-induced thermoelastic effects: the first study for indirect radiation. In: 2015 IEEE World Haptics Conference (WHC), pp. 374–380, June 2015. https://doi.org/10.1109/WHC.2015.7177741
17. Jun, J.-H., et al.: Laser-induced thermoelastic effects can evoke tactile sensations. Sci. Rep. **5**(1), 11016 (2015). https://doi.org/10.1038/srep11016
18. Spelmezan, D., Sahoo, D.R., Subramanian, S.: Sparkle: hover Feedback with touchable electric arcs. In: Proceedings of the 2017 CHI Conference on Human Factors in Computing Systems, pp. 3705–3717, May 2017. https://doi.org/10.1145/3025453.3025782
19. Adel, A., Micheal, M.M., Self, M.A., Abdennadher, S., Khalil, I.S.M.: Rendering of virtual volumetric shapes using an electromagnetic-based haptic interface. In: 2018 IEEE/RSJ International Conference on Intelligent Robots and Systems (IROS), pp. 1–9, October 2018. https://doi.org/10.1109/IROS.2018.8593699
20. Weiss, M., Wacharamanotham, C., Voelker, S., Borchers, J.: FingerFlux: near-surface haptic feedback on tabletops. In: Proceedings of the 24th Annual ACM Symposium on User Interface Software and Technology, pp. 615–620, October 2011. https://doi.org/10.1145/2047196.2047277
21. Boldu, R., Jain, S., Forero Cortes, J.P., Zhang, H., Nanayakkara, S.: M-Hair: creating novel tactile feedback by augmenting the body hair to respond to magnetic field. In: Proceedings of the 32nd Annual ACM Symposium on User Interface Software and Technology, pp. 323–328, October 2019. https://doi.org/10.1145/3332165.3347955
22. Rakkolainen, I., Freeman, E., Sand, A., Raisamo, R., Brewster, S.: A survey of mid-air ultrasound haptics and its applications (2021). https://doi.org/10.1109/TOH.2020.3018754
23. Digital worlds that feel human | Ultraleap. https://www.ultraleap.com/. Accessed 15 Feb 2023
24. Marzo, A., Corkett, T., Drinkwater, B.W.: Ultraino: an open phased-array system for narrowband airborne ultrasound transmission. IEEE Trans. Ultrason. Ferroelectr. Freq. Control **65**(1) (2018). https://doi.org/10.1109/TUFFC.2017.2769399
25. Shen, V., Shultz, C., Harrison, C.: Mouth haptics in VR using a headset ultrasound phased array (2022). https://dl.acm.org/doi/pdf/10.1145/3491102.3501960. Accessed 8 Feb 2023
26. Singhal, T., Phutane, M.: Elevating haptics: an accessible and contactless elevator concept with tactile mid-air controls (2021). https://doi.org/10.1145/3411763.3451574
27. Singhal, Y., Wang, H., Gil, H., Kim, J.R.: Mid-air thermo-tactile feedback using ultrasound haptic display (2021). https://doi.org/10.1145/3489849.3489889
28. Freeman, E.: Enhancing ultrasound haptics with parametric audio effects (2021). https://doi.org/10.1145/3462244.3479951

29. Hung, G.M.Y., John, N.W., Hancock, C., Hoshi, T.: Using and validating airborne ultrasound as a tactile interface within medical training simulators. In: Bello, F., Cotin, S. (eds.) Biomedical Simulation. ISBMS 2014. LNCS, vol. 8789, pp. 30–39. Springer, Cham (2014). https://doi.org/10.1007/978-3-319-12057-7_4

30. Hung, G.M.Y., John, N.W., Hancock, C., Gould, D.A., Hoshi, T.: UltraPulse - simulating a human arterial pulse with focused airborne ultrasound. In: 2013 35th Annual International Conference of the IEEE Engineering in Medicine and Biology Society (EMBC), pp. 2511–2514, July 2013. https://doi.org/10.1109/EMBC.2013.6610050

31. Fu, Y., Lin, W., Yu, X., Rodriguez-Andina, J.J., Gao, H.: Robot-assisted teleoperation ultrasound system based on fusion of augmented reality and predictive force. IEEE Trans. Ind. Electron., 1–8 (2022). https://doi.org/10.1109/TIE.2022.3201322

32. Harrington, K., Large, D.R., Burnett, G., Georgiou, O.: Exploring the use of mid-air ultrasonic feedback to enhance automotive user interfaces. In: Proceedings of the 10th International Conference on Automotive User Interfaces and Interactive Vehicular Applications, pp. 11–20, September 2018. https://doi.org/10.1145/3239060.3239089

33. Shakeri, G., Williamson, J.H., Brewster, S.: May the force be with you: ultrasound haptic feedback for mid-air gesture interaction in cars. In: Proceedings of the 10th International Conference on Automotive User Interfaces and Interactive Vehicular Applications, pp. 1–10, September 2018. https://doi.org/10.1145/3239060.3239081

34. Limerick, H., Hayden, R., Beattie, D., Georgiou, O., Müller, J.: User engagement for mid-air haptic interactions with digital signage. In: Proceedings of the 8th ACM International Symposium on Pervasive Displays, pp. 1–7, June 2019. https://doi.org/10.1145/3321335.3324944

35. Corenthy, L., et al.: Touchless tactile displays for digital signage: mid-air haptics meets large screens. In: Extended Abstracts of the 2018 CHI Conference on Human Factors in Computing Systems, pp. 1–4, April 2018. https://doi.org/10.1145/3170427.3186533

36. Georgiou, O., et al.: Mid-air haptic interfaces for interactive digital signage and kiosks. In: Extended Abstracts of the 2019 CHI Conference on Human Factors in Computing Systems, pp. 1–9, May 2019. https://doi.org/10.1145/3290607.3299030

37. Makino, Y., Furuyama, Y., Inoue, S., Shinoda, H.: HaptoClone (Haptic-Optical Clone) for mutual tele-environment by real-time 3D image transfer with midair force feedback. In: Proceedings of the 2016 CHI Conference on Human Factors in Computing Systems, pp. 1980–1990, May 2016. https://doi.org/10.1145/2858036.2858481

38. Kervegant, C., Raymond, F., Graeff, D., Castet, J.: Touch hologram in mid-air. In: ACM SIGGRAPH 2017 Emerging Technologies, pp. 1–2, July 2017. https://doi.org/10.1145/3084822.3084824

39. Hoshi, T., Takahashi, M., Iwamoto, T., Shinoda, H.: Noncontact tactile display based on radiation pressure of airborne ultrasound. IEEE Trans. Haptics 3(3), 155–165 (2010). https://doi.org/10.1109/TOH.2010.4

40. Matsubayashi, A., Makino, Y., Shinoda, H.: Direct finger manipulation of 3D object image with ultrasound haptic feedback. In: Proceedings of the 2019 CHI Conference on Human Factors in Computing Systems, pp. 1–11, May 2019. https://doi.org/10.1145/3290605.3300317

41. The Unreal Garden: Multiplayer Mixed Reality | Ultraleap, Ultraleap (2020). https://www.ultraleap.com/company/news/case-study/unreal-garden/. Accessed 15 Feb 2023

42. Fallen Planet Deepen VR Immersion with Mid-Air Haptics | Ultraleap, Ultraleap (2020). https://www.ultraleap.com/company/news/case-study/fallen-planet-affected/. Accessed 15 Feb 2023

43. Orlosky, J., Itoh, Y., Ranchet, M., Kiyokawa, K., Morgan, J., Devos, H.: Emulation of physician tasks in eye-tracked virtual reality for remote diagnosis of neurodegenerative disease. IEEE Trans. Vis. Comput. Graph. 23(4) (2017). https://doi.org/10.1109/TVCG.2017.2657018

Author Index

Published by Springer Nature Switzerland AG 2024. All Rights Reserved
M. Clayton et al. (Eds.): INTETAIN 2023, LNICST 560, pp. 223–224, 2024.
https://doi.org/10.1007/978-3-031-55722-4

Printed in the United States
by Baker & Taylor Publisher Services